Parole in Canada

LAW AND SOCIETY

Law and Society Series

W. Wesley Pue, General Editor

The Law and Society Series explores law as a socially embedded phenomenon. It is premised on the understanding that the conventional division of law from society creates false dichotomies in thinking, scholarship, educational practice, and social life. Books in the series treat law and society as mutually constitutive and seek to bridge scholarship emerging from interdisciplinary engagement of law with disciplines such as politics, social theory, history, political economy, and gender studies.

For a complete list of titles in the series go to www.ubcpress.ca. Recent titles include:

Sarah Turnbull

PAROLE in CANADA

Gender and Diversity in the Federal System

UBCPress · Vancouver · Toronto

25 24 23 22 21 20 19 18 17 16   5 4 3 2 1

Printed in Canada on FSC-certified ancient-forest-free paper (100% post-consumer recycled) that is processed chlorine- and acid-free.

Library and Archives Canada Cataloguing in Publication

Turnbull, Sarah, author
   Parole in Canada: gender and diversity in the federal system / Sarah Turnbull.

(Law and society)
Includes bibliographical references and index.
Issued in print and electronic formats.
ISBN 978-0-7748-3193-2 (hardback). – ISBN 978-0-7748-3195-6 (pdf). –
ISBN 978-0-7748-3196-3 (epub). – ISBN 978-0-7748-3197-0 (mobi)

   1. Parole – Canada. 2. Discrimination in criminal justice administration – Canada. 3. Women parolees – Canada. 4. Parolees – Canada. 5. Criminal justice, Administration of – Canada. I. Title. II. Series: Law and society series (Vancouver, B.C.)

HV9308.T87 2016   364.6'20971   C2016-901504-1
                                                                 C2016-901505-X

Canadä

UBC Press gratefully acknowledges the financial support for our publishing program of the Government of Canada (through the Canada Book Fund), the Canada Council for the Arts, and the British Columbia Arts Council.

This book has been published with the help of a grant from the Canadian Federation for the Humanities and Social Sciences, through the Awards to Scholarly Publications Program, using funds provided by the Social Sciences and Humanities Research Council of Canada.

UBC Press
The University of British Columbia
2029 West Mall
Vancouver, BC V6T 1Z2
www.ubcpress.ca

Contents

Acknowledgments

Parole in Canada would not exist without the early support and encouragement of Kelly Hannah-Moffat, to whom I am immensely thankful. I would like to thank those who participated in the study as informants and took time out of their busy days to speak with me. Thanks as well to Randy Schmidt and the editorial team at UBC Press and to the two anonymous reviewers whose feedback improved the book. I completed *Parole in Canada* while holding a postdoctoral research fellowship at the University of Oxford through Mary Bosworth's European Research Council Starting Grant (2012-2017), no. 313362. I have benefited from the support of fantastic colleagues at the Centre for Criminology at Oxford, in particular, Ines Hasselberg, Julia Viebach, Alpa Parmar, and Ambrose Lee. I am grateful to Kelly Hannah-Moffat and Dawn Moore for their ongoing encouragement and mentorship. I thank Armel and my fabulous friends for believing in me. I also thank my mother, father, and sister for their unconditional love and support.

Parole in Canada

Introduction

On January 17, 2012, several Canadian news outlets reported on an upcoming parole hearing for Gregory Bromby, a "Haitian-born" Canadian man convicted in 1997 of the rape and murder of a fifteen-year-old girl (CBC News 2012a; Hopper and Wilton 2012). A central focus of the news stories was that Bromby had been granted an elder-assisted hearing, a special type of parole hearing typically reserved for Aboriginal prisoners. The media coverage highlighted the fact that Bromby was Haitian-born, not Aboriginal, yet was permitted to have an Aboriginal hearing. Two days later, on January 19, 2012, the same news outlets reported that Bromby had been denied parole, while also highlighting the victim's father's view that Bromby's access to an elder-assisted hearing was disrespectful to Indigenous peoples in Canada (CBC News 2012b; Giroday 2012). One article cited an e-mail statement by the press secretary for then minister of public safety Vic Toews, which said that the parole system had been left "in a state of disarray" by the previous government because now "any inmate, regardless of heritage, [could] claim that they [were] aboriginal and receive *benefits*" (Giroday and Wilton 2012, n.pag; emphasis added).

This example raises a number of questions about penality in contemporary Canada, pointing to the intersection of concerns around identity, rights, and entitlements in the context of how we punish those who transgress the law. Within a society characterized by growing racial, cultural, and ethnic "divers-ity,"[1] greater attention to women's rights, and attempts to make (post)colonial reparations with Aboriginal peoples, notions of "fair" and "appropriate" punishment are changing. In Canada's penal system, it is not "business as usual." Using the federal parole system as a case study, I explore this shifting penal landscape. More specifically, I examine how concerns about Aboriginality, gender, and the multicultural ideal of diversity are interpreted and used to alter parole (conditional release) policy and practice. Of particular interest are how offender "diversities" are identified, understood, and incorporated into the policies and practices governing parole at the national level. I trace how certain "differences," and categories of offenders, are constituted as targets for "accommodation" or as having "special needs." I consider how penal institutions like the Parole Board of Canada (PBC) frame "culturally relevant" and "gender-responsive" policy and, in the process, constitute the identities of particular groups of offenders. Importantly, I demonstrate the limitations inherent in approaches that fail to challenge the underlying fabric of a penal system in which ideas around gender, race, and Aboriginality are interwoven, producing exclusion, discrimination, and differential outcomes.

Penal Reform and the Turn to Diversity

The scholarship on penal reform over the past twenty years has produced a large body of literature theorizing and otherwise accounting for the various ways that punishment has changed since the early 1970s. Although there is overwhelming agreement in the literature that most western countries' penal systems have shifted, the underlying reasons – and scope – of these reforms are debated among scholars. Extant literature focuses on the punitive nature of contemporary penal policy, including debates about the emergence of a "new" penal order and the "death" of rehabilitation as a central feature of modern punishment (e.g., Garland 1990, 1996, 2001, 2003a; Feeley and Simon 1992, 1994; O'Malley 1999; Pratt 2000; Simon and Feeley 2003; Sparks 2003; Tonry 2004; Brown 2005; Hallsworth 2005; Pratt et al. 2005; Simon 2007; Harcourt 2007). Other scholars consider the rise of risk-based penalities and associated reforms to penal policy based on the logics of risk and "what works" (e.g., Feeley and Simon 1992, 1994; Ericson and Haggerty 1997; Hannah-Moffat 1999, 2005; Garland 2003b; Hudson 2003; Kemshall 2003; O'Malley 2004; Maurutto and Hannah-Moffat 2006; Carlen 2008). A large body of scholarship examines the implications of the so-called "punitive turn," including mass incarceration (e.g., Caplow and Simon 1999; Tonry and Petersilia 1999; Blumstein 2003; Petersilia 2003; Haney 2004; Tonry 2004) and its gendered, racialized, and classed character (e.g., Kruttschnitt and Gartner 2003, 2005; Tonry 2004; Wacquant 2003, 2005; Sudbury 2005).

Within this broader context, a small but growing body of literature is examining penal change in relation to issues of diversity within penal populations, including various approaches taken by penal systems to help ameliorate gender discrimination and historical legacies of discrimination against Indigenous peoples (e.g., Cunneen 2006; Murdocca 2007, 2009, 2013; Spivakovsky 2008, 2013; Hannah-Moffat and Maurutto 2010; Martel et al. 2011). Although the literature on reforms to the punishment of women is well developed and covers several jurisdictions, including Canada (e.g., Hannah-Moffat 2001; Hannah-Moffat and Shaw 2000; Hayman 2006), the United Kingdom (e.g., Carlen 2002a; Corcoran 2010; Hedderman 2010), and the United States (e.g., Kruttschnitt and Gartner 2005; Shaylor 2009), fewer studies have considered questions of racial, ethnic, or cultural diversity in relation to penal change or how specific diversity initiatives, such as legal requirements or policy changes designed to ameliorate formal and systemic discrimination in penal policy and practices, has affected these regimes (although see Russell and Carlton 2013). This may be because not many jurisdictions undertake diversity initiatives – for example, because of funding issues or punitive sentiments (Zellerer 2003) – and/or because the initiatives that do exist are relatively new and not yet the subject of much academic research. The research that does exist shows a number of unintended consequences resulting from efforts to address systemic discrimination through institutional reforms that involve adding diversity initiatives to existing processes and structures (e.g., Hannah-Moffat 2001, 2004a; Carlen and Tombs 2006; Hayman 2006; Martel and Brassard 2008; Schoenfeld 2010; Martel et al. 2011; Pollack 2011; Russell and Carlton 2013). More specifically, there is a possibility that recent initiatives to make incarceration and parole sensitive and responsive to notions of gender, race, ethnicity, and/or culture will reaffirm these structures as necessary or suitable for managing deviance, thereby strengthening the "carceral pull" of these institutions (Carlen and Tombs 2006, 339; see also Shaylor 2009; Russell and Carlton 2013), particularly as they appear responsive to various groups of offenders and their needs.

In the Canadian context, federal penal institutions in recent years have placed greater emphasis on the need to recognize diversity and to respond to differences in the offender population. These changes can be situated within a broader context whereby organizations – from government institutions to corporations – have faced increasing pressure to accept and promote gender, racial, and cultural diversity from various sources, including human rights, employment equity, and multiculturalism law. Yet, as I discuss throughout *Parole in Canada*, diversity is not formally defined by government officials or within government texts but, rather, emerges as a fluid term that, most commonly, is used to signal non-whiteness and sometimes non-maleness. Herring (2009, 209) notes that "generally, 'diversity' refers to policies and practices that seek to include people who are considered, in some way, different from traditional members." Within the literature, diversity is also linked to groups that are typically covered under human rights, affirmative action, or equal employment opportunity legislation or policy (Edelman et al. 2001; Ahmed et al. 2006; Kalev et al. 2006; Herring 2009; Dobbin et al. 2011). In this book, I use the term "diversity" as a construct that includes racialized and/or culturalized difference, as constituted in relation to white Anglo- and Franco-Canadian norms that remain dominant in the white settler nation-state known as Canada.

At the federal level in Canada, diversity within the offender population has, for the most part, been identified as belonging to three groups: Aboriginal, women, and so-called "ethnocultural" offenders.[2] These groups are constituted as "different" in relation to the normative white male offender. The historical and systemic ways that ideas about gender and race are entwined into the penal system have produced certain forms of exclusion and discrimination. Aboriginal, women, and ethnocultural offenders are thus seen as other, as having special needs that cannot be met through the status quo and that, consequently, require certain accommodations, which range from the development of new programs to the creation or alteration of physical structures (e.g., healing lodges and special ranges within penitentiaries) to special formats for parole hearings (e.g., elder-assisted hearings).

As I illustrate in *Parole in Canada*, key legislative changes, such as the 1992 *Corrections and Conditional Release Act* (*CCRA*), and developments in case law have mandated that federal penal institutions be responsive to specific differences. For instance, the Supreme Court of Canada's decision in *R. v. Gladue* [1999], an important court case that I discuss in more detail in Chapter 2 and throughout, specified a different approach for sentencing Aboriginal offenders and has been used by the penal system to guide its policies and practices. In addition to legal stipulations requiring institutions to take into account cultural differences – or perhaps because of them – there is increasing recognition that the "success" of penal responses (e.g., in the rehabilitation and reintegration of offenders) is based on their ability to be responsive to issues of diversity. It is therefore important to consider how current penal systems and practices of punishment – which are based on and have "privileged white male nativist norms" (Flavin and Bosworth 2007, 218) – respond to what they perceive to be, and constitute as, the concerns or needs of those who are not white or male.

The institutionalization of diversity mandates and subsequent changes in penal policy and practice raise interesting questions for scholars of punishment, particularly given that much of the mainstream theorizing focuses on transformations that are highly punitive in nature and preoccupied with the management of risk. Although often occurring in tandem with well-documented punitive and risk-based policies, diversity-related reforms that accommodate gender, ethnic, and cultural diversity are shaping the punishment of offenders in the pursuit of a variety of penal goals, such as the (post)colonial amelioration of racial injustice through reductions in the incarceration rates of Indigenous peoples and the creation of gender-responsive models of justice. Such changes are very much specific to certain jurisdictions based on their unique historical, social, and political contexts; issues of injustice and discrimination are different across borders. It is therefore worthwhile to study the implications and outcomes of local initiatives.

Parole in Canada is a qualitative study of how concerns about gender and diversity are historically and politically constituted as problems that mandate changes to existing penal policy and practice. I examine the various meanings, impacts, and implications of penal transformations that aim to construct what appear to be fair, culturally appropriate, and/or gender-responsive penal policies and practices. My central focus is on how the ideal of diversity is interpreted and used to alter parole policy and practice. I draw on the ground-breaking work of Sara Ahmed and others who have critically examined the uptake of diversity in institutions and the ways in which the diversity framework reinforces, rather than challenges, racism and other forms of inequality. The research I present in *Parole in Canada* provides a nuanced understanding of how well-meaning penal reforms are institutionalized and the nature of their outcomes. I document some of the complexities of operationalizing abstract ideals of substantive equality and the amelioration of discriminatory practices that have yet to be sufficiently examined in the literature on punishment and society. I explore the following questions: How are certain differences and categories of offenders constituted as targets for "accommodation" or as having "special needs"? And, more broadly, how do penal institutions frame culturally relevant or gender-responsive policy and, in so doing, use normative ideals and selective knowledge of gender, race, culture, ethnicity, and other social relations to constitute the identities of particular groups of offenders?

I consider these questions by tracing the history of policy discussions about gender and facets of diversity within legislation and penal and parole policies and practices as well as the current approaches to managing offender differences used by the PBC. I argue that the incorporation of diversity into the federal parole system fulfills several organizational objectives. These include: satisfying the legislative mandate of the *CCRA* to recognize and respond to diversity;

meeting expectations of fairness; observing human rights ideals and, increasingly, the interests of victims; managing reputational risk to protect the organization from legal challenges and/or negative public opinion; conforming to managerial logics as a means of measuring and tracking diversity and showing that it is being done at the organization level; instituting "effective" correctional practice in order to reduce risk and to increase public safety; and addressing issues of representation in such a way that board members and staff reflect the diversity of the Canadian population.

I argue that the accommodation of gender and diversity provides a narrative of parole and an institutional framework that positions the PBC as responsive to the diverse needs and/or experiences of non-white and non-male offenders. In the (post)colonial Canadian context,[3] the penal system strives to deliver fair punishment through the selective inclusion of difference and without altering or reconsidering fundamental structures, practices, and power arrangements. Diversity and difference are instead added onto and/or incorporated into pre-existing penal policy and logics, including risk management and managerialism. The organizational approach to difference is focused on the production of knowledge about the other in an attempt to be culturally (or gender) sensitive. In addition, the rhetoric of diversity does work for the PBC as such initiatives become auditable products that demonstrate diversity is being practised within the organization. In this way, racism, neocolonialism, and sexism remain unrecognized and unaddressed.

Some Background

For federally sentenced offenders, parole and conditional release are the last stage of the penal system in Canada. The *CCRA* requires that all federally sentenced offenders be considered for some type of conditional release during their sentence. There are four types of release: temporary absence, day parole, full parole, and statutory release (PBC 2010a). This system has been largely rationalized as a means of enabling gradual release so that prisoners may return to their communities under the supervision of parole officers to serve the remainder of their sentence. Gradual and supervised release are viewed as promoting public safety by allowing for the monitoring of released offenders as they attempt to (re)establish themselves in their communities, thereby by permitting corrective actions (e.g., parole suspensions or revocations) if their behaviours become "risky" to the public. As a penal practice, parole is one strategy for managing the transition from the highly regulated environment of the federal penitentiary to the comparably "free" space of the community. The application of conditions to release facilitate this re-entry by targeting the behaviours, activities, and associations connected to the risk to reoffend (see Turnbull and Hannah-Moffat 2009).

The PBC is an independent administrative tribunal that has, under the *CCRA*, exclusive decision-making power to grant or deny release (with the exception of statutory release, which is set by law), apply conditions, suspend and revoke release, detain offenders until the completion of their sentence, and consider appeals of its decisions (PBC 2011a).[4] Established in 1959 through the *Parole Act*, the organization makes conditional release decisions for all federally sentenced offenders in Canada as well as for prisoners in the provinces and territories that do not have parole boards.[5] The PBC is also responsible for making decisions related to pardons and clemency; however, its program of conditional release accounts for most of its work. Board members are the individuals responsible for conditional release decision making.[6] The PBC headquarters are located in Ottawa and there are offices located in the five regions: Pacific, Prairies, Ontario/Nunavut, Quebec, and Atlantic. The organization is part of the Public Safety Canada portfolio and is headed by a chairperson who reports to Parliament through the minister of public safety (PBC 2011a).

The *CCRA* and its *Regulations* comprise the legislative framework for the PBC's policies, operations, training, and decision making (PBC 2011a). The *CCRA* outlines the principles guiding the PBC and the criteria for conditional release decision making. As per the *Act*, the protection of society is the paramount principle guiding the work of the organization. The assessment of whether an offender, if s/he reoffends, poses an "undue risk" to society is the primary focus of release decision making, along with the belief that her or his gradual release would contribute to public safety (PBC 2011a). The *CCRA* also mandates the organization to adopt policies to guide decision making, which the PBC has done through its Policy Manual (see PBC 2015). The Policy Manual, in turn, reflects the prescriptive elements of the *CCRA* that guide decision making, such as the stipulation in section 151(3) of the *CCRA* that these policies respect "gender, ethnic, cultural and linguistic differences and be responsive to the special needs of women and aboriginal peoples, as well as to the needs of other groups of offenders with special requirements."

The PBC has several partners that assist it in carrying out its mandate. These include law enforcement, the courts, provincial and territorial corrections, community groups, and non-governmental agencies. The PBC's primary partner is the Correctional Service of Canada (CSC), "which is responsible for the custody, programming, and case management of offenders serving two years or more and for their supervision in the community on conditional release, and for case preparation and parole supervision in provinces/territories without their own parole boards" (PBC 2010b, n.pag). According to the PBC (2000a), its ability to make "quality decisions" rests on the information provided to the organization by the CSC. More recently, this includes the provision of "cultural information" to the PBC regarding Aboriginal offenders, including assessments by elders, offenders' progress in Aboriginal programs, and/or institutional behaviour within Aboriginal-specific ranges or institutions (PBC n.d.-a).

As I demonstrate, issues of diversity are taken up within the PBC in a variety of different contexts. Diversity – that is, Aboriginal, ethnocultural, and female difference – is understood to be relevant to formal policies and practices, including those relating to decision making, hearing formats, and risk assessment. Diversity issues also emerge in relation to the training of board members and staff so as to improve communications and information gathering during hearings, thereby contributing to more "appropriate" decision making. Another way that diversity is taken up relates to the membership of the PBC and the extent to which board members are representative of the community. Diversity issues are also tracked in relation to the organization's corporate performance monitoring and reporting activities (e.g., how it implements the *Canadian Multiculturalism Act*). Other organizational practices, like community consultations, outreach activities, and research agendas, also reflect the uptake of diversity issues.

Simon (1993, 11) aptly characterizes parole as "a unique enterprise," one that "must provide an account of how dangerous people can be secured in the community, and thus of the relationship among criminal dangerousness, penal technologies, and public safety." As a decision-making body with a prescriptive mandate under the *CCRA*, the PBC is required to navigate this terrain and do its work in a social and political context that is increasingly risk averse. Yet, exactly how the PBC carries out its mandate is largely unknown. Indeed, the literature on parole in Canada is sparse, particularly in relation to the creation of the *CCRA*, the development of the conditional release system over time, and the establishment of the PBC as the federal decision-making body. Although a few Canadian studies consider the gendered and racialized nature of conditional release decision making (e.g., Hannah-Moffat 2004a; Silverstein 2005; Turnbull and Hannah-Moffat 2009) and the reintegration of female offenders on parole (e.g., Maidment 2006; Pollack 2007, 2008, 2009, 2011), to my knowledge no study examines how the PBC as a penal institution has responded to and managed diversity over time. In *Parole in Canada*, I bring together Foucauldian, anti-racist feminist, and critical organizational literatures to help advance our understanding of penal change and the consequences of institutional responses to difference in the context of Canadian penality.

Organization

I draw on a multi-method approach involving the analysis of interview data, documents acquired through public channels (e.g., libraries, the internet, etc.), and documents obtained through the filing of requests to the PBC under the *Access to Information Act* (*ATIA*). Access to the PBC was limited, therefore the use of publicly available and institutionally held documents helped fill in some gaps undoubtedly left by the small number of interviews and vice versa. This triangulated approach aims to provide a rich account based on the best available data. I conducted semi-structured interviews with a total of thirteen individuals – twelve public servants and one member of the voluntary sector – before my research access was halted by the PBC by denials of my requests for further interviews with staff, including parole board members. These individuals can be classified as belonging to two groups: (1) key informants, who provided background and contextual information on the development of legislation as well as various policies and practices, and (2) practical informants, who provided information on the day-to-day operation of the PBC as well as its institutional history.

I gained access to unreleased and/or unpublished documents produced by the PBC through sixteen formal requests made under the *ATIA*.[7] These requests were filed in 2009 and 2010. Using the *ATIA* allowed me to go beyond the surface of the organization to gain access to documents that are not publicly available and thus fall outside the ways in which the PBC imagines and portrays itself as an organization through its website.[8] These requests allow researchers to get at what Walby and Larsen (2011, 625) term the "live archive" – the multitude of texts produced within governments on a daily basis. Written documents produced by the PBC thus comprise a significant portion of the data analyzed in this study. These documents include mission and vision statements, policy manuals, training manuals and workbooks, newsletters, assessment reports, institutional performance reports, corporate strategies and analyses, and pamphlets and descriptive materials. Some of these documents are specifically related to diversity, including policies, commitment statements, newsletters, assessment reports, and explanatory materials, while others were more general in nature (e.g., performance reports, annual reports, corporate strategies, policy manuals, etc.). I use these documents to fashion a historical record (in the absence of any other) and to consider how the organization constitutes and responds to the problem of diversity. The focus of my analysis is the institutional representations, narratives, and discourses within institutionally produced documents that speak to notions of gender and diversity.

In Chapter 1, I trace the previously undocumented historical moments of recognition, articulation, and development of responses to gender and diversity within Canadian conditional release since the 1970s. In undertaking this project, I found that my research was restricted by the absence of a formal institutional history of parole in Canada. I therefore offer a contribution to the field by documenting changes to conditional release over the past four decades. To do this, I examine various government and non-government reports, key pieces of legislation, and case law that provide insight into how issues of difference were constituted, which problems were identified and how they were framed, and the types of solutions that were imagined. I explore how gender and diversity emerge as institutionally important in the current context, including how diversity is constituted through various forms of knowledge that frame the problem of difference as manifested in certain penal populations and as related to particular policies and practices. I aim to provide a historical context for the institutional responses to diversity at the PBC by tracing the emergence of diversity as an object of penal concern. I argue that the initial framings of diversity within legislation and policy debates, and the constitution of the "problems" facing certain offender populations, shape the types of legislative and organizational solutions that are imaginable and practicable.

In Chapter 2, I focus more directly on the PBC and trace its organizational approaches to gender and diversity. I use anti-racist feminist, sociology of organizations, and management studies literatures to position the PBC's own "diversity work" (Ahmed 2007a, 237) within a broader context within which organizations are increasingly required to respond to gender and diversity issues. I discuss the creation of the PBC's Aboriginal and Diversity Initiatives section and the types of diversity work it carries out. I suggest that how diversity is constituted within the PBC shapes its diversity work. The organizational policies and initiatives that respond to, or attempt to accommodate, diversity can be seen as technologies of power for organizing difference and producing knowledge about those defined as different. Organizational attempts to be culturally, racially, and/or gender sensitive may work to reproduce institutional whiteness and maleness and dominant conditional release approaches based on white male offenders as the standard.

In Chapter 3, I focus on three organizational knowledge practices designed to produce to "appropriate" conditional release decisions for offenders who have been identified as different along lines of gender, race, and culture: (1) diversity training, (2) the interpretation of *R. v. Gladue*, and (3) attempts to "Indigenize" risk. I suggest that these knowledge practices can be understood as organizational attempts to "know" certain populations and the ways in which difference is applicable to issues of risk assessment in the context of decision making. The cultural and gendered knowledges of offenders circulated through these practices reveal the complexities of accommodating difference in the pursuit of appropriate decisions.

In Chapter 4, I examine the PBC's diversity work specifically in relation to Aboriginal offenders. I explore the genesis of the elder-assisted hearing (EAH) and community-assisted hearing (CAH) approaches and their contemporary manifestations as well as the implications of how "Aboriginality" and the role of the elder are constituted vis-à-vis these practices. I also consider how the *R. v. Gladue* decision was implemented within the organization. I contend that EAHs and CAHs are two instances of a reconfigured contemporary penality in which standard practices (i.e., parole hearings) are "Aboriginalized" in order for hearings, and the parole process more generally, to be perceived and experienced as fair, effective, and culturally appropriate. In addition, the PBC's implementation of the *R. v. Gladue* decision illustrates how the organization is grappling with issues of Aboriginal difference. I argue that Aboriginal offenders are confined to the realm of culture, with EAHs and CAHs remaining exceptional and peripheral to the normal program of conditional release.

In Chapter 5, I look at diversity work in relation to those offenders defined as "ethnocultural." I show how notions of difference within the context of institutionalized multiculturalism have shaped the development of responses to non-white, non-Aboriginal offenders. I consider various institutional documents that attempt to define, understand, and rationalize this population as targets of ethnicized parole policies and practices. By analyzing four institutional practices – (1) the adaptation of hearing models originally designed for Aboriginal offenders, (2) the refocused efforts on interpretation services for offenders who do not speak English or French, (3) a regional project developed specifically for African Canadian offenders, and (4) the production of cultural fact sheets to advise decision makers – I show how the PBC has grappled with issues of ethnocultural difference. I argue that organizational responses to ethnocultural offenders works to maintain institutional whiteness and masculinity through the attribution of diversity to those who are non-white. I also reveal the lack of consideration given to gender issues.

In Chapter 6, I focus on the organizational responses to female offenders. I examine the attempts to create a corporate strategy for this group as well as one regional initiative designed to better familiarize female offenders with the hearing process. Although the PBC recognizes that gender influences criminal offending and parole outcomes and that female offenders are different from male offenders, it struggles with the practical application of exactly how gender (or, perhaps more accurately, femininity) figures into conditional release decision making. I argue that organizational responses to diversity are unable to consider gender as one intersecting aspect of difference. Gender issues are also translated as being solely applicable to female offenders. Moreover, the partitioning of racial and/or cultural difference from gender has resulted in the constitution of female offenders as a largely homogeneous group, whereby Aboriginal women and racialized women exist as afterthoughts or appendages to dominant approaches to this offender population.

I conclude with some reflections on the limitations of the politics of inclusion and the framework of diversity in the federal parole system, including the potential for "inclusive" measures to reinforce the same systems of inequality connected to the criminalization and punishment of Indigenous, racialized, and other marginalized people. I suggest that the analysis presented in *Parole in Canada* supports a more critical engagement with the ideals of diversity, cultural appropriateness, and gender responsiveness in the development and implementation of penal policies and practices.

1

Putting Gender, Race, and Culture on the Penal Agenda

Since the late 1960s, the federal parole system, like other government institutions, has been the target of numerous reform efforts, primarily as a result of increased public criticism and subsequent governmental scrutiny. And, largely beginning in the 1970s, Aboriginal and feminist lobbies brought similar pressures to reform based on the perceived differences and different needs of Aboriginal peoples and women in conflict with the law. In particular, concerns began to be raised about the failure of the justice system in relation to Aboriginal peoples – as evidenced by their vast overrepresentation in the penal system – as well as the lack of appropriate facilities, programs, and approaches for both Aboriginal and female offenders. The momentum towards reform was also strengthened by the introduction of the *Charter of Rights and Freedoms* in 1982 and several key government and non-government reports throughout the 1970s and 1980s highlighting the particular disadvantages faced by Aboriginal and female offenders caught in the carceral net.[1] The enactment of the *Corrections and Conditional Release Act* in 1992 marks the first time issues of gender, ethnicity, and Aboriginality were recognized in corrections and parole (conditional release) legislation, thereby mandating the institutional recognition of diversity within the federal offender population.

In this chapter, I explore reforms to the parole system in Canada, focusing on efforts directed towards issues of gender and diversity.[2] I do not intend to offer a comprehensive history of penal reform in Canada over the past forty years; rather, my aim is to provide an account of key changes to parole and the broader penal context as a result of diversity issues. Importantly, this chapter offers one of the first accounts of the changes in parole leading up to and following the enactment of the CCRA. I explore how diversity becomes institutionally important, including how it is constituted through various forms of knowledge that frame the "problem" of difference as manifested in certain penal populations and related policies and practices. As Garland (2001, 26) observes, "every 'solution' is based upon a situated perception of the problem it addresses, of the interests that are at stake and of the values that ought to guide action and distribute consequences." By examining the process of penal reform over the past four decades, we can see how the problem of diversity is framed and made actionable in particular ways. These "solutions" reflect a selective incorporation of diversity as only certain knowledges and approaches are taken up and integrated into policies and practices. As I show, diversity issues cannot be ignored; through the enactment of the CCRA, penal institutions face legal risks for their failure to respond to difference. At the same time, there is genuine interest on the part of many individuals in creating penal systems that take issues of diversity into account.

This discussion is situated within the broader context of penal change as shifts in the area of parole and conditional release are by necessity connected to correctional reform. Among the official documents (e.g., commissions of inquiry, parliamentary committees, government task forces and initiatives, etc.) analyzed here, the primary problem identified for Aboriginal offenders relates to their overrepresentation within the correctional population, with related concerns raised around the lack of culturally relevant punishment. For female offenders, the main problem relates to their underrepresentation in the penal system, something that was seen to be related to discriminatory treatment due to the lack of gender-appropriate punishment. These documents frame both the problems and solutions to difference and produce particular knowledges of Aboriginal and female populations upon which to base reforms and strategies of governance. I argue that the historical framing of the problems related to Aboriginal and female offenders is important because it shapes their solutions, thereby excluding alternative visions for change that are not consistent with how these problems are understood. This framing limits the scope of change and directs the focus towards "fixing" aspects of legislation, policy, and practice to make the penal system more "responsive" to certain offender differences and not to others. By tracing the emergence of diversity as an object of penal concern, the following provides a context for the institutional responses to difference that I discuss in subsequent chapters. The developments considered here are

Putting Gender, Race, and Culture on the Penal Agenda

indicative of the challenge of bringing about penal change within complex systems that must handle multiple objectives (Houchin 2003), of which gendered and cultural approaches are only a part.

The Problem of Indigeneity: Overrepresentation, Parole Failure, and Cultural Difference

The challenges facing Aboriginal peoples in conflict with the law have been a subject of ongoing issue for the last forty years. During this time, a key policy concern at the federal level was the continuing overrepresentation of Aboriginal offenders within the penal system and the identification and implementation of possible remedies that could reduce the rate of imprisonment while making punishment fairer through culturally appropriate programs and practices. Efforts to create "culturally sensitive" penal policies were based on the recognition of Indigeneity, or Aboriginal difference, as shaping the relations between Aboriginal offenders and the criminal justice system. Aboriginal peoples were understood as being culturally different from non-Aboriginals and as having unique perspectives and needs. This section considers the ways in which the "problems" facing Aboriginal peoples were framed as a way to situate the types of "solutions" created. I argue that Indigeneity presented its own problem to the penal system by illuminating the whiteness of normative practices and processes, and troubling assumptions that "fair" or "equal" treatment was equated with "same" treatment. The various governmental reports and inquiries discussed herein can be seen as producing knowledge about Aboriginal offenders and their needs as targets of reform efforts, yet the basic assumptions about parole and punishment remain largely unquestioned.

Although *Indians and the Law* (Canadian Corrections Association 1967) was one of the first reports to consider the relationship between Aboriginal peoples and the criminal justice system, it was during the 1970s that the federal government began to recognize the particular problems faced by Aboriginal offenders (Ekstedt and Griffiths 1988). The issue of overrepresentation – that is, the fact that numbers of Aboriginal offenders in both federal and provincial correctional institutions are disproportionately high compared to their numbers in the general Canadian population – emerges as particularly salient in governmental texts.[3] This problem was identified consistently in nearly all reports of various commissions, inquiries, and initiatives since the 1970s that examined federal penal regimes and was occasionally linked to systemic discrimination. Additional problems cited included the lower rates of conditional release for Aboriginal offenders, their poor performance while on parole, the lack of culturally relevant approaches and practices, and little Aboriginal representation among staff employed by Canada's penal institutions.

The 1974 report of the Standing Senate Committee on Legal and Constitutional Affairs, chaired by Carl Goldenberg, was among the first to identify Aboriginal offenders and their needs (Canada 1974), although a mere two pages were devoted to these issues. The Goldenberg Report highlights the disproportionate number of Aboriginal offenders within the federal correctional system and the challenges they faced when on parole. Concerns about Aboriginal offenders' poor parole performance were echoed in the *Solicitor General's Study of Conditional Release: Report of the Working Group*, published in 1981, which discusses, albeit briefly, their lower rate of release yet higher rate of revocation. However, the report notes that this

> is not an indicator of racism in corrections, but in many cases reflects a lack of release plans considered appropriate by releasing authorities. Native offenders sometimes consider this judgment of their release plans to be an insistence by authorities that Natives try to adapt their plans and post-release lifestyle to a standard appropriate for white offenders, but not necessarily for Natives. (Solicitor General 1981, 117-18)

This excerpt recognizes the problem of cultural difference as leading to parole failures for Aboriginal offenders, where the whiteness of the system results in inappropriate decision making around release plans. The normative criteria and decision-making practices that produce discriminatory results are not viewed as racist but merely as inappropriate as they reflect white standards.

A pivotal report for penal reform related to Aboriginal offenders is that of the Task Force on the Reintegration of Aboriginal Offenders as Law-Abiding Citizens (hereafter the Task Force). This report lays the foundation for future policy initiatives directed towards Aboriginal offenders. The Task Force was created in March 1987 by the Solicitor General of Canada,[4] and its mandate was to

> examine the process which Aboriginal offenders (status and non-status, Indians, Metis, and Inuit) go through, from the time of admission to a federal penitentiary until warrant expiry, in order to identify the needs of Aboriginal offenders and to identify the ways of improving their opportunities for social reintegration as law-abiding citizens, through improved penitentiary placement, through improved institutional programs, through improved preparation for temporary

absences, day parole and full parole, as well as through improved and innovative supervision. (Solicitor General 1988a, 5)

The *Final Report: Task Force on Aboriginal Peoples in Federal Corrections* (hereafter the Final Report) was released in 1988 and contains sixty-one recommendations for change to existing policy, institutional structure, and programming.

The impetus behind the Task Force was the government's recognition of a number of problems, which include: the overrepresentation of Aboriginal people within federal corrections, the lack of Aboriginal people as correctional staff, the differential parole grant and revocation rates for Aboriginal offenders, and the complexity created "by the fact that Aboriginal offenders are not a homogeneous group" due to their different constitutional and legal statuses and cultures (Solicitor General 1988a, 5). The Task Force also noted that assessment practices have been developed based on non-Aboriginal offenders and, as such, have questioned the "capability of an individual from a particular sociocultural, economic and professional background to assess individuals who do not share the same background and perceptions" (ibid.). Here, the presence of Aboriginal difference illuminates the whiteness of normative practices and processes and their disparate impact on Aboriginal offenders. Again, the focus is on cultural difference rather than on the effects of racism and colonialism.

Also in 1988, the Standing Committee on Justice and Solicitor General, chaired by David Daubney, released the report *Taking Responsibility*, which reviews sentencing, conditional release, and corrections (Canada 1988). As with other official documents, the central problem identified in *Taking Responsibility* with regard to Aboriginal offenders is their overrepresentation in custody, with additional problems related to lower levels of participation in programs, their more frequent waiving of parole opportunities, and their lower rates of parole compared to other offenders. The Daubney Committee also noted the perception on the part of Aboriginal offenders that "the National Parole Board [was] not always sensitive to the needs of Native offenders or the environment to which they [were] to be conditionally released" (Canada 1988, 215). The two main contexts used to illustrate this lack of sensitivity are explained as follows:

One of these [contexts] is to refuse to accept a release plan because there is no parole supervision capacity in the area to which the inmate is to be conditionally released – often a reserve or remote village where the offender has come from or where there is a community willing to take him back. The other is to impose the standard disassociation condition of release saying that the offender is not to have contact with anyone with a criminal record. (ibid.)

Here, the problem is located in PBC decision-making practices that are insensitive to cultural difference and that may result in unfair decisions for Aboriginal offenders. In this context, decision-making policies and practices are not identified as discriminatory but, rather, as in need of being more sensitive.

Locating Solutions, Making Exceptions

The pursuit of culturally sensitive penal practices emerges as a primary solution to the problem of Aboriginal difference as manifested in the overrepresentation of Aboriginal offenders, their poor performance while on parole, and their cultural needs. As I show in the following, the types of solutions offered to address the problems facing Aboriginal offenders remain consistent over time and reflect an approach to diversity that is about making exceptions. In this sense, reform efforts were focused on making minor adjustments to the penal system so that Aboriginal difference could be accommodated without fundamental change in structures or dominant practices. These solutions are framed as cultural accommodations, thereby deflecting focus from issues of systemic racism within the justice system and failing to consider that the system itself is not "appropriate" for Aboriginal peoples (Monture 2006, 77). As exceptions, these solutions reflect a selective incorporation of Aboriginal knowledges and practices into corrections and parole policy.

One of the solutions to the problems facing Aboriginal peoples put forth by numerous reports is the increased involvement of them and their organizations in all facets of the penal system. The presence of Aboriginal individuals within penal institutions was thought to result in improvements to the system's handling of Indigenous peoples and to provide more appropriate penal responses. For instance, the Goldenberg Report recommended increasing the number of Aboriginal staff in order to assist Aboriginal offenders with pre-release planning as well as having parole authorities contract with Aboriginal organizations for the delivery of aftercare services (Canada 1974). The 1975 National Conference on Native Peoples and the Criminal Justice System also advocated for the increased involvement of Aboriginal groups in the planning and delivery of programs and services, the greater recruitment of Aboriginals into positions throughout the justice system, and the establishment of Aboriginal committees, consultations, and commissions to advise federal government ministries on

Aboriginal justice issues (Solicitor General 1975). These recommendations were restated nearly ten years later in an advisory committee's report on ways to reduce violent incidents in federal penitentiaries (Solicitor General 1984). According to the report, the use of Aboriginal staff would help reduce "difficulties in staff/inmate relationships," while contracting with Aboriginal groups "would provide programming which [would be] more sensitive to the needs of native inmates" (27). Such organizational adjustments, which better reflect the specific needs and circumstances of Aboriginal offenders, were linked to improved management, thereby reducing tensions and improving relations among prisoners and staff. Within these reports, issues of Aboriginal overrepresentation, parole failure, and cultural difference could be addressed through the greater involvement of Aboriginal peoples in the penal system as staff and program deliverers.

The Task Force on the Reintegration of Aboriginal Offenders as Law-Abiding Citizens (Solicitor General 1988a) and the Daubney Committee (Canada 1988) also supported the greater participation of Aboriginal peoples in corrections and conditional release. In order to allow for "equitable decision-making and equivalent opportunities for [the] successful reintegration" of Aboriginal offenders, the Task Force found that there must be greater participation of Aboriginal peoples within the correctional system, including increased Aboriginal control over programs and services for Aboriginal offenders (Solicitor General 1988a, 10). Likewise, the Daubney Committee called for Aboriginal-specific programming that was designed and delivered by Aboriginal peoples (Canada 1988). Increased hiring was thought to "assist in good communications and greatly enrich the professional treatment of Aboriginal offenders" (Solicitor General 1988a, 38). The Task Force also recommended an increased number of Aboriginal board members to heighten "trust between the National Parole Board and Aboriginal offenders" and to "lead to parole decisions which are consistent with conditions in the North and Aboriginal communities" (41). Furthermore, a greater representation of Aboriginal staff at both regional and national offices was seen as a way to ensure all locations had "Aboriginal expertise" available (42). The inclusion of diverse staff consequently emerges as a key institutional strategy to provide a more culturally appropriate environment. Yet, although the integration of Aboriginal staff and organizations into penal institutions may be a practice of inclusion, it is also selective, emphasizing certain attributes (e.g., spirituality and cultural practices) and neutralizing others (e.g., demands for Aboriginal control of justice processes) (Jaccoud and Felices 1999, 86). I address this issue in greater detail in Chapter 4, where I discuss elder-assisted hearings and community-assisted hearings.

Both the Daubney Committee (Canada 1988) and the Task Force (Solicitor General 1988a) recommended greater participation of Aboriginal communities and agencies in the parole and conditional release process. More specifically, the Task Force advocated the greater participation of Aboriginal organizations and/or community councils in the supervision of Aboriginal offenders and post-release services as a way of improving their chances on conditional release (Solicitor General 1988a). Without the involvement of Aboriginal communities and organizations, the PBC "often has no option but to reject their release plan if it involves returning to those communities" (73). In order to improve the likelihood of Aboriginal offenders being accepted back into their communities, the Task Force recommended greater participation of Aboriginal community leadership in release decision making, such as through the provision of advice on release conditions (76-77). Similarly, the Daubney Committee (Canada 1988) recommended that the PBC enable Aboriginal communities that want to accept returning offenders to assume responsibility for reintegrating them. I discuss the idea of greater involvement of Aboriginal communities in the parole process in more depth in Chapter 4, where I suggest that these solutions, among other things, shift the onus away from the government and onto Aboriginal communities, which are expected to assume responsibility for Aboriginal offenders as a practice of culturally appropriate punishment (Andersen 1999).

Another solution put forth in several official documents relates to training for non-Aboriginal staff, such as orientation training on Aboriginal issues (Solicitor General 1975) and sensitization and awareness education for staff so that the specific cultural and spiritual needs of Aboriginal offenders can be met (Solicitor General 1984; Canada 1988). Training was viewed as a necessary mechanism for promoting acceptance of cultural difference as a means of being responsive to Aboriginal offenders' needs (Solicitor General 1984, 51). The Task Force also recommended cultural awareness and sensitivity training based on a perceived "lack of understanding on the part of decision-makers about Aboriginal Peoples and Cultures" as well as "uneasiness" on the part of Correctional Service of Canada and Parole Board of Canada personnel due to difficulties gauging the "reactions of Aboriginal offenders in an interview situation" (Solicitor General 1988a, 44). The solution of sensitivity training stems from the initial framing of the problem facing Aboriginal offenders as a matter of insensitivity – that is, insensitive parole boards and conditional release practices have contributed to poor parole performance among Aboriginal offenders (I analyze the issue of training in Chapter 3).

In terms of unique solutions to the problem of Indigeneity, the Task Force recommended including Aboriginal elders in decision-making processes at the

PBC (Solicitor General 1988a). The Final Report indicates that, for three reasons, Aboriginal elders were seen to provide more accurate assessments of Aboriginal offenders than were PBC personnel. These had to do with:

(a) an Elder's understanding of Aboriginal communities and their degree of acceptance of a released inmate; (b) an understanding of Aboriginal spiritual and cultural programs, and whether the inmate has benefited from those programs; and (c) the willingness of Aboriginal inmates to discuss their problems and aspirations with Elders who, in turn, listen to the inmates in an appropriate manner. (37-38)

However, it appears that not all members of the Task Force agreed that elders were capable of making more accurate assessments of Aboriginal offenders or that their assessments of conditional release decision making should replace those of other professionals. Instead, the Task Force recommended that elders, if requested by the offender, be allowed to submit assessments to the PBC on behalf of the offender and that these be considered on par with those of other professionals. The Task Force noted that this would lead to more equitable decision making (Solicitor General 1988a, 38) as elders' assessments could provide more accurate information about Aboriginal offenders and their release plans. As noted in the previous section, concerns were raised that inappropriate decision making was occurring with regard to Aboriginal offenders in cases in which (white) board members were using non-Aboriginal standards to assess them (see Solicitor General 1981; Canada 1988). Here, the Task Force presents an argument for integrating new forms of knowledge into conditional release decision making and for broadening the scope of expertise recognized by the PBC – a recommendation that was eventually implemented (see Chapter 4).

Reinforcing the Need for Change

The Task Force's report was debated in a session of the House of Commons on November 27, 1990, with then NDP member of Parliament John Brewin making a motion for the government to immediately implement the Task Force's recommendations (Canada 1990a, 15820). The ensuing discussion of the report reflected general agreement among the MPs participating in the debate that the situation of Aboriginal peoples needed to be addressed. However, from the perspective of the government, voiced by Benno Friesen, then parliamentary secretary to the Solicitor General of Canada, actions were already being taken to implement the recommendations, including an "accelerated implementation plan" by the CSC (Canada 1990a, 15824).[5] The CSC was viewed by several MPs

– with the exception of Brewin – as being capable of bringing about change through adjustments to its operating procedures, including its strategic planning and mission statement. The motion was subsequently dropped from the Order Paper.

Non-governmental voices also pressed for reforms to improve the situation of Aboriginal peoples in the penal system. The report of the Canadian Bar Association (CBA) Committee on Imprisonment and Release, entitled *Locking Up Natives in Canada* (Jackson 1988), reinforced several of the solutions raised by the Task Force and Daubney Committee. However, the CBA Committee was more forceful in its critique of the criminal justice system's treatment of Aboriginal peoples and pushed for more fundamental structural and organizational changes. For instance, it situated the overrepresentation of Aboriginal peoples within the correctional system in the context of poverty, racist stereotyping, colonization, and alcoholism, noting that "the prison has become for many young native people the contemporary equivalent of what the Indian residential school represented for their parents" (3-4). In addition, the CBA Committee argued for Aboriginal self-determination and for creating Indigenous justice systems rather than solely accommodating Aboriginal difference within the mainstream criminal justice system – the approach advocated by the Task Force.

Like the Task Force and Daubney Committee, the CBA Committee was also supportive of the PBC working with Aboriginal communities to ensure that offenders could be released on parole to their communities (Jackson 1988, 101). However, it favoured legislative changes that required penal programming to be "particularly suited to serving the spiritual and cultural needs of Aboriginal offenders" (109). Interestingly, the CBA Committee observed that some Aboriginal-led initiatives have been thwarted by correctional authorities – for example, when programs become "transformed ... through the process of fitting into" the correctional bureaucracy (96-97). For instance, the CBA Committee noted that the proposals put forth by Aboriginal organizations tended to be modified through negotiations with penal institutions prior to implementation. This being the case, it argued that programs should be designed and delivered in consultation with Aboriginal offender groups and community organizations, presumably as a way to mitigate the co-optation of these initiatives.

Importantly, the CBA Committee report illustrates alternative knowledges regarding how to resolve the problems experienced by Aboriginal offenders. These knowledges offer solutions based in the context of Aboriginal self-determination and are ensured through legislative changes rather than solely

Putting Gender, Race, and Culture on the Penal Agenda

through reforms to institutional policies and practices (Jackson 1988). The framing of Aboriginal difference by the CBA Committee favours creating Aboriginal models of punishment rather than modifying mainstream practices in order to accommodate Aboriginality. However, as I show, these solutions have not been adopted within the *CCRA*. The dominant framing of Aboriginality as something that can be accommodated within the existing system limits the options for reform.

Gender Discrimination and the Partitioning of Difference

The last few decades of the twentieth century also saw increasing concern about the imprisonment of female offenders and the lack of gender-appropriate policies and practices. In Canada during the 1970s and 1980s, specific focus was directed towards the impact of incarceration on female prisoners as a result of the conditions at the Prison for Women in Kingston, Ontario. The growing awareness of issues faced by female offenders was associated with the larger women's movement in Canada and the increasing number of feminist interventions through the courts (Hayman 2006). The greater involvement of women in the realm of policy making within government also focused attention on women's equality struggles (Rankin and Vickers 2001). In relation to penal change, "feminist penal reformers began to actively pursue liberal, rights-based equality strategies to secure equal access to prison and community programs for female offenders and to improve their conditions of confinement" (Hannah-Moffat 2001, 134). Reformers and advocates also pressured the government to develop "appropriate" responses to female prisoners based on the recognition of gender differences among women and men. In the following, I analyze the discussions about female offenders emerging from key governmental reports and inquiries. I argue that the framing of the problem as one of gender discrimination functions to partition various aspects of difference, such that certain female offenders (e.g., Aboriginal women) are viewed as doubly disadvantaged when racial discrimination is added to gender discrimination. This framing prevents an intersectional analysis of the various problems facing female offenders as a diverse population.

Although the problem for Aboriginal peoples was their overrepresentation in the penal system, for female offenders it was underrepresentation – they were "too few to count" (Adelberg and Currie 1987).[6] The small number of women in prison was viewed as the main factor in their inequitable treatment (Ekstedt and Griffiths 1988). Most government-led correctional initiatives focused on female offenders during the 1970s and 1980s examined the problems faced by women prisoners due to their small numbers. In particular, the primary concern was the Prison for Women, including issues of geographic dislocation and the lack of gender-appropriate programming and services (Hannah-Moffat 2001; Hayman 2006). However, concerns around the Prison for Women were nothing new. As Ekstedt and Griffiths (1988, 336) note, "every major correctional inquiry in Canada has recommended closure of the Prison [for Women]," including Archambault (in 1938), Fauteux (in 1956), and Ouimet (in 1969), although, as Hayman (2006, 20) observes, these calls took place within broader discussions of federal imprisonment rather than specific discussions of female offenders.

The 1970s and 1980s also witnessed greater attention to the female offender as an object of knowledge, or what Snider (2003, 354) calls a "punishable subject." As with Aboriginal offenders, so with female offenders: the proliferation of governmental reports and inquiries work to constitute them in particular ways through knowledge claims about who they are and what they need. One of the earliest reports to comment on the specific circumstances of federally sentenced women was the Royal Commission on the Status of Women in 1970. Although the commission's report made a number of recommendations, of interest here are its calls for revisions of the *Prisons and Reformatories Act* to eliminate discriminatory provisions, promote greater cooperation with Aboriginal communities, create halfway houses for female offenders, and ensure the availability of appropriate services and programs for Aboriginal and francophone female offenders (Hannah-Moffat 2001; Hayman 2006).

The commission's recommendations were echoed in subsequent reports and reviews in the late 1970s that examined, and made recommendations on, the issue of the female offender. For example, in 1977, the National Advisory Committee on the Female Offender echoed themes raised by the commission's report, including the "need for more community-based residences, temporary release, and better institutional programs linked (wherever possible) to the community" (Ekstedt and Griffiths 1988, 336). A year later, in 1978, the National Planning Committee on the Female Offender, in its assessment of the Advisory Committee's report, recommended the creation of regional federal facilities and the development of community-based residential centres (CBRCs) for women. Also in 1978, the Joint Committee to Study Alternatives for the Housing of the Federal Female Offender was convened by the Commissioner of Corrections to examine the issue of correctional facilities for women offenders. Like the Planning Committee, the Joint Committee also advocated for the increased use of CBRCs for women as well as exchange of service agreements with the provinces to allow for the housing of federally sentenced female prisoners in provincial facilities (Ekstedt and Griffiths 1988). These recommendations echo the approaches put forth for Aboriginal offenders in that the solutions to female difference could be accommodated within the existing system through minor adaptations, such as increased aftercare services and improved programming.

Concerns about female offenders and the problems posed by the Prison for Women continued to be raised in several government reports related to parole and conditional release during the 1980s. For instance, the *Solicitor General's Study of Conditional Release: Report of the Working Group*, published in 1981, points to the difficulties created through the geographic centralization of the Prison for Women and the lack of meaningful correctional programming and conditional release planning (Solicitor General 1981). It recommends further study of three possible changes to the system to help alleviate these difficulties:

> First, more liberal use could be made of parole by exception and day parole to move women closer to their home communities under correctional supervision. Second, government funds could be made available to finance releases to areas distant from PW [Prison for Women]. Third, there may be a need for a special caseworker at PW to help deal with the special release planning and coordination problems experienced by women. (153)

The recommendations signal an approach to reform that encourages minor tweaking of the system and exceptions that would enable female offenders to be better accommodated through special activities within existing structures and practices. Concerns about the Prison for Women continued in the mid-1980s, with the Advisory Committee to the Solicitor General of Canada on the Management of Correctional Institutions recommending the regionalization of "the accommodation of federal female offenders across the country" to reduce geographic isolation (Solicitor General 1984, 42).

Both the *Final Report of the Task Force on Aboriginal Peoples in Federal Corrections* (Solicitor General 1988a) and the Daubney Committee (Canada 1988) report were critical of the centralized nature of women's imprisonment at the Prison for Women. The Daubney Committee's tour of the Prison for Women cemented its acceptance of the Canadian Association of Elizabeth Fry Societies' submissions on the prison's geographical isolation, overly high security level, and unequal provision of programs. A potential solution to the latter problem was for correctional programs to "be responsive to the needs, aspirations and potential of women offenders" (Canada 1988, 235, emphasis removed). The Daubney Committee also chastised the CSC for its reluctance to expand halfway houses for women offenders because their numbers were too small and were therefore viewed as not being cost-efficient. To best address the needs of female offenders, the Daubney Committee recommended the creation of a task force on federal female offenders to plan for the closure of the Prison for Women and to address the problems associated with programming for female offenders (Canada 1988).

The Task Force and Daubney Committee reports identify Aboriginal women offenders as experiencing additional difficulties due to their gendered and racialized identities. Aboriginal women offenders are constituted as a special group of women within the female offender population and are framed as dually discriminated against. This framing reflects an additive approach that understands "women" as a disadvantaged group due to gender, while non-white women are even more disadvantaged as a group due to race; additional disadvantages (e.g., class, ability, sexuality, etc.) can be tacked on as appropriate (Grabham et al. 2009). For example, according to the Daubney Committee, "imprisoned Native women are triply disadvantaged: they suffer the pains of incarceration common to all prisoners; in addition they experience both the pains Native prisoners feel as a result of their cultural dislocation and those which women prisoners experience as a result of being incarcerated far from home and family" (Canada 1988, 237). Consistent with this framing, the Task Force notes that Aboriginal women offenders encounter additional difficulties, including a lack of specific (i.e., cultural) programming and day parole facilities (Solicitor General 1988a). Scholars such as hooks (1981), Razack (1998), Yuval-Davis (2006), and Grabham et al. (2009) argue that the framing of inequalities as additive, rather than as intersectional, works to partition differences and reinforce approaches to women that tend to privilege one form of difference over others. A similar process appears to be occurring here through the framing of gender and cultural difference as being additive and resulting in dual or triple disadvantage. Yet the Daubney Committee also observes that programming should "be appropriate to Native female offenders in terms of both culture *and* gender" (Canada 1988, 237, emphasis in original) in order to address dual discrimination. Here, the committee hints at the importance of programming that addresses the intersectionality of culture and gender, but it does not consider exactly how these issues should come together.

Towards Gender Justice[7]
During the late 1980s and early 1990s, several feminist-inspired reform efforts continued to push for change in the treatment of female offenders. The deteriorating conditions at the Prison for Women, including the suicides of several Aboriginal prisoners, helped spark the launch of a *Charter* challenge against

Putting Gender, Race, and Culture on the Penal Agenda

the CSC by the Women's Legal and Education Fund (LEAF) in 1987 (Hannah-Moffat 2001). In LEAF's view, the CSC's treatment of female offenders violated their section 15 rights on the basis of sexual discrimination. According to Hannah-Moffat (2001), this *Charter* challenge was postponed in anticipation of the release of a key reform document intended to address the problems facing women prisoners: the report of the Task Force on Federally Sentenced Women (TFFSW), *Creating Choices*. This reform document encapsulates feminist knowledges that constitute female offenders as different and in need of "women-centred" models of punishment (Hannah-Moffat 2001, 2002; Hayman 2006).

The TFFSW was created in 1989 by the Solicitor General with the mandate "to examine the correctional management of federally sentenced women from the commencement of sentence to the date of warrant expiry and to develop a plan which will guide and direct the process in a manner that is responsive to the unique and special needs of this group" (TFFSW 1990, n.pag, emphasis removed). Its terms of reference were later amended to "stress the over-representation of Aboriginal people in the Canadian criminal justice system as well as the significant impact of Aboriginal experience in clarifying the un-resolved problems affecting federally sentenced women" (ibid.). The TFFSW's primary goal was closing the Prison for Women and regionalizing women's imprisonment in Canada.

Of the government initiatives discussed so far in this chapter, the TFFSW and its report, *Creating Choices*, published in 1990, has received the most critical scholarly attention (see, for example, Hannah-Moffat and Shaw 2000; Hannah-Moffat 2001, 2002; Hayman 2006). The TFFSW was unique in that it was comprised of representatives from both government and feminist non-profit advocacy organizations (Hannah-Moffat and Shaw 2000; Hayman 2006). It was also attentive to the unique issues faced by Aboriginal women offenders. Al-though much of *Creating Choices* focuses on creating a holistic and women-centred model of corrections, it touches upon issues related to conditional release. The TFFSW proposed a community release strategy that would allow for additional accommodation for women on conditional release, such as half-way houses, Aboriginal centres, home placements, and multi-use women's centres, which provide women-centred and Aboriginal-specific programming and services. This strategy would also permit community support workers to assist women offenders to create personal plans during their incarceration so that they could prepare for release as soon as they were eligible (TFFSW 1990).

In relation to the larger reform movement, *Creating Choices* makes a strong argument for the recognition of women (not necessarily gender) and Aboriginality within the operation and design of the country's penitentiaries for women. The TFFSW recognized that legislative change was needed in order to meet its goals and bring its recommendations to fruition; however, its mandate was limited by the requirement for it to "develop a plan which [could] be implemented within current legislation" (TFFSW 1990). As noted in its report, this

> created severe constraints. It obligated the Task Force to exclude from full consideration provincially sentenced women, the impact of the pre-sentence period and the issue of Aboriginal self-determination with respect to corrections. In addition, the legislative limitations precluded the formulation of a community-based correctional system. (ibid.)

It is therefore interesting that the TFFSW's mandate was limited to making recommendations within the legislative framework existing in the late 1980s, when, at the same time, the federal government was undertaking a comprehensive correctional law reform project.

Penal Reform in Action: The Correctional Law Review

Taken together, the increased focus on Canada's correctional system as a whole during the 1970s, 1980s, and early 1990s brought greater attention to the parole system as well as to the specific issues faced by Aboriginal peoples and women under penal control, eventually leading to a large-scale reform process on the part of the federal government to revamp the legislation governing corrections and conditional release. The coalescing of diversity and gender agendas enabled these reforms to move forward in a temporal moment characterized by both institutional and broader public concern about the rights of these groups to more fair and appropriate punishment. As one informant recalled, there was growing recognition that "what's fair for everybody isn't always fair for certain groups that have particular needs or particular problems or just react differently [because] their circumstances are different" (Interview 9). At the same time, the existence of new legal mechanisms – such as the *Charter* – allowed for right claims if institutions did not respond to calls for changes, as seen with LEAF's challenge on behalf of federally sentenced women (Hannah-Moffat 2001). The *Charter* and the resultant Correctional Law Review project (part of the larger Criminal Law Review) were significant factors in the enactment of a new piece of legislation, the *CCRA*, on June 18, 1992. In this section, I consider the reform efforts led by the Correctional Law Review, paying specific attention to how issues of diversity and gender are taken up and incorporated into the new legislation.

The roots of the *CCRA* lie in the Criminal Law Review project, which began in 1979, and its policy document, *The Criminal Law in Canadian Society*, published in 1982 (McPhail 1999). The Criminal Law Review was launched after a federal-provincial meeting of ministers responsible for criminal justice in October 1979. The ministers agreed that a thorough review of the *Criminal Code* was needed in order to enact "a modern, responsive and effective Canadian criminal law" (Canada 1982, 10). In addition, the review was deemed necessary to address what McPhail (1999, 2) calls a "crisis of legitimacy" of the law and the criminal justice system, largely due to the public's fear of crime and increased burdens on the system in the 1970s. This more general context for the Criminal Law Review points to issues of accountability and reputation for the government, whose failure to bring about a coherent and modern approach to criminal justice "would be met, at best, by public ambivalence and, at worst, by disrepute" (McPhail 1999, 2-3). Griffiths (1988) contends that the Criminal Law Review was created in part due to increasing judicial scrutiny of corrections and conditional release operations during the late 1970s and early 1980s.

According to one informant, *The Criminal Law in Canadian Society* comprised a "policy framework for criminal law" that "articulated a lot of principles about sentencing and corrections, [such as] the use of restraint in application of criminal law to solve social problems, restraint in the number of people we send to prison, and asked a number of questions" (Interview 1). These questions focused on determining "the proper scope, purpose and objectives of the criminal law" (Canada 1982, 2). *The Criminal Law in Canadian Society* recognizes the importance of the *Charter*, both in terms of its broader impact on human rights legislation and the issue of compliance of law and policy with *Charter* principles. Interestingly, the document concludes by noting that the treatment of Aboriginal offenders and female offenders received no discussion because such issues were considered to be peripheral to its scope rather than to be central aspects of criminal law. In this way, issues of culture and gender were relegated to the sidelines of penal reform. This initial framing is important as it reinforces the designation of non-white and female offenders as other, such that difference becomes a "special project" to be managed outside the "real" work of penal institutions.

Building off *The Criminal Law in Canadian Society*, and as part of the larger Criminal Law Review, the Correctional Law Review (CLR) project was established to focus specifically on issues related to corrections and conditional release law. As one informant reveals,

> there was a recognition that the *Penitentiary Act* and *Parole Act* had not kept up with developments ... They had been amended along the way but it had

been piecemeal reform, so the decision of the government was to launch this thing called the Correctional Law Review to think about what should a modern legislative framework look like. (Interview 1)

This ad hoc development and the lack of a clear statement of principles or philosophy in these pieces of legislation constituted the key problems addressed by the CLR (Solicitor General 1986b, 57-58).

The CLR was conducted by a team working in the Policy Branch of the Solicitor General of Canada, along with the aid of a working group comprised of members from the CSC, PBC, and Department of Justice (McPhail 1999). The CLR was carried out between 1986 and 1988 and yielded nine working papers that outlined the ideas, principles, and philosophies that were to guide and influence the development of corrections and conditional release law and policy. These working papers fed into the government's proposals, *Directions for Reform*, published in 1990, which formed the basis of the *CCRA*. Reflecting back on the CLR, one informant notes that "it was an exciting time to put it mildly ... it was just a massive exercise and taken very seriously" (Interview 1). The CLR focused on the consolidation of five pieces of federal legislation – *Solicitor General Act, Penitentiary Act, Parole Act, Prisons and Reformatories Act,* and *Transfer of Offenders Act* – as well as certain sections of the *Criminal Code*. It also consulted widely with provincial and territorial jurisdictions, victims' groups, non-profit service agencies, academics, members of the public, all levels of the court, inmates, and correctional staff in order to garner feedback on its proposals (McPhail 1999).

The working papers of the CLR, which total nearly five hundred pages, cover a number of philosophical and substantive issues related to correctional and conditional release law in Canada. The first two working papers outline the guiding philosophy for corrections and the framework for the CLR. The remaining papers focus on substantive issues, including conditional release, inmate rights, the powers of correctional staff, Aboriginal peoples, federal-provincial issues, and mental health services for inmates. These papers reflect the impact of the *Charter* on corrections and conditional release law. Indeed, one of the principal tasks of the CLR was "to ensure that all correctional legislation and practice conform with the *Charter*" (Solicitor General 1986b, 61).[8] The reform process was geared towards the production of legislation that avoided or minimized litigation on the basis of *Charter* rights and the common law duty of fairness.[9] Litigation was seen as "costly, slow and (often for reasons of slowness alone) ineffective to serve as an adequate remedy for the hundreds of decisions made daily by correctional authorities in relation to inmates" (Solicitor

Putting Gender, Race, and Culture on the Penal Agenda

General 1986a, 32). The creation of new legislation was one way the government could minimize the legal risks posed by litigation, particularly in relation to human rights complaints.

The CLR's working papers on conditional release (Solicitor General 1986a) and Aboriginal peoples (Solicitor General 1988b) highlight many of the same concerns related to Aboriginal offenders raised in early government reports. The problems of overrepresentation, cultural difference, and poor parole performance emerge once again as dominant themes and are framed as key areas in need of reform. Governmental concern around Aboriginal offenders is positioned in relation to the recognition of this population as a special "group warranting specific attention both because of the special legal status of Aboriginal peoples and because of the serious ongoing problem of their substantial overrepresentation in the correctional system and other manifestations of their situation as a traditionally disadvantaged group" (352). The working paper functions to constitute Aboriginal offenders' difference vis-à-vis non-Aboriginal offenders "in terms of their attitudes, values, interests, identities and backgrounds" (355). The cultural uniqueness of Aboriginal offenders is framed as making things difficult for conventional methods, such as those related to pre- and post-release planning (Solicitor General 1986a, 95). The framing of Aboriginal offenders within this document suggests that they are understood to have special cultural, spiritual, and social needs that can be accommodated as add-ons to the mainstream penal system (Monture 2006).

In relation to parole and conditional release, the CLR identifies several problems for Aboriginal offenders. First, there is the tendency of more Aboriginal than non-Aboriginal offenders to waive their rights to parole hearings, suggesting that the former are not able to benefit from gradual release as are the latter. Second, the CLR points to the unique challenges for successful reintegration within Aboriginal communities due to the exclusion of Aboriginal communities from effective participation in the parole preparation process and the development of reintegration plans for Aboriginal offenders (Solicitor General 1988b). In other words, Aboriginal communities have not been able to participate in the parole process. Concerns are also raised about the appropriateness of parole decision-making practices related to Aboriginal offenders as well as a lack of Aboriginal representation among PBC board members and staff. This lack of representation is linked to a limited understanding of Aboriginal offenders and inappropriate and inadequate parole planning, criteria, and assessments.

These failures are connected to concerns over potential *Charter* challenges if the PBC's "decisions, procedures and conditions of parole could be demonstrated to de facto discriminate against Native inmates" (Solicitor General 1988b, 365). More generally, the uniqueness of Aboriginal offenders due to their treaty rights and specific provisions in various constitutional documents is identified as a potential source of litigation, particularly in cases involving claims of systemic discrimination. According to the CLR, "even where a law or program is apparently neutral on its face, it may have a different impact on some minority groups than on the mainstream" (ibid.). The CLR recognizes the potential for discriminatory treatment to arise from legislation or policies that appear fair or non-biased but that, in practice, work to the detriment of Aboriginal offenders. Consequently, a key focus for the CLR was to propose strategies to reduce the risk of litigation.

The working papers propose some legislative and policy approaches to alleviate the aforementioned problems facing Aboriginal offenders. More specifically, one working paper makes a case for the new legislation to include specific provisions for this population:

> The unique status of Canada's aboriginal peoples, and their acute problems once they arrive in correctional care suggests that there is merit in statutory entrenchment of appropriate protections. Legislation in this area would clearly demonstrate the government's concern to improve the situation of aboriginal people in corrections ... Grounding aboriginal corrections policy in legislation gives such policy greater authority, and provides explicit protection for specific entitlements such as religious freedom. (Solicitor General 1988b, 374)

This excerpt is illustrative in several ways. First, the focus on "appropriate protections" and "specific entitlements" reflects the framing of Aboriginal difference as something that can be accommodated within the mainstream justice system (Monture 2006). It also works to downplay difference, so that entitlements are restricted to things like religious freedom. Second, the statement about governmental concern hints at an orientation towards diversity that is connected to issues of reputation and the imperative to appear responsive to the plight of disadvantaged groups of offenders, as would be expected given the political nature of the document. The entrenchment of Aboriginal corrections policy within legislation also speaks to the need to compel penal institutions to address Aboriginal offenders' needs, such as in cases in which desire to do so is lacking. The grounding of such policy in legislation would also provide an opportunity for advocates to hold institutions to account through litigation.

Based on the framing of the problems for Aboriginal offenders in relation to conditional release, as noted above, the proposed reforms are unsurprising.

For instance, the CLR proposes a provision in correctional law allowing Aboriginal communities greater participation in conditional release planning, programming, and supervision (Solicitor General 1988b). Given the concerns over inappropriate parole decision-making practices, the issues of staff recruitment and training are raised, along with the recommendation of a provision requiring that "specific Native awareness training [be provided] to all staff coming into contact with Native offenders" (381). The possibility of a legislated requirement for an affirmative action program to increase the hiring and promotion of Aboriginal staff is also considered. Ostensibly, these reforms would increase Aboriginal representation among PBC board members and staff and subsequently improve organizational knowledge and understanding of Aboriginal offenders and appropriate parole planning, criteria, and assessments. Of note is the lack of attention that the CLR and its working papers pay to the issue of gender, or female offenders (more specifically), or to the issues of race, ethnicity, or culture (with the exception of Aboriginal offenders). Absent from the working papers is any discussion of principles that reflects the need of the correctional and parole systems to take into account the specific needs of female offenders. As discussed above, significant consideration was given to Aboriginal-specific provisions within the proposed legislation so as to help ameliorate the disadvantages experienced by this population.

Setting the Stage: Directions for Reform

The CLR working papers outlined several proposals for reform in relation to Aboriginal offenders, with a notable lack of attention to gender or other forms of racialized difference. The preceding discussion attempts to show how the constitution of problems facing Aboriginal and female offenders are eventually made actionable in "ways that fit with the dominant culture and the power structure upon which it rests" (Garland 2001, 26). In this section, I consider the framing of key issues related to diversity within the broader context of reform efforts directed at corrections and conditional release. The compartmentalization of difference can be seen in the tendency to approach certain differences (e.g., gender *or* Aboriginality) separately and as being relevant to specific contexts (e.g., programming or services).

In 1990, the federal government published a green paper entitled *Directions for Reform: A Framework for Sentencing, Corrections and Conditional Release* (Canada 1990b), which was accompanied by the papers *Directions for Reform in Corrections and Conditional Release* (Canada 1990c) and *Directions for Reform in Sentencing* (Canada 1990d). As one informant recalls, *Directions for Reform* "was intended to be a comprehensive response to the Daubney Committee, to the various inquiries into [the] community tragedies, and to be roll up of the Correctional Law Review" (Interview 1). Taken together, the green papers formed a consultation package that outlined proposals for policy and legislative changes related to sentencing, corrections, and conditional release. According to the same informant, *Directions for Reform* reflects the idea that any reforms to the criminal justice system must approach the system as a whole: one "can't think about corrections without also thinking about what's going on at sentencing, and what criminal justice should be about" (Interview 1). In this sense, the green papers reject "patchwork, *ad hoc* approaches" to criminal justice reform and espouse the CLR's goal of "creating a coherent, integrated set of rules in corrections" (Canada 1990b, 10).

In the introduction to *Directions for Reform*, the government notes a number of problems with sentencing, corrections, and conditional release systems, including poor public perception, unmet concerns of victims, lack of information sharing between agencies, lack of non-carceral programs, sentencing disparities, over-reliance on incarceration, treatment and assessment of offenders, rehabilitation, and public concern about conditional release (Canada 1990b, 2-3). It also recognizes the special needs of Aboriginal and women offenders as well as of long-term offenders, sex offenders, and mentally disordered offenders. The proposed reforms are contextualized in relation to the *Charter* and speak to the criticisms and recommendations raised by the Daubney Committee.

Directions for Reform is significant in that it makes some strong statements about gender and diversity, particularly in relation to corrections and conditional release.[10] It states:

> It can be said that our prison system is geared to managing a homogeneous population of offenders. As much as it has inadequacies in its primary focus, its shortcomings are unfortunately even more acute for women, Aboriginal People, ethnic groups, the mentally disturbed, and other distinct groups. The effectiveness of our system, its fairness, and its even-handedness are called into question by our approach to these groups. (Canada 1990b, 10)

The reference to "a homogenous population" once again illuminates the whiteness – and maleness – of the penal system. In relation to women offenders, the paper points to the small number of federally sentenced women as the main reason for the lack of facilities and programs for them. For Aboriginal offenders, it notes the overrepresentation of Aboriginal people among the penitentiary population and suggests this disparity is likely to increase if steps are not taken

Putting Gender, Race, and Culture on the Penal Agenda

to prevent the incarceration of Aboriginal people in the first place. The paper also argues that the special needs of Aboriginal offenders – and the doubly special needs of Aboriginal women offenders – must be met in order to reduce recidivism and to ensure fair treatment in the conditional release process (Canada 1990b). According to the government, "part of the solution must lie in recognizing that traditional Aboriginal community, spiritual and cultural values are not the same as those of non-Aboriginal communities" (11). Ostensibly, these differences must be taken into account in order to "deal fairly and effectively with Aboriginal offenders" (ibid.). As such, the government proposed a principle for corrections that requires correctional policies, programs, and practices that "respect gender, ethnic and cultural differences, and [that] should be responsive to the needs of women and Aboriginal People, as well as [to] the needs of other groups of offenders with special needs" (18). No such provision is suggested for sentencing or conditional release.

The companion paper, *Directions for Reform in Corrections and Conditional Release*, outlines proposals for policy and legislative changes related to these key areas. It states that the "fundamental goal of corrections and conditional release reform is to improve public safety, correctional effectiveness, and public confidence," which can be accomplished through a "clear set of rules, as well as effective practices" (Canada 1990c, 1). The paper indicates that the paramount consideration for the corrections and conditional release systems is the protection of the public. Issues of gender and diversity are not raised within this companion paper in relation to conditional release. They do, however, appear in the chapter on corrections and, more specifically, in connection to programming. In this way, difference is compartmentalized as being relevant to only some aspects of punishment and not others. The paper notes that the correctional system has been criticized by women's groups and other organizations "for failing to rectify the disparity in treatment between male and female inmates in relation to the availability of programs and services, geographic location and security classification" (35). It mentions the TFFSW and states that the government "will be making proposals in relation to programs, facilities and resources for female offenders once it has had an opportunity to consider the Task Force Report, as well as other opinions and recommendations in this area" (ibid.). However, the paper also indicates that the new legislation will contain provisions requiring that correctional programs and services be "particularly suited to serving the needs of female offenders" (ibid.). In these ways, gender issues are reduced to concerns around gender-specific programming and services.

The issues facing Aboriginal peoples are largely discussed in relation to programming and service contracts with Aboriginal communities or agencies so that they can take up some of the punishment of Aboriginal offenders. Here, Aboriginal communities can be responsibilized for addressing the structural and systemic problems facing Aboriginal offenders (Andersen 1999). The paper also emphasizes the importance of consulting with Aboriginal groups so that the CSC can better respond to the special needs of Aboriginal offenders. In particular, it argues that these consultations will aid in the development and implementation of programs and address the problem of the disproportionate numbers of Aboriginal peoples within the correctional system. In relation to conditional release, the government proposes training workshops for PBC members so that they have increased sensitivity towards, and better knowledge of, Aboriginal issues as well as requiring that all new policies be assessed as to their impact on Aboriginal offenders (Canada 1990c, 35).

The aforementioned papers were put forth for consultation among interested members of the public, academics, criminal justice professionals, service providers, and inmates. As one informant recalls, there was "a team of people dedicated to [consultations] ... we just wanted to hear from all perspectives because, you know, in criminal justice there's no single right answer usually, there's a lot of competing points of view, and the idea was to try to find the right balance" (Interview 1). The *CCRA* was the end product of the CLR and this final consultation process.[11]

The Corrections and Conditional Release Act

Bill C-36 was presented in the House of Commons for its second reading on November 4, 1991,[12] by Doug Lewis, then solicitor general of Canada. In his presentation of the bill to Parliament, Lewis stressed the paramount focus on public safety, stressing that "if the release of an offender threatens society, the offender will not be released" (Canada 1991, 4430). The proposed legislation was framed in relation to the "plight of victims" and the need for the system to better meet victims' needs and to restore public confidence (ibid.). The specific issues facing female and Aboriginal offenders were noted briefly towards the end of Lewis's remarks. In particular, Lewis mentioned the closure of the Prison for Women and the construction of regional facilities as well as the expansion of correctional programming for Aboriginal offenders (4434) as key initiatives to address gender and Aboriginal difference supported by the proposed legislation.

The *Corrections and Conditional Release Act* is significant because, for the first time, the legislation recognizes – albeit partially and selectively – gender, cultural, and ethnic issues. Part I of the *CCRA*, which focuses on "Institutional and Community Corrections," lists among its principles "that correctional policies, programs and practices respect gender, ethnic, cultural and linguistic differences and be responsive to the special needs of women and aboriginal peoples, as well as to the needs of other groups of offenders with special requirements" (s.4(h)). Part I also outlines the special considerations for programs for women offenders, such that the CSC should ensure the provision of programs that address their needs (s.77(a)), and are (in theory) to be developed in consultation with women's groups and others who have experience with, and expertise on, female offenders (s.77(b)). Similarly, Part I of the *CCRA* addresses the special circumstances of Aboriginal offenders. Sections 80 to 84 call for the provision of programs developed on the basis of Aboriginal offenders' needs, the creation of advisory committees to provide advice to the CSC on Aboriginal issues in consultation with local Aboriginal communities, the recognition of Aboriginal spirituality and spiritual leaders as being on par with other religions and religious leaders, and the provision of information to Aboriginal communities about prisoners' parole application, such that the communities can aid in their integration.

Part II of the *CCRA*, entitled "Conditional Release, Detention and Long-Term Supervision," interestingly, does not contain a specific principle related to gender and/or ethnic or cultural issues. However, the Organization of the Board section contains a clause requiring that PBC policies "respect gender, ethnic, cultural and linguistic differences and be responsive to the special needs of women and aboriginal peoples, as well as to the needs of other groups of offenders with special requirements" (s.151(3)). It remains to be seen why the drafters of the *CCRA* did not include the above clause as part of its general principles, as in Part I. However, as I discuss later on in this book, it appears that the PBC has interpreted the *CCRA* in such a way that gender and diversity have become increasingly relevant to the institution's policies and practices. More specifically, through the creation of the Aboriginal and Diversity Initiatives section, the PBC is attempting to respond to the "growing ethnocultural diversity within Canada's federal offender population" and the *CCRA*'s directive that the PBC must "develop policies and processes which are sensitive to [Aboriginal offenders'] circumstances and needs" (PBC 2010c, n.pag).

The compartmentalization of gender and diversity as being applicable to certain contexts (e.g., programming and community consultation) enables institutions to narrowly interpret when and how diversity matters. In addition, several informants expressed some reservation as to the ability of the *CCRA* to bring about change in relation to the special needs related to gender, Aboriginality, and ethnoculturalism. One informant noted that the *CCRA* only contains one paragraph "that speaks to women, Aboriginal, whatever, in Part II, and it's only in relation to our policies" (Interview 7). The same informant believed that the principle would be more effective if it were broadened beyond PBC policies to include its approaches. Another informant felt that the *CCRA*, as a whole, did not have enough "meat" to compel the PBC to "look at ethnicity" or "women," which was viewed as a shortcoming, especially given the changing "Canadian mosaic" and the increasing "multicultural aspect of the prison population" (Interview 13). According to a different informant, at the time the *CCRA* was enacted, "the multicultural development of Canada had not impacted to the same degree [and] had not created the same level of concerns" that currently exist around ethnocultural offenders (Interview 6). So although the legislation is fairly specific around Aboriginal offenders, some informants viewed it as being unable to adequately "force" the PBC to properly address the needs of other diverse groups, including ethnocultural and female offenders. In a different vein, another informant was sceptical about the inclusion of gender and diversity in law more broadly, arguing instead that, as an "add-on" to the "big system," the accommodation of particular groups "is undermined by the big policy picture" (Interview 9). For this informant, "you cannot have broad social policy, you know, that has a destructive effect on minorities and then try to make up with it with minor policies that still fall under that." From this informant's perspective, the clauses in the *CCRA* that address diverse populations are add-ons with limited ability to bring about change.

The Post-*CCRA* Context

Since the enactment of the *CCRA* in 1992, issues of gender, race, and Aboriginality within Canadian penality have continued to garner attention. Although the consideration of diversity issues tends to be focused on corrections rather than on parole and conditional release, these ongoing discussions have highlighted how penal institutions have accommodated (or failed to accommodate) gendered and racialized difference. In this section, I provide a brief overview of key developments after the passage of the *CCRA* that relate to issues of gender and diversity within Canada's penal system. The intent of this overview is not to be exhaustive but, rather, to highlight some of the important developments that involve diversity issues. Some of these developments reflect general concerns around diversity that were happening at the time, while others more directly touch upon the legislative mandate of the *CCRA* and the purview of the PBC. A key development in this context is the Supreme Court of Canada's decision in *R. v. Gladue* [1999], which supports an approach to decision making that takes into account Aboriginal difference.

Five-Year Review of the *CCRA*

In 1998, a comprehensive review of the *CCRA* was initiated, as per section 233, which requires a parliamentary committee to review its provisions and operations after five years. In support of this review, the solicitor general released a consolidated report examining the provisions of the *CCRA* and other issues (Canada 1998). This report highlights "special groups" of offenders with "special needs" as one of four "thematic lines" that guided legislative reform, with the other three being public safety and reintegration, openness and accountability, and fair processes and equitable decisions (v). The report describes how the CSC and the PBC have implemented the provisions in the *CCRA* that mandate action in relation to policies and programs for Aboriginal and female offenders. It also examines statistical data related to incarceration and parole rates for these groups that reflect their racialized and gendered difference. The report details specific organizational initiatives that aim to tackle "longstanding challenges" related to Aboriginal and female offenders (142), several of which are discussed in later chapters. This report underscores the legislative requirement that Canada's federal systems of corrections and conditional release address special offenders groups and their needs, which, in this context, are identified as Aboriginal and female.

In November 1998, the Standing Committee on Justice and Human Rights established the Sub-Committee on Corrections and Conditional Release with a mandate to conduct the review of the *CCRA*. In May 2000, the sub-committee released its report, which is entitled *A Work in Progress: The Corrections and Conditional Release Act* (Canada 2000). While the review was comprehensive in scope, several recommendations were made in relation to "special groups with special needs," the first of which was to broaden the *Act*'s provisions (i.e., section 4(h) and subsection 151(3)) to include offenders who are young, elderly, or have serious health problems (Canada 2000, para. 3.33). The sub-committee indicated that the CSC and the PBC had already been taking the needs of these groups into consideration; inclusion in the provision of the *CCRA* would further solidify these activities. The bulk of the sub-committee's recommendations for "special groups with special needs," however, focused on Aboriginal and female offenders. As will be seen, the sub-committee pointed to the same issues that have been raised time and again in government reports over the past several decades. In relation to female offenders, the sub-committee concentrated on the issue of programming, including the need for the CSC to provide "services that will facilitate their reintegration into the community as law-abiding citizens," despite the fact that the organization faces "difficulties" due to the relatively small number of federally incarcerated female offenders (para. 3.42). In other words, the number problem could not be used as an excuse for failing to meet female offenders' needs in this regard.

Regarding Aboriginal offenders, the sub-committee pointed to their over-representation among federally sentenced offenders and the tendency for Aboriginal offenders to spend more time incarcerated and be subject to the detention provisions of the *CCRA* in comparison to non-Aboriginal offenders (Canada 2000). The sub-committee also reiterated the requirement within the *CCRA* that rehabilitation and reintegration programming be "sensitive to Aboriginal culture" (para. 3.45). Services and programming that reflected Aboriginal offenders' needs were seen to promote their reintegration as law-abiding citizens. The sub-committee recommended the creation of a position of deputy commissioner for Aboriginal offenders who could both champion and problem solve in relation to issues affecting this population. The position was envisioned as akin to the existing deputy commissioner for women, including participation in the CSC's executive committee (para. 3.48).

The sub-committee discussed several other issues relating to Aboriginal and female offenders but in relation to *CCRA* provisions pertaining to the CSC (e.g., segregation, security classification, etc.). The report did not assess how the PBC had responded to diversity-related provisions of the *Act*. The sub-committee, however, did observe "based on its institutional and other visits that the ethno-cultural make-up of the offender population [had] changed in the last number of years" (Canada 2000, para. 9.13). Due to the increased diversity of the offender population, the sub-committee recommended that both the CSC and the PBC continue their programs of recruitment and training to respond to the changing offender demographics. In sum, then, the five-year review of the *CCRA* highlighted most of the same issues affecting Aboriginal and female offenders that had been raised prior to its enactment. The matter of the increasing diversity of the offender population – in terms of its ethnocultural (i.e., non-white) make-up – emerges as a more novel concern. The sub-committee's five-year review of the *CCRA* focused primarily on correctional issues in relation to issues of diversity, with little said about the PBC's policies and approaches for non-white and female offenders.

Maintaining Momentum on Issues of Offender Diversity

For female offenders, the mid-1990s and early 2000s comprise a significant time period due to the notable reconfigurations in the punishment of federally sentenced women. More specifically, it was during this time that the "women-centred" vision of *Creating Choices* was implemented through the establishment of new regional prisons and the closing of the Prison for Women.[13] This time period is also marked by several developments that drew attention to the issues facing federally sentenced women, including systemic failures on the part of the Canadian penal system to address their needs. The first development was a commission of inquiry headed by Louise Arbour in response to a series of high-profile events at the Prison for Women in 1994 (Canada 1996a; see also Faith 1999; Shaw 1999; Hannah-Moffat and Shaw 2000; Hannah-Moffat 2002; Jackson 2002). The report details Arbour's findings in relation to the events at Prison for Women, including abuses of power and violations of prisoners' rights. She also outlines recommendations to address systemic problems within the correctional system and instill a culture of rights within the CSC (Canada 1996a).

The second development was the Canadian Human Rights Commission (CHRC) "review of the treatment of federally sentenced women on the basis of gender, race and disability" (CHRC 2003, Preface). This review was conducted after the CHRC was approached in March 2001 by the Canadian Association of Elizabeth Fry Societies and Native Women's Association of Canada as well as other organizations, such as the Canadian Bar Association, the Assembly of First Nations, and the National Association of Women and the Law. These organizations raised concerns about the treatment of female offenders by the federal corrections system, including both prison and community corrections services (CHRC 2003). Although the review focuses on the CSC, the CHRC's findings highlight more general issues related to bringing about organizational change within a system that was created for white male offenders. According to the CHRC, "differences between individuals and groups that relate to prohibited grounds of discrimination must lead to changes in how systems are designed, how policies are developed, and how practices are implemented" (71). More specifically, it argues that penal institutions must go beyond making "special measures" in order to transform the system into one that is inclusive, with an "equal opportunity" for all offenders "to benefit from the rehabilitative purpose of the correctional system" (ibid.). The CHRC observed that, to be gender responsive, the penal system had to both create services based on the "underlying differences among women and men" and recognize that not all female offenders are alike (ibid.). In particular, Aboriginal women and female offenders with disabilities may have different needs in relation to rehabilitation and reintegration. Aboriginal women were also identified by the CHRC as being overrepresented within the correctional system, likely due, at least in part, to their over-classification by security assessments. The CHRC's report is noteworthy as it argues for the penal system to be transformed so that it is compliant with human rights.

For Aboriginal offenders, issues of overrepresentation, discrimination, and access to culturally appropriate treatment continued to be raised at the federal level during the 1990s and 2000s. A key development was the Royal Commission on Aboriginal Peoples (RCAP) and the release of its five-volume report in 1996 (Canada 1996b). The RCAP was created in 1991 by the federal government with an extensive mandate that included helping to mend and to build a more just relationship between Aboriginal and non-Aboriginal people in Canada. One of the mandated focal points was the justice issues facing Aboriginal peoples. The RCAP explored the overrepresentation of Aboriginal peoples within the justice system at length in its report *Bridging the Cultural Divide* (Canada 1995). It identified three explanations of this overrepresentation: culture clash, socio-economic, and colonialism. However, it concluded that colonialism was the best explanation for the overrepresentation of Aboriginal peoples, especially because it best explained the ongoing reality of disadvantage and discrimination. The RCAP observed: "The Canadian criminal justice system has failed the Aboriginal peoples of Canada – First Nations, Inuit and Metis people, on-reserve and off-, urban and rural – in all territorial and governmental jurisdictions" (309). It explained that the "principal reason for this crushing failure is the fundamentally different world views of Aboriginal and non-Aboriginal people with respect to such elemental issues as the substantive content of justice and the process of achieving justice" (ibid.). This conclusion bluntly questions the ability of the mainstream justice system to meet the needs of Aboriginal peoples and points towards doing something different in relation to punishment rather than simply tinkering with existing practice.

A second important development during the 1990s relates to the addition of section 718.2(e), one of the sentencing reforms that came into effect in 1996, to the *Criminal Code*. This amendment is particularly significant as it introduces a sentencing provision intended to help address the overrepresentation of Aboriginal offenders within the justice system. In this way, the criminal law is being used to address racial oppression and the historical legacy of colonialism as it applies to Aboriginal peoples through the recognition of difference (Kramar and Sealy 2006). Section 718.2(e) stipulates that "all available sanctions other than imprisonment that are reasonable in the circumstances should be considered for all offenders, *with particular attention to the circumstances of aboriginal offenders*" (emphasis added). The latter part of this clause reflects the intent to reduce the imprisonment of Aboriginal offenders by requiring sentencing judges to use their discretion to consider non-custodial options, including more creative and restorative sentences (Roach and Rudin 2000; Pelletier 2001; Kramar and Sealy 2006; Murdocca 2013).[14] Although the directed focus on the circumstances of Aboriginal offenders may encourage more contextualized sentencing decisions, it is less clear how these circumstances matter or what they mean for policy development. The application of section 718.2(e) was subject to review for the first time by the Supreme Court of Canada through a 1996 appeal in *R. v. Gladue* (Roberts and Melchers 2003). In the following section, I briefly introduce the Court's 1999 decision in this case; in Chapters 3 and 4, I examine in more detail the impacts of this decision on the PBC.

Attempting to Ameliorate Racial Injustice: The Application of *R. v. Gladue*
The Supreme Court's *Gladue* decision is an important development with regard to the formalization of responses to Aboriginal offenders within the Canadian justice system. As I discuss in subsequent chapters, the *Gladue* decision constitutes part of the legal framework that shapes the institutional responses to diversity at the PBC and creates opportunities for litigation for discriminatory treatment if institutions fail to consider and accommodate, where feasible, Aboriginal uniqueness. The Court's decision acknowledges the impacts of systemic discrimination within the criminal justice system that have contributed to the overrepresentation of Aboriginal peoples. It also recognizes that Aboriginal offenders who live off-reserve, such as in urban contexts, deserve to be treated like other Aboriginal offenders (Roach and Rudin 2000). Notably, the decision can be understood as an attempt to ameliorate historical and contemporary instances of racial and cultural injustice by encouraging remedial and contextual sentences (Roach and Rudin 2000; Kramar and Sealy 2006; Murdocca 2007, 2009, 2013; Williams 2009). However, although the Supreme Court's decision requires that attention be paid to Aboriginal offenders' circumstances, there is less clarity around how these contexts matter and, more important for the PBC, what this means for policy.

The case of *Gladue* involved an appeal of an Aboriginal woman's sentence of three years' imprisonment and a ten-year weapons prohibition for manslaughter in the death of her common-law partner. In imparting the sentence, the provincial court judge of the Supreme Court of British Columbia determined that section 718.2(e) did not apply to Gladue because she lived within an urban, off-reserve environment and therefore was not a member of an Aboriginal community. This was the key issue upon which the case was appealed to British Columbia's Court of Appeal (Kramar and Sealy 2006). According to Roach and Rudin (2000), the trial judge based his decision to discount Gladue's Aboriginal status on myths and stereotypes about Aboriginal offenders. The appeal court ruled that section 718.2(e) was relevant to Gladue despite her living off-reserve, yet upheld the sentence due to the seriousness of the crime (Kramar and Sealy 2006). In the appeal to the Supreme Court, the sentence was not revisited because Gladue had been paroled. However, the Court used the case to interpret the legislative intention behind the provision.[15]

The decision in *Gladue* is significant because it calls upon judges to remedy "injustice faced by aboriginal peoples in Canada" (*Gladue* 1999, para. 65). The decision provides a "framework for analysis" for sentencing that requires judges to consider "the unique background and systemic factors which may have played a part in bringing the particular offender before the courts" (para. 69). The Supreme Court notes various factors that "figure prominently in the causation of crime by aboriginal offenders," including "low incomes, high unemployment, lack of opportunities and options, lack or irrelevance of education, substance abuse, loneliness, and community fragmentation" (para. 67). In order to help remedy such injustices and reduce the incarceration of Aboriginal peoples, judges are authorized "to employ creative methods" when sentencing Aboriginal offenders (Williams 2009, 85), even if the alternatives are not culturally focused (Roach and Rudin 2000). The *Gladue* decision is therefore noteworthy because it reflects an attempt to recognize and respond to Aboriginal difference in the context of decision making. In addition, several courts in subsequent cases have drawn on *Gladue* to apply the sentencing provision to non-Aboriginals, including African Canadian offenders (e.g., *R. v. Hamilton* [2003]) (see Kramar and Sealy 2006).

Conclusion

This chapter grows out of my attempt to identify and understand the reforms to the conditional release system in Canada that have taken place since the early 1970s and that are directed towards issues of gender and diversity. I analyze how problems and solutions to Aboriginal and female difference are constituted and framed within official documents linked to penal change, including the key transformations in conditional release leading up to and following the enactment of the *CCRA*. In particular, I show that Aboriginal and female differences are narrowly framed within homogeneous categories of Aboriginality and woman, which works to reduce a range of diversities to uncomplicated constructs. The constitution of these differences matters because the framing identifies the "problems" that need to be addressed through policy reform. For Aboriginal offenders, the framing of Aboriginality directs policy reform to concentrate on issues of overrepresentation rather than on more insidious forms of systemic discrimination that may emerge as a consequence of the dominant risk-based approach to conditional release. In the case of female offenders, the focus on gender difference partitions various aspects of difference (e.g., gender from race), which prevents an intersectional analysis of the various problems facing female offenders as a diverse population. Although gender and cultural differences are recognized as affecting conditional release processes, the dominant policy framework remains unchanged. In other words, legislative and policy initiatives to address issues of difference have largely been brought into conformity with existing approaches and "established patterns of operation" (Houchin 2003, 143; see also Carlen 2002b).

By examining the processes of penal change over the past four decades, it is possible to see how the problem of diversity in the offender population is framed and made actionable in particular ways. This reflects a selective incorporation of diversity as only certain knowledges and approaches are taken up and integrated into policies and practices. Gender and Aboriginal difference are constituted as being relevant to specific contexts (e.g., programming or services) and tend to be compartmentalized (e.g., gender *or* Aboriginality) and treated separately. To create legislation and policy in response to offender diversities outside of this dominant framework would, in the words of Murdocca (2013, 78), "require recognition of the ways in which histories of colonial violence, genocide, and systemic racism [and sexism], along with global and economic relations of labour and production, interweave with government policies in criminal justice at the local and national level." Such a conceptualization necessitates moving beyond the cultural (and gender) difference model that frames "inclusion," through minor tweaks to the system, as the solution to the effects of long-standing structural inequalities experienced by non-white and female offenders. What, then, does the institutionalization of diversity look like at the PBC?

Responding to Diversity
Organizational Approaches to Managing Difference

The Parole Board of Canada's responses to diversity occur in a context within which "public institutions [are required] to acknowledge, rather than ignore or downplay, cultural [and ethnic] particularities" (Dhamoon 2009, 3). Institutions are expected to accommodate certain forms of difference through the recognition that fair treatment does not mean identical treatment. In other words, institutional responses to diversity are premised on substantive as opposed to formal equality arguments. The accommodation of difference is also justified on the basis that institutions should reflect the diversity of Canada's (post) colonial, multicultural population in order to be more inclusive of difference. As discussed in the previous chapter, for the PBC, section 151(3) of the *Corrections and Conditional Release Act* mandates that it attend to gender, cultural, and ethnic differences, including the special needs of Aboriginal and female offenders. Importantly, however, the law does not specify what differences matter or how they are relevant to conditional release policy. Part of the organizational process of accommodating diversity, then, is determining which specific differences matter and in what ways.

In this chapter, I analyze the organizational responses to diversity, including how the PBC has responded to diversity over time, the creation of the present-day Aboriginal and Diversity Initiatives section of the PBC, and other initiatives undertaken at the organization to address the problem of difference. Drawing on the work of Sara Ahmed and other anti-racist feminist scholars, I consider some of the implications of the recognition, inclusion, or accommodation of difference and diversity within the PBC as a penal institution, including the degree to which the diversity of the offender population challenges institutional policies and practices based on white male norms. I argue that these penal policies and initiatives can be seen as technologies of power for defining differences in particular ways and for determining how to manage them.

The Language of Diversity

The term "diversity" is a vacuous construct: its given meaning and definition varies within institutional contexts. Yet the vagueness of the term is likely what facilitates its operationalization within policy and practice. Puwar (2004, 1) notes that the "language of diversity is today embraced as a holy mantra across different sites," and yet "what diversity actually is remains muffled in the sounds of celebration and social inclusion." Similarly, Ahmed and colleagues (2006, 7) observe that the "word 'diversity' is difficult to pin down" because it is often "used to refer both to individuals and to everyone" (see also Edelman et al. 2001; Ahmed and Swan 2006; Herring 2009) as well as to "signal a well-intentioned stance against prejudice" (Dhamoon 2009, 6), often in lieu of other language used to describe issues of equality. Edelman and colleagues (2001, 1590) point to the expansive power of diversity discourses, which enable the concept to "include a wide array of characteristics not explicitly covered by any law." Indeed, it is the fluid nature of diversity that makes the study of its incorporation into organizational contexts interesting. In the context of penality, the languages used to recognize and respond to diversity among offenders helps shape the responses to the problems that this diversity poses, both to a dominant framework based on white male offenders and to ideas about what constitutes "fair" punishment for those deemed diverse.

The shift towards the language of diversity means that other languages are no longer used or are at least shifted to the periphery of policy debates (Benschop 2001; Ahmed et al. 2006; Ahmed and Swan 2006; Dhamoon 2009; Phillips 2007; Swan and Fox 2010; Ahmed 2012). Described as the "turn to diversity" (Ahmed and Swan 2006, 96), this move reflects "the way that diversity as a concept and set of practices has replaced or supplemented the concepts and practices of equal opportunities" (Swan and Fox 2010, 570). The language of diversity is believed to differ from identity-based categories such as gender and race because it "does not so powerfully appeal to our sense of justice and equality" (Benschop 2001, 1166). The turn to diversity thus reflects the appeal of the "celebratory" aspects of difference that the term evokes. The languages of equality, social justice, or anti-racism are increasingly absent from policy debates around difference and diversity, largely because these terms have "complex histories" linked to political actions such as the women's and civil rights movements (Ahmed et al. 2006, 33). In contrast, fluid and abstract terms like "diversity" are easily mobilized and can be defined and used in many ways. Although diversity may not appeal to notions of justice or equality (Benschop 2001), the term is attractive because it can make people "feel good" (Ahmed 2007a, 245). Diversity is something that can be celebrated and even consumed, especially when it is framed as enriching organizational environments. Conversely, terms such as "equality" or "anti-racism" are more challenging as they point to structural elements.

The uptake of diversity, then, signals the need for considering how such discourses may displace alternative framings or strategies such as those of equality, anti-racism, anti-colonialism, or anti-sexism; be complicit with racism and other forms of discrimination (Razack 1998; Jaccoud and Felices 1999; Bannerji 2000; Puwar 2004; Ahmed et al. 2006; Phillips 2007); and/or simply exist as "something that can be implemented without necessarily changing the underlying structure of the institution and its day-to-day operations" (Brayboy 2003, 73). This is because the language of diversity may have the potential to skirt around power relations and fail to bring about meaningful organizational and policy change. Yet it is important to consider the organizational processes and structures in order to help explain how diversity is taken up (Edelman et al. 2001; Kalev et al. 2006; Herring 2009; Dobbin et al. 2011). By focusing on institutional practices, it is possible to understand why organizational change is difficult to bring about, particularly in relation to equality and anti-discrimination agendas. Corporate cultures play an especially important role in promoting (or suppressing) diversity initiatives. For example, diversity rhetoric tends to intersect with managerial knowledges to transform legal ideals and to reframe understandings of law, thereby converting diversity into a managerial concern rather than seeing it as a legal issue (Edelman et al. 2001). The institutionalization of diversity, then, is a complex and contested process (Schneiberg and Soule 2005) that is shaped by organizational processes and structures (Edelman et al. 2001; Kalev et al. 2006; Dobbin et al. 2011).

Diversity within Organizations

Within organizations, overwhelmingly, the term "diversity" has come to refer to a workforce that contains a variety of individuals from different gender, racial, and/or ethnic backgrounds (Puwar 2004; Ahmed 2006, 2012; Ahmed et al. 2006). Diversity is seen to "arrive" within organizations via the inclusion of people who look "different" (i.e., women and non-white peoples). This arrival is important as it has the potential to disturb the status quo and to shed light on the racialized and gendered norms upon which dominant institutional processes are based (Puwar 2004). Such is the case with increasing numbers of non-white and non-male offenders in the penal system and calls for greater representation of this diversity among staff and decision makers. However, the physical presence of gendered and/or racialized individuals does not mean that an organization is therefore diverse or that this necessarily leads to more inclusive penal policy or regimes.

During the initial stages of this research project, it became apparent, through interviews with informants and within PBC documents, that the term "diversity" implicitly refers to race and ethnicity and sometimes gender (read: women). I could not locate any formal or explicit definition of the term within internally produced documents. I asked one informant what was meant by diversity at the PBC:

> We would define it among ourselves, we would define it as everything but white males, really, know you, just in our internal conversations, that's the populations that we dealt with. We certainly wouldn't have gone out in the public and said that, but that's really the populations that we felt that we were responsible for. (Interview 8)

As this quote illustrates, diversity is understood (internally) as pertaining to female and non-white male offenders as these are the populations that have been identified as in need of greater attention (e.g., PBC 2010b, 2010c). Through this framing, diversity works as a shorthand signifier of difference as being that which is not white maleness.

The recognition of diversity in corrections and conditional release policy provides an opportunity to consider the constitution of difference in relation to the universal norm (i.e., the white male) that circulates in discourses about offenders as well as in discourses about staff and board members. If diversity presumes a multiplicity of difference, then it begs asking, different from what? (Bannerji 2000, 41). According to Puwar (2004), the notion of difference helps illuminate the gendered and racialized norm and how this norm operates within organizations.[1] Several scholars examine the implications associated with the locating of diversity within non-white and non-male individuals (e.g., Brayboy 2003; Puwar 2004; Ahmed et al. 2006; Hunter 2010). They note that the primary implication is the reproduction of institutional whiteness and masculinity, and the hyper-visibility of clientele and staff who are not white or male. However, more interesting analytical questions can be considered by shifting the focus to the implications of an organization's engagement with diversity and how it makes diversity actionable through various policies and initiatives.

Several scholars express concern as to how notions of difference are conceptualized and put into practice in the context of criminal justice (e.g., LaRocque 1997; Andersen 1999; Jaccoud and Felices 1999; Cowlishaw 2003; Phillips and Bowling 2003; Hannah-Moffat 2004a, 2004b; Bosworth et al. 2008; Hudson 2008a; Murdocca 2009; Hannah-Moffat and Maurutto 2010). Writing about the move to establish culturally relevant models within the criminal justice system, LaRocque (1997) argues that it is important to consider how ideas about tradition, culture, and healing are taken up in policies and practices that aim to be culturally appropriate. The integration of such ideas into policies and practices is not straightforward as the underlying meanings are complex and contested and often do not adapt well to penal contexts. Other scholars, such as Andersen (1999), show how notions of tradition and difference work to constitute and govern Aboriginal offenders and communities in particular ways. For instance, difference is something the Canadian state encourages Aboriginal peoples to embrace and to be proud of, with the result that ideas about culture and spirituality become incorporated in Aboriginalized technologies of governance and utilized to encourage certain Aboriginal subjectivities. Similarly, in their examination of the recruitment of racialized groups in Canadian police forces, Jaccoud and Felices (1999, 87) argue that integration policies function more as a process of racialization that attributes difference to certain others than they do to reduce social inequality.

In Canada, the idea that the penal system should be responsive to difference is now commonly expressed within government documents and websites as well as being mandated by the *CCRA*. The recognition of, and response to, difference is generally accepted as necessary when dealing with a variety of penal concerns, including effective and appropriate programming, decision making, and training (Brady 1995; Zellerer 2003; Martel et al. 2011). It has resulted in attempts to create appropriate, sensitive, and/or relevant policies and practices that respond to difference, whether this difference be cultural, ethnic, or gender. In this sense, punishment is increasingly constituted as something that should be carried out in gender-specific and culturally appropriate ways. These differences pose a formidable challenge to institutional policies and practices derived from Eurocentric values (Comaroff and Comaroff 2004), including those premised on treating offenders alike. Within liberal democracies such as Canada and penal institutions such as the PBC, a key issue that emerges is how difference is recognized and responded to, and in what ways. In the remainder of this chapter, I consider the various recognitions of, and responses to, diversity at the PBC.

The Aboriginal and Diversity Initiatives Section

The following discussion examines the Aboriginal and Diversity Initiatives section of the PBC's national office as a key unit within the organization that is charged with doing what Ahmed (2007a, 237) calls "diversity work" – the various activities and practices related to attempts to put diversity into action within institutional contexts. The present-day Aboriginal and Diversity Initiatives section originated out of the position of manager of diversity issues, which was created in September 1998 to focus on Aboriginal issues, women, and ethnocultural issues (PBC 2006a, 12). According to one informant, the chairperson at that time thought the PBC should have a counterpart to the diversity work being done at the CSC's Aboriginal Initiatives section (Interview 7). Initially, it was to focus solely on "Aboriginal issues," but section 151(3) of the *CCRA* broadened its scope to include other groups (e.g., women and other special needs offenders) (Interview 7). In addition, the national office sought to ensure it could provide a measure of consistency for the organization's response to diversity concerns. As one informant explained, the PBC "wanted to have national visibility and to work with the regions and not to be overly influenced ... by Prairie traditions" (Interview 7). This is because the Prairie Region was active in its attempts to address the needs of Aboriginal offenders due to their significant overrepresentation within the jurisdiction.

The same informant noted that the position of manager was created largely through "the political will within the Parole Board" (Interview 7). In other words, the impetus for creating the manager position (and then the Diversity Issues section) came primarily from the interest of the chairperson at the time, who directed the executive vice chairperson and the executive director to "make it happen" (ibid.). Initially, Aboriginal initiatives were a "standing agenda item" at Executive Committee meetings so that the regions could provide updates.[2] According to the same informant, this ensured that all regions, rather than just the Prairie Region, had to consider Aboriginal issues, and that, and in doing so, this provided a type of accountability mechanism for action. The informant explained that the requirement for all regions to report on their diversity initiatives "made a really big difference" because, "after a while, all the regions were engaged in talking about all of these areas ... and actively pursuing initiatives." The reporting requirement thereby helped ensure that the responsibility for diversity initiatives was distributed more evenly across the PBC.

Previous research on the uptake of diversity within organizations points to several different determinants of the degree to which diversity programs and initiatives gain ground. For Ahmed and colleagues (2006), the commitment of leaders within organizations is crucial to what gets done and to the overall success of integrating diversity. They argue that the "commitment of the leadership is what makes policies legitimate, true and real, as what 'comes down' the organisation" (115). Without the support of senior management, it is much more difficult to do diversity work and to bring about organizational change. When commitment wanes, the allocation of resources may also be affected, thereby reducing the ability of staff to carry out diversity work (Ahmed et al. 2006). However, the focus on leadership does not tell the whole story. Corporate culture is particularly important for the support and implementation of diversity initiatives (Dobbin et al. 2011). More specifically, organizational cultures that are "pro-diversity" are more likely to promote diversity policies and programs, particularly if such practices reflect industry norms and in cases in which there are women managers who internally advocate for change.

Interviews with two informants highlighted the importance of senior management in determining what got done in relation to diversity. According to one informant, the PBC's "political will" waxed and waned due to changes in senior management, some members of which were seen to have "no interest in any of that work" (Interview 7). As a result, diversity issues were removed as a standing agenda item at Executive Committee meetings. The removal of the reporting requirement suggests that diversity issues were not effectively integrated into the existing organizational structure of the PBC but, rather, were constituted as peripheral to the organization's "real" work. In other words, concerns about diversity were simply added to the mix of interests and priorities and were subsequently reliant on the sustained commitment of individual actors. Diversity issues were treated more as a special project than as an ongoing aspect of day-to-day organizational processes.

Another informant noted that the PBC has "scaled back a lot of the work that Aboriginal Initiatives" does and that the section is "no longer represented on senior management or Executive Committee" (Interview 8). When asked why this was the case, the informant explained that there "was no will from senior management to keep that going." At the time of writing, two individuals make up the Aboriginal and Diversity Initiatives section.[3] The same informant noted an organizational tendency to pay "lip service" to issues of gender and diversity, where commitment exists in words rather than in the actions of the institution. For this informant, the PBC's commitment to diversity was reflected in the actions of senior management rather than being emblematic of the PBC's corporate culture.

As the above quotes from informants regarding the creation and evolution of the Aboriginal and Diversity Initiatives section demonstrate, the "personal commitment" of senior managers is very much related to "organizational commitment" (Ahmed et al. 2006, 115). The section was started due to the interest and commitment of a previous chairperson, yet in recent years the reported lack of commitment from senior management may be reflected in waning organizational commitment. This, of course, assumes that commitment to diversity is reflected through particular actions, such as in the staffing of the section, its representation on decision-making bodies, and allocation of resources in such a way that it can do its work. There may be other reasons (i.e., financial or political pressures) for the ebb and flow of commitment to diversity, as represented by its actionable elements; however, during the course of my research, personal commitment emerged as the key issue identified by informants.

The apparent inability of diversity issues to stick as key aspects of the organization's structures and practices can be linked to how the problem of diversity was framed in the first place. The working definition of diversity as being everything but white male offenders and staff (i.e., the norm) constitutes differences as relating to non-white and female offenders and staff (i.e., the others) (Puwar 2004; Ahmed et al. 2006; Ahmed 2007a). This process of othering positions diversity as outside the norm, thereby increasing the likelihood that difference will be seen as peripheral to the organization's primary work and as something that can be accommodated by special projects rather than as something that demands the rethinking and reworking of structures, policies, or practices. Senior management's refusal to provide adequate funding for the organization's diversity work is one way that diversity agendas are regulated (see also Phillips 2007).

Organizationally, the national Aboriginal and Diversity Initiatives section is part of the Policy, Planning and Operations Division of the PBC.[4] Its current mandate is to meet the "challenges" posed to the PBC by the "growing ethnocultural diversity within Canada's federal offender population," "increasing ethnicity and gender issues," and the "long-standing challenges related to Aboriginal offenders" (PBC 2010c, n.pag), such as their overrepresentation. The PBC (2008a, 221) indicates that the section's "energies are particularly focused on developing national strategies and initiatives aimed at enhancing informed conditional release decision-making, in relation to Aboriginal, women, and ethnocultural/racial offenders, to ensure public safety." As such, its work feeds into various organizational processes for responding to gender, cultural, and racial diversity within the PBC's existing legislative parameters. To do so, the section undertakes "research production and analysis, awareness-building and community outreach that pertains to Aboriginal, ethnocultural and women offenders in the federal correctional system" (PBC 2010c, n.pag). It also provides "corporate expertise" on these groups and leads on board member training and policy development and implementation. It also works with the regional offices, partner departments, and stakeholders on diversity issues (PBC 2008a, 221). In sum, the Aboriginal and Diversity Initiatives section is primarily focused on knowledge production about certain aspects of offender diversity – that is, female, Aboriginal, and ethnocultural difference.

The Prairie Region is the only region that has its own Aboriginal and Diversity Initiatives unit. According to one informant, the unit "was not something that was funded by the national office, it was identified as a need by the region" because it has a "vastly higher Aboriginal population than any of the other regions" (Interview 11). As the informant explained, "in all the other regions the Regional Manager of Community Relations and Training would take care of their job as well as the Aboriginal and Diversity Initiatives, whereas in [the Prairie Region] it's just not possible for them to do all of it." The Prairie Region's Aboriginal and Diversity Initiatives unit's main focus is on Aboriginal programs like elder-assisted hearings and training "board members and staff to be culturally sensitive." Because of the low number of Aboriginal board members in the region, the unit wants to ensure "that they're very aware of Aboriginal culture and why there's so many Aboriginal offenders incarcerated," as called for by the Supreme Court's decision in *Gladue*. The creation of this regional unit points to the links between organizational commitment to diversity and the resources necessary to conduct diversity work.

In relation to the importance of the national office's Aboriginal and Diversity Initiatives section, one informant remarked: "[The PBC] can do its job without having a diversity unit, you know, they can make decisions on parole with or without, you know, the most credible information or the most appropriate information" (Interview 8). However, it was this informant's belief that diversity initiatives "were vital to helping board members get a better understanding of the person sitting in front of them." In this sense, the section is seen as playing an important role in ensuring better decision-making practices through the recognition of difference. Yet, within the organization, the compartmentalization of diversity as being the purview of the Aboriginal and Diversity Initiatives section and its regional counterpart is shaped by the constitution of difference as belonging to non-white and non-male individuals. The creation of a special section with seemingly limited staffing and inclusion in organizational processes may reflect a lack of institutional integration of diversity. These data suggest that the incorporation of diversity into standard organizational approaches and practices is by no means straightforward. Several barriers pose a challenge to the creation of inclusive institutions, including a lack of political will, the organizational culture, and financial constraints. In the next section, I explore the sorts of diversity work undertaken at the PBC.

Forms of Diversity Work

As suggested above, what gets done within organizations is shaped by how diversity, and its associated problems and issues, gets defined (Ahmed 2007a). A canvassing of the activities of the Aboriginal and Diversity Initiatives section and some regions suggests that diversity work focuses largely on raising awareness related to particular groups of offenders, communities, and victims. These forms of diversity work can be viewed as strategies for managing difference and representing the organization as diverse and inclusive. In this context, difference is acknowledged and accommodated in ways that do not challenge dominant institutional practices. Said differently, diversity is confined to certain activities – committees, newsletters, and community outreach – that remain peripheral to the organization's day-to-day functioning and real work.

Diversity Committees

Diversity committees emerged during the late 1980s based on organizational experts' recommendations that oversight and advocacy groups were needed within institutions to spearhead and monitor diversity initiatives (Kalev et al. 2006). Typically, diversity committees are comprised of individuals who represent different areas of the organization and have different professional backgrounds. Yet, as the following discussion illustrates, the work of diversity committees is shaped by how diversity is conceptualized by the organization in the first place. In the case of the PBC, diversity is framed as relating to non-white (and occasionally female) offenders and staff, thereby resulting in these groups being the focal points for diversity committees. As a consequence, diversity issues are not seen as relevant to white male offenders and staff.

Some of the regional PBC offices have diversity committees. For instance, the Atlantic Region has informal committees focused on Aboriginal and African Canadian issues that involve interested staff, elders, and the African Canadian cultural liaison officer. The committees create work plans for training and community outreach with the overall goal of helping both the community and offenders by making the parole process more substantively fair to particular groups. According to one informant, "these committees for women, for Aboriginals, for black offenders have a lot of merit in the decision-making process" and "can help keep our communities safe" (Interview 10). The Prairie Region's diversity committee is also "staff focused" (Interview 11). The same informant explained that the purposes of the committee are to promote "staff and Board member awareness of diversity issues facing [PBC] offices in Canada as a whole" and to "be inclusive of all staff and Board member contributions and to provide information about community cultural events." The Ontario/Nunavut Region's Diversity Committee consists of volunteer board members and staff. Its stated mandate "is to promote diversity and equality within the region" (PBC 2005a). As per its terms of reference, the committee's work focuses "on providing advice on policy and training initiatives with respect to historically disadvantaged groups in our society and address[es] inequalities based on sex, race, ethnic origin, disability, sexual orientation, age, religion and income" (ibid.). These terms of reference clearly identify the facets of inequality that are to be addressed, thereby linking diversity to equality. This is unique as diversity tends to be neither organizationally defined nor connected directly to historical disadvantages.

However, from the interviews it appears that these regional committees exist largely as a result of personal interest in, and commitment to, diversity issues (Interview 10). Previous research on diversity work within organizations suggests that commitment to diversity is unevenly distributed, with responsibility for diversity often located in some individuals and units more than in others (Brayboy 2003; Ahmed et al. 2006; Ahmed 2007a; Smith and Roberts 2007). Processes of racialization and gendering tend to result in making non-white and female staff responsible for diversity work, which may free the organization from having to do this work when there are "diversity champions" for this purpose (Ahmed 2007a, 250). Yet, without diversity champions, it is unlikely this work would get done at all, or at least to the same extent. Personal interest in, and commitment to, diversity issues is probably what drives the diversity agenda within organizations, especially in cases in which there is more lip service than action, such as in the allocation of resources (Ahmed 2007a, 249).

This is not to say that diversity committees do not serve important functions within the PBC. Indeed, such committees may push the diversity agenda forward and work to address pressing issues. However, because the distribution of responsibility for diversity is uneven, it may result in others being able to give it up as well, even as the organization can claim or show that it is responding to diversity (Ahmed 2007a). Consequently, diversity becomes something that only certain individuals and units do rather than being the responsibility of all members of the organization, as in the case of the ideal of "mainstreaming" (e.g., Squires 2005; Eveline et al. 2009) or of the "full" integration of diversity (e.g., Smith and Roberts 2007). Yet, on the other hand, "the project of 'integrating diversity' by not having a diversity unit, which works on the principle that 'everyone' should be responsible for diversity, does not seem to work" (Ahmed 2007a, 250). This is likely because "'everyone' quickly translates into 'no one'" (ibid.). Mainstreaming diversity does not succeed because diversity and equality are not mainstream (252), hence the need for drivers and supports, such as diversity committees. This connects to the operational definition of diversity as pertaining to female and non-white difference and to its being framed as a special project within conditional release policy and practice.

Diversity Newsletters

Newsletters can be seen as techniques used by the PBC to produce knowledge about certain differences and to communicate diversity issues among staff and board members. Diversity newsletters also work to promote an image of the organization as being conscious and committed – one that is doing something about diversity and that is therefore responsive to advocate and stakeholder calls for reform. In other words, these documents help manage reputational risk – that is, the potential harms to reputation that could result from inactivity on the diversity front. Additionally, newsletters reflect and reinforce the organization's understanding of diversity as relating to non-white and female populations through a process of othering. Difference is constituted against white and male norms and dominant organizational practices, thereby framing these populations as objects to be "known." Newsletters provide a vehicle for knowledge about these others to be disseminated while simultaneously reinforcing a view of diversity as a special project that is peripheral to the organization's real work.

For a short period of time, the Aboriginal and Diversity Initiatives section of the national office produced a newsletter intended to "be a forum to share information between the regions and national office"; "provide updates on various initiatives, meetings and conferences" and upcoming events; and impart some "fun facts and educational information" (PBC 2007a, 3). This information focused on Aboriginal, female, and ethnocultural groups. The newsletter was originally slated to be distributed quarterly, but only three issues were produced between 2007 and 2008 (personal communication). The Prairie Region also publishes the *Diversity Committee Newsletter* (PBC 2009a), which aims to assist in the sharing of information and networking (Interview 11). This newsletter is intended to be a monthly publication of the region's diversity committee (PBC 2008a, 221).

These newsletters represent a form of diversity work that attempts to put diversity into action. Conceptualized as a mechanism to share and transmit information and activities related to diversity, these newsletters involve the translation of diversity into certain formats that will appeal to the intended audience of PBC staff and board members. Part of the work here is "selling" issues related to ethnicity, women, and Aboriginal peoples as matters of importance for all members of the organization. For instance, although much of each newsletter was devoted to summaries of various initiatives, meetings, or conferences related in some way to the PBC and diversity (e.g., female and non-white) groups, space was given to upcoming events as well as to "did-you-know" and recipe sections (PBC 2007a, 2008b, 2008c). The newsletter format is one way to communicate information in ways that feel good rather than bad. In other words, diversity is framed in terms of cultural enrichment. It is something that can be celebrated and even consumed (Ahmed 2007a) – for example, through the sections highlighting community events (e.g., Black History Month, International Women's Day, the International Day for the Elimination of Racial Discrimination, National Aboriginal Day, Multiculturalism Day, Saint-Jean Baptiste Day, and Chinese New Year) and offering recipes as a means "sharing one's culture" (PBC 2007a, 11).

The newsletters are reflective of Canadian liberal multiculturalism, which involves "the celebration of diverse cultures and their festivities, clothes, food, and music" (Dhamoon 2009, x). As hooks (1992, 21) argues, with the commodification of otherness or difference, "ethnicity becomes spice, seasoning that can liven up the dull dish that is mainstream white culture." The discourse of cultural enrichment encourages everyone to participate in the celebration and experience of difference. The newsletters share knowledge about gender and diversity as things requiring sensitivity and awareness, and as special issues that are peripheral to the PBC's real work. Again, this is reflective of how diversity is operationalized within the organization.

Advisory Committees
In addition to diversity committees, some regions also have joint Correctional Service of Canada-PBC advisory committees devoted to diversity issues. These committees are techniques for creating legitimacy around organizational approaches to diversity and fostering perceptions of inclusiveness. As with diversity committees, advisory committees function as a way of generating and managing the PBC's reputation as an organization that is concerned about, and committed to, diversity. These forms of diversity work show that something is being done about offender and staff differences, albeit only those that are institutionally

recognized as different in relation to the white male norm. Advisory committees also operate as a form of "inclusion," inviting others "in," yet at the same time setting the parameters of this inclusion (see Ahmed 2012).

The Pacific Region's Ethnocultural Advisory Committee is one example of an advisory committee. It was formed to provide assistance, advice, and recommendations to the regional deputy commissioner (of the CSC) and regional director (of the PBC) on issues related to ethnocultural offenders (CSC-PBC n.d.). These issues include the identification of "the needs and cultural interests of offenders belonging to ethnocultural minority groups," the development and maintenance of "programs and services to meet the cultural needs of offenders who are incarcerated or on conditional release," and the promotion of a "better understanding" within both organizations of "related/pertinent ethnocultural issues including, but not limited to, employment equity, discrimination in the workplace and multiculturalism" (1). According to the PBC (2008a, 222): "The Minutes from the various meetings are widely shared within the Board as a means of sharing ideas and best practices."

As described in its terms of reference, the committee's scope is extended to issues affecting offenders (e.g., addressing needs), communities (e.g., building partnerships), and organizations (e.g., education and awareness in the workplace) (CSC-PBC n.d., 1). Although not explicitly defined, ethnocultural offenders appear to be those from "ethnocultural minority groups," which ostensibly means non-white offenders who are different from the presumed cultural majority of white Canadians. The lack of attention to gender within the terms of reference further suggests that the (default) focus of the committee is non-white male offenders. This follows an observable pattern within the institution whereby difference is implicitly constituted vis-à-vis the unstated white masculine norm.

Unlike organizational committees that are made up of staff and board members, the Pacific Region's Ethnocultural Advisory Committee membership consists of a chairperson and at least "seven people selected from the community who are *familiar with ethnocultural issues* and who *represent ethnocultural communities* reflecting the diversity of Pacific Region's ethnocultural offender population" (CSC-PBC n.d., 2, emphasis added). The conditions of inclusion are set by the PBC and the CSC: a member must both "represent" (i.e., look like a minority community) and "know the issues" (i.e., be able to speak to ethnicity and culture). The terms of reference specify that "non-ethnocultural candidates" may be considered for appointment to the committee if they have "extensive experience working with [minority group] issues" (CSC-PBC n.d.). The notion of a non-ethnocultural person is interesting in this context as it signals how processes of racialization work to designate some people and communities as having ethnicity or culture but others as not having them. Whiteness is largely unacknowledged except as being non-ethnocultural; in other words, whiteness is by default defined as a lack of race, ethnicity, or culture. It is the norm through which the difference of ethnocultural offenders and their communities is constituted. Awareness and knowledge of those who are different is positioned as a potential solution to this difference. Advisory committees address this need by sharing information about the relevance of diversity to corrections and conditional release as well as by bolstering the PBC's image as an inclusive organization that is committed to diversity issues.

Community Outreach

Another form of diversity work carried out by the PBC is community outreach, especially with Aboriginal communities. The targets of community outreach echo how the concept of diversity is operationalized within the organization as pertaining to racialized individuals and communities. As with the above-mentioned committees and newsletters, outreach can be seen as a technique of building reputation and demonstrating that the organization is committed and responsive to diversity.

Several rationales for conducting community outreach are apparent from the PBC's documents. One is that this initiative supports the organization's strategic outcomes for "safeguarding Canadian communities and public safety" (PBC n.d.-b, n.pag). In this sense, diversity work is linked to matters of public safety. The PBC contends that

> Aboriginal communities are generally less informed about the correctional process and would benefit from greater understanding of the system. A better informed community means better quality community involvement in Section 84 *CCRA* releases, better informed decision-makers about these communities and ultimately better safeguards for public safety. (ibid.)

Outreach therefore helps educate Aboriginal communities, the aim being to increase their involvement in community-assisted hearings and/or the supervision of Aboriginal offenders on conditional release. This outreach is perceived as necessary given the overrepresentation of Aboriginal offenders in federal penitentiaries and their lower rates of conditional release compared to non-Aboriginal offenders. In Chapter 4, I consider community-assisted hearings in detail, including the ways in which Aboriginal communities are involved in the conditional release process.

Community outreach is often done at the regional level in order to respond to regional issues and needs. For instance, the Atlantic Region office does outreach with Aboriginal communities to explain the CAH model and to give presentations on the pardon function of the PBC (Interview 10). The region hired a consultant to do outreach with Aboriginal victims because there are "not a lot of Aboriginal victims who are registered with the Board and [the organization] has been trying to figure out why" (ibid.). This issue was also identified by the Prairie Region, which does outreach and works to raise awareness of the reasons "it would be less desirable to identify [oneself] as a victim" within an Aboriginal community (Interview 11). Community outreach via education and information sharing is one way the organization attempts to bring Aboriginal communities in line with its normative practice of victim registration.

The PBC (n.d.-b) views community outreach as a mechanism for increasing the organization's profile with Aboriginal communities. Outreach helps the PBC to build reputation through its workshops and forums for educating Aboriginal (and other) communities about its mandate. Within PBC documents, community outreach is framed as supporting the organization's strategic goals and obligations, such as building and bolstering partnerships with other government departments, like the CSC and the Royal Canadian Mounted Police (PBC n.d.-b). Community outreach and consultation are also viewed as contributing to the PBC's "openness" and "accountability," whereby it must share both "successes" and "failures" as indicators of its performance (PBC 2009b, 17). In order to manage reputation, organizations "must understand their constituencies, consider their significance and possible impact, and develop and implement a strategy for communicating with them" (Power 2007, 145). Community outreach requires knowledge of particular communities as the targets of outreach such that the organization can effectively communicate with them. The evaluation of outreach activities becomes a risk-based practice in the service of organizational reputation as the organization can show that it is responding to the needs or concerns of diverse communities. Although community outreach likely serves multiple organizational functions, little is known about how community consultations are carried out, such as whether they are ongoing negotiated process of developing practices, one-time events that cement particular practices in place (Hyndman 1998), and/or tied to performance outcomes (Power 1997).

Aboriginal Circle
In addition to diversity and advisory committees, which appear focused on ethnocultural offenders, the PBC has a unique Aboriginal-focused working

group called the Aboriginal Circle. The mandate of the Aboriginal Circle is to provide "strategic advice to PBC's Executive Committee on any matter related to policy, training or operations arising from the Board's mandate for conditional release, pardons, [or] clemency that will improve the efficiency and effectiveness of the Board in meeting the needs of Aboriginal offenders, victims and communities" (PBC 2009c, n.pag). The Aboriginal Circle was established after a March 1999 meeting of PBC representatives from all regions as well as with the national office (PBC 2006a).[5] Initially, the participants were, for the most part, Aboriginal board members and staff, although non-Aboriginals were also in attendance as representatives from those regions that did not have any Aboriginal board members or staff (PBC 2005b). The PBC observes that, "for most Aboriginal participants, this was the first opportunity to come together in a national forum as Aboriginal people, to share individual and regional experiences as [PBC] staff and decision-makers" (1).[6] The meeting resulted in a number of recommendations, one of which was for the group to meet annually "to promote the use of the Board's internal resources in terms of [participants'] expertise on Aboriginal issues and to contribute to the [PBC]'s vision as it concerns Aboriginal people" (ibid.). As a form of diversity work, the Aboriginal Circle was to be a key resource to drive the agenda forward on so-called, yet undefined, "Aboriginal issues."

Approval for the creation of this working group of Aboriginal board members and staff was given by the Executive Committee (PBC 2005b, 2006a). The Aboriginal Circle was to meet annually, typically for two days, and act as an advisory body to make recommendations to the chairperson and Executive Committee regarding Aboriginal issues (PBC 2006a, 2008a). In the 2004-05 fiscal year, the Aboriginal Circle held a strategic planning meeting to "discuss concrete plans for the direction of the Aboriginal Circle," including its role, vision, and priorities (PBC 2005b, 1). The resulting document from this meeting outlines a strategy for the Executive Committee in relation to Aboriginal issues (see PBC 2005b). This document also contextualizes the Aboriginal Circle within an environment characterized by the overrepresentation of Aboriginal peoples in the justice system; government priorities that support mechanisms or approaches that meet the needs of Aboriginal peoples and communities; a legislative mandate to address the conditional release needs of Aboriginal offenders; the findings rendered in the Royal Commission on Aboriginal People and the *Gladue* decision; and the PBC's vision for Aboriginal offenders. In this sense, the document lays out the rationale for the existence of the Aboriginal Circle as an entity that supports various priorities aimed at addressing the needs of Aboriginal offenders and their communities.

According to its vision statement, the "Aboriginal Circle is a body of knowledge and expertise about Aboriginal culture, people, and communities; it is a body of knowledge on the conditional release process; it is a body who can review areas of concern relating to Aboriginal offenders" (PBC 2008d, 4). The Aboriginal Circle has been viewed as "a golden opportunity for the Board to remain sensitive to aboriginal culture and sensitivities in delivering its mandate"; however, as the Aboriginal Circle's strategy document notes, the circle's role as an advisory group to the PBC has been "informal in nature" (5). The Aboriginal Circle therefore recommended that the group be formally recognized so as to "engender understanding and recognition from the broader organization," particularly in relation to the importance of its work "vis-à-vis Aboriginal issues" (ibid.). The group also sought to have "Aboriginal concerns" be part of the PBC's "day-to-day business in order for the Board to collectively move forward" (ibid.). The Aboriginal Circle's strategy document is one way the group sets its priorities and accompanying "strategies for action" (ibid.). The committee's push for inclusion through formal, as opposed to informal, recognition by senior management reflects the positioning of diversity as outside the organization's main functioning and the struggle of diversity groups to bring it inside.

The current terms of reference for the Aboriginal Circle outline the membership for the committee (PBC 2009d). Following an assessment of the committee in 2008 (see PBC 2008d), the nature of membership was altered, thereby shifting the Aboriginal focus to a broader organizational representation. In its initial articulation (e.g., PBC 2005b), as discussed above, the Aboriginal Circle provided a space for predominantly Aboriginal staff and board members to share experiences and to strategize on ways for the organization to respond to Aboriginal issues. Ostensibly, such a space was needed for Aboriginal staff and board members and other interested individuals to consider issues that were not garnering attention from the organization. According to one informant, this particular membership structure "was sometimes not necessarily as clear, so [for example] there was some people that maybe were not contributing at all" (Interview 4). The informant also explained that there was a need "to reach out for people that are not necessarily Aboriginal but have a contribution to make because of their capacity [i.e., position]" that involves work related to diversity or Aboriginal issues. The recently altered membership raises the possibility that organizational priorities and interests, rather than those of Aboriginal staff and board members, will steer the Aboriginal Circle.[7]

The current terms of reference state that "membership will be comprised of permanent and rotating members, with each region being represented by at least one member, and *ensuring adequate representation of Aboriginal staff or*

Board members" (PBC 2009d, 1, emphasis added). The notion of "adequate representation" is not defined. Rotating members participate in the committee for two years. Membership in the Aboriginal Circle consists of:

- a chairperson who is a member of the Executive Committee and designated by the Chairperson of the PBC;
- four permanent members who are representatives of the PBC and include the Directors of Policy, Planning and Operations and Professional Development and Decision Processes, the Manager of Aboriginal and Diversity Initiatives, and the Regional Manager of Aboriginal and Diversity Unit;
- six rotating members who are representatives of the PBC and include a Regional Director, a Regional Manager of Community Relations and Training, and "up to 4 Aboriginal Board Members (regional rotation; always with at least 1 Board Member from the Prairie region)";
- a CSC partner who has "expertise in Aboriginal issues" in the spheres of corrections and conditional release;
- a rotating elder/cultural advisor;
- two or three external members who are representatives from Aboriginal organizations that have experience with the work of the PBC; and
- observers whose presence is permitted at the discretion of the chairperson (PBC 2009d, 1).

At least one in-person meeting is to be held annually, with additional meetings to be determined by the committee's chairperson. S/he must also approve any alternate representatives for the meetings.

This membership structure raises some questions as to how adequate representation of Aboriginal persons may be obtained and how issues of power play out within the Aboriginal Circle. It is unknown how the Aboriginal organizations are selected, although it could be surmised that these are organizations that are ideologically compatible with the PBC and/or have pre-existing or working relationships with the organization. Although such an approach potentially broadens the organizational responsibility for Aboriginal issues by reducing the responsibility for diversity from Aboriginal board members and staff and shifting it to "everyone" (Brayboy 2003; Ahmed et al. 2006; Ahmed 2007a), the new membership structure may work to reduce the critical edge of the Aboriginal Circle as a vehicle for holding the PBC accountable for how it handles or responds to Aboriginal issues. Yet, as a form of diversity work, the Aboriginal Circle represents an important institutional process for integrating and/or including Aboriginal difference in the organization and conditional release policy and practice. It serves as an oversight body that may increase the accountability of the PBC with regard to how it deals with issues pertaining to Aboriginal offenders, even as it sets the terms of this inclusion (Ahmed 2012).

Other Diversity Work

In relation to other forms of diversity work at the PBC, the Atlantic Region has developed a "resource guide about each Aboriginal community" for board members that explains the size of the reserve, its population, and the available services to assist with decision making (Interview 10). The creation of resource guides works to constitute Aboriginal communities in particular ways, as certain types of communities, containing certain individuals and resources. As a knowledge product, each guide is necessarily based on imperfect and selective information. Additionally, complex histories and issues are simplified so that the information can fit within a short-hand guide format. It is unknown whether these guides are created with community input, with opportunities for dialogue and feedback, or whether they are the result of a top-down initiative. Although this information is thought to help board members make decisions because it will enable them to know "what this community is [like] and what's available to the offender," the resource guide may inadvertently impose normative criteria on Aboriginal communities in relation to reintegration. Indeed, this same informant viewed the resource guide as an effective way for board members to learn about Aboriginal communities given that it was financially impossible for them to travel to each community: the guide is "kind of a way [the organization] brings [the community] to them." As I discuss in Chapter 5, the PBC has also developed cultural fact sheets that profile certain countries in order to assist board members in decision making for immigrant and non-citizen offenders. These short-hand guides aim to provide quick cultural information for busy board members, but they produce racial knowledge about certain offenders and their "home" countries. Similar to the other forms of diversity work discussed above, the resource guides and fact sheets generate knowledge about specific differences and are reflective of how diversity is operationalized at the PBC.

Responding to Diversity

The previous section examines the creation of Aboriginal and Diversity Initiatives and the diversity work of the PBC. The following discussion highlights the various responses to diversity at the PBC as articulated by informants and within key documents. This includes the impetus for the organization to change, how diversity is believed to affect risk assessment and decision making, and how the

organization is committed to diversity. I show that the process of institutionalizing diversity is complex and marked by competing ideas as to how and why
diversity matters. Despite the uptake of diversity within the PBC, exactly *how*
knowledges of difference and sensitivity to diversity are used to make gender
or culturally appropriate decisions remains less clear. Concerns about certain
offender differences come up against dominant policies and practices, such as
the assessment of risk, where the integration and understanding of diversity
issues are limited. Diversity is defined and taken up in ways that fit into existing
organizational structures.

Impetus to Change

Informants identified the *CCRA* as a vital development that led to changes at
the PBC with respect to diversity. Several of the PBC's documents also point to
compliance with the law as a driver for change (e.g., PBC 2008a, 2010c). More
specifically, the PBC (2008a, 220) indicates that section 151(3) of the *CCRA*
"guides the Board's work in relation to Aboriginal and diversity initiatives" and
comprises its "legislated responsibility." The *CCRA* "dictates that [its] policies
must respect gender, ethnic, cultural and linguistic differences and that the Board
must be responsive to the needs of women, Aboriginal peoples, and of other
groups of offenders with special requirements" (ibid.). The PBC is mandated
by law to consider diversity in its policies. The organization's key documents
(e.g., PBC 2009b, 2010e) frame its institutional commitment to issues of diversity
in terms of compliance with law. Importantly, the focus on legal compliance
positions the organization as responding to diversity in order to militate against
legal risks and potential risks to reputation. Compliance with the law is also
one among several competing expectations about how gender and diversity
should be included in organizations and the goals of diversity work.

Impetus to change was also internally generated. Several informants noted
that Aboriginal board members and staff pressured the organization to be more
responsive to the needs of Aboriginal offenders during the parole and conditional release process. One informant said that the PBC was "fortunate ... to
have on the Board First Nations individuals in the Prairie Region and in the
British Columbia Region who were strong advocates within [the organization's]
consultations and discussions for the unique interests" (Interview 6). Another
informant also pointed to the work of certain staff and board members, particularly in the Prairie Region, to "connect with Aboriginal communities" and to
apply internal "pressure" (Interview 13). These staff and board members were
therefore important advocates for change, pressing the PBC from within to

respond to diversity and to take into account issues of ethnicity, culture, and/ or gender in institutional policies and practices.

Several informants noted the changing ethnic composition of the Canadian population as an important driver for the increased attention to diversity within the PBC, both in terms of responses to ethnocultural offenders and in terms of the organization's hiring of board members to ensure proper "representation." As one informant put it, "we can't just keep doing our regular business, it's changing out there" (Interview 7). This sentiment was echoed by another informant who indicated that justice system responses to ethnocultural groups are a result of the "changing pace of the Canadian population ... As the Canadian population changes, you can usually see, sometimes it's a generation delayed, but you can usually see it reflect in those populations having a period within our criminal justice system where they are in conflict" (Interview 2).

The idea that changes to the national population's demography creates pressures within organizations to consider diversity is supported in research from other areas (e.g., Jaccoud and Felices 1999; Ahmed and Swan 2006). The changing ethnic make-up of the Canadian population was said to require the PBC to adopt different approaches to assessing offenders' risk:

> We have a vast myriad of peoples from different cultures and you cannot apply the uh, you know, white Anglo-Saxon filter because it doesn't fit ... [T]he diversity is such within the offender population, as well as in Canada, that you cannot do that anymore. (Interview 5)

This diversity was also seen to have affected the PBC's hiring practices, as explained by another informant:

> The Parole Board has always tried to reinforce with the government of the day the need for diversity within [its] board member appointments. The legislation clearly identifies that it's a community board, that the members collectively represent the values and beliefs of the Canadian population. So this was a way of reinforcing the need to reflect that in the board members. (Interview 2)

Similarly, a different informant noted that the PBC tries to reach out to diverse groups because the organization is supposed to be representative of the Canadian population and have a "balance" of these groups (e.g., women and men, Aboriginal and non-Aboriginal, etc.) appointed to the board (Interview 4). To ensure "balanced representation," the PBC (2011b, n.pag) states that it "makes every effort to recruit individuals from a wide variety of cultural, ethnic, and professional backgrounds" and that it "promot[es] a balanced gender representation." For the PBC, its "effectiveness" in serving diverse communities is linked to "the recruitment, selection and appointment of qualified members and staff from these communities" (PBC 2010b, n.pag). One informant noted that the PBC has focused on "trying to have more Aboriginal people appointed, particularly in the Prairie Region" (Interview 3). Ostensibly, the inclusion of more Aboriginal or non-white board members and staff will, among other things, help to improve the organization's performance and effectiveness (Jaccoud and Felices 1999).

A representative parole board was also seen as being important to offenders in terms of providing respect for the diversity of "life conditions." As one informant explained:

I think it's important that justice be perceived as being accessible and in tune with those it's supposed to serve. If you appoint only people, uh, people from only upper-middle class, white, in their late fifties, you will not have that necessary – you have to have a connection to the people you're supposed to be serving. (Interview 5)

As this quote reveals, a more representative board, in terms of its class, racial, and age make-up, was seen to enable greater connections with the offender (and victim) population and therefore make board members more accessible and responsive to diverse needs, experiences, and backgrounds. Yet, as Jaccoud and Felices (1999) contend, practices of representation and the integration of diversity within an organization necessitate the designation of the other. According to them, "designation is not only reproduction, but production, of otherness to the extent that one or several characteristics are selected out of a complex set of statuses and identities" (86). Consequently, for the groups selected for increased representation, it is their ethnic or cultural identities that are deemed relevant. This works to privilege one aspect of identity or form of difference over others, thereby limiting recognition of the simultaneity and multiplicity of identity (Dhamoon 2009).

The PBC (2011b, n.pag) states that knowledge of "the societal issues impacting on the criminal justice environment including gender, Aboriginal and visible minority issues" is part of the criteria used to select board members. However, given the nature of the appointment process (i.e., the fact that the PBC can only make recommendations to Cabinet as to who should be appointed),[8] several informants suggested that the PBC was limited in what it could do as an organization to increase its diversity – that is, the visible representation of individuals within the organization that look different in terms of their racial and/or ethnic background. As one informant elucidated:

> If only one visible minority applies [to be a board member] and he flunks the written test, then that's the end of the visible minority... [The PBC has] no control of input on who applies and ... no control over who succeeds as well. (Interview 5)

This same informant offered the recruitment process for 2008 as an example of the difficulty associated with increasing board member diversity:

> [The PBC] had 416 people who applied to become parole board members, of which we had twenty-five Aboriginal people and twenty-three visible minorities. So the initial pool was a little bit more than 10 percent of the total number of applicants was either Aboriginal or visible minority, five and five, good? And then we have, uh, we screened in twenty and seventeen, but only five and five survived the written test and then ended up at an interview. And we ended up with two and two qualified. So out of sixty-two qualified candidates we only have four who are either Aboriginal or visible minority, which is lower than the original proportion, but we have no control over the quality of the candidates. (Interview 5)

These comments reflect a type of "institutional inertia" (Ahmed et al. 2006, 75) whereby the lack of a representative board can be explained away and, in a sense, justified as an unfortunate but inevitable situation. The idea that the PBC has "no control over the quality of candidates" explains the lack of representation from non-white people. Yet, according to the same informant, the PBC tries "to have [qualifying] tests that are culturally sensitive" (Interview 5),[9] which presumably means tests that do not privilege the knowledges and experiences of white Canadians. The informant also recognized that the PBC is "far from having reached that [greater representation], you know, the typical board member is still somebody in, on average, in their fifties" and the organization is "still predominantly white, central Canadians." The focus on the representation of organizational diversity as the presence of racialized individuals as staff reinforces the idea that this presence alone can change policies and practices.

However, in relation to its gender (i.e., [white] women) composition, the same informant suggested that the PBC was doing "not bad," with the ratio of approximately forty-five women to fifty-five men (Interview 5).[10] Another informant concurred with this assessment, noting that women were very well represented as PBC staff, including those in higher-level positions and as members of the Executive Committee (Interview 12). Ahmed et al. (2006, 78) suggest that "it is only certain kinds of difference that are acceptable" within organizations, such that "assimilable" differences are preferred over "unassimilable" differences. Perhaps in the case of white women, this group's difference is more open to assimilation and less likely to challenge shared organizational values than are non-white women and men.

Diversity and Risk Assessment

All informants agreed that sensitivity to difference was a necessary condition for making decisions and conducting parole hearings, both of which are centred on the assessment of risk. As noted in Chapter 1, the assessment of risk is mandated by the *CCRA* and focuses on whether or not the offender presents an "undue risk" to reoffend. Several informants highlighted the issue of communication between board members and offenders and how this can affect risk assessment.

> A lot of it comes down to communication, to make sure that everybody's understanding the same vocabulary, and when you ask a question, people are understanding what you ask and you understand what they are saying to you. I mean, there's all kinds of examples of how men and women communicate differently, so this is important when we're doing interviewing techniques, we actually spend some time on looking at the issues that could impede communication cross gender, cross cultural ... and that in turn will have, can have an impact on your risk analysis. If you think someone is being evasive in answering your questions, but they come from a culture where giving you a direct answer is rude and they believe that, then you have to find another way of communicating because you could be misinterpreting their answers. (Interview 2)

> For one thing it's all about the gathering of information to base their decision on, so it's all these pieces of the puzzles. So the more that they can understand about the person in front of them, and you know, getting them to realize that they can actually learn from that person, will just give them more information, you know, on which to base their decision. (Interview 7)

> In terms of training it's a big issue, how to approach interviews ... [B]asically the purpose of the hearing is to try to get a sense of the offender and if you can't connect with the offender at the hearing, then you've lost your chance and the offender has lost her chance. (Interview 13)

Aboriginal offenders and other offenders from various ethnic groups were viewed as less able and/or willing to communicate, or "spill their guts," at hearings, thereby impeding the information-gathering process. The idea that offenders should share openly during parole hearings reflects expectations around the presentation of a certain kind of self that conforms to the communication style preferred by the PBC (see Razack 1998; McKim 2008). The idea that the PBC's regular hearing approach was not working for all offender groups (i.e., non-white, non-male) was evident in the lack of communication between offenders and board members.[11] As the above quotes reveal, diversity is believed to affect the hearing process, thereby requiring board members to be cognizant of offender differences, including those related to gender, ethnicity, and culture. Yet the belief that diversity matters does not necessarily mean that board members know *how* to apply knowledge of offender difference to their decision making (e.g., Hannah-Moffat 2004a; Hudson and Bramhall 2005; Silverstein 2005). This point is discussed in further detail in subsequent chapters.

Several informants raised sensitization to difference as being central to making quality release decisions, arguing that understanding various differences would contribute to improved information gathering and assessments of risk. According to one informant, "unless you understand what you're dealing with you don't make an informed decision" (Interview 13). It is therefore important to be sensitized to the issues facing particular racialized or ethnicized communities – for example, knowing where people are returning to upon release and "where they [came] from." For instance, another informant noted:

> [Board members need an] awareness of the [offender's] community, what's
> unique to the community, what may be the impediments to communications,
> what may be the impediments to the cultural impediments to change. I mean,
> if you're returning to a community that holds values that are in conflict with
> our law, with Canadian law, then it's important to understand how that can be
> managed if the individual's returning to a community. Or whether it presents
> a risk that can't be managed.

Awareness of, and sensitivity towards, cultural and community differences – particularly those that deviate from Canadian norms and standards – were important for properly assessing risk. Sensitivity was also deemed necessary for understanding how different offenders react at parole hearings. In relation to female offenders, one informant noted that special interviewing approaches were needed because women were more emotional at hearings than were men and that many "just freak[ed] out" due to fear (Interview 13). In this particular example, it is possible that gender stereotypes helped to shape the types of situations requiring sensitivity to difference.

Several informants viewed sensitivity as a necessary condition for treating offenders fairly and appropriately, arguing that differences among offenders mattered in the context of release decision making. But to take gender or culture into account, one had to "know something or be sensitized to something that was going to assist the person" (Interview 12). Knowledge of the other was viewed as essential to the process of assessing risk and making decisions.

> I mean, you don't do a hearing of someone that is a Chinese, for example, a Chinese offender, without knowing what's the background, the cultural background, because – and their own experience of their community – because you can interpret completely out of context the way they talk to you, the way they look or don't look at you, and things like that. (Interview 4)

> As a board member you come to an appreciation that there are different paths to reducing risk and to changing behaviour. (Interview 3)

For these informants, sensitivity to offender diversity is linked to the ideal of a fair and culturally sensitive process, one that helps to ensure that parole hearings are handled properly based on offenders' differences. One technique for attending to difference that was raised by several informants involved "put[ting] yourself in someone else's shoes, to be able to understand where someone else came from and where they're going back to" (Interview 8). Informants also spoke of the need to recognize culture and gender as filters that shape how people see the world and how such filters can influence decision making. Board members therefore need to be "aware of their own perception and how it colours, can colour, their assessment and their decision" (Interview 4).

In sum, being responsive to diversity through sensitization to, and awareness of, difference was perceived as a benefit as it contributes to what many informants identified as quality decision making. Although informants did not define the term explicitly, in the context of the interviews quality or appropriate decision making emerges as a practice that requires board members to ensure that they are able to effectively communicate with offenders across gender and/or cultural lines in order to gather information upon which to base their decisions. Several informants saw inaccurate or misconstrued information based on a lack of cultural or gender sensitivity or awareness as impeding decision making and potentially leading to unfair decisions. Officially, a "quality decision" is guided by eight "hallmarks," one of which is "a responsiveness to diversity" (PBC 2011c,

Ch. 2.2, 23).[12] Attention to diversity is therefore something required by policy, linking issues of sensitivity and awareness to notions of accountability in decision making.

Exactly *how* knowledges of difference and sensitivity to diversity are used to make quality or appropriate decisions remains less clear.[13] As previous research has shown, the interpretation and application of cultural and gendered knowledges in practice is often problematic (see Hannah-Moffat 2004a; Hudson and Bramhall 2005). The focus on sensitization leaves unquestioned the existing decision-making criteria and processes (these issues are explored in greater detail in Chapter 3). Indeed, this knowledge of the other was viewed critically by one informant, who was worried about how it would be taken up and applied during hearings:

> I guess I was always worried ... in relation to Aboriginal offenders, oh yes, they got training about [how] Aboriginal people don't look you in the eye, they don't do this, they don't do that. Well, sorry, some do look you in the eye, and if they do, I was always worried that board members would think, hmm, this is a high risk, look at that, he has no respect for me, he's looking me right in the eye, you know, kind of a thing. (Interview 7)

By drawing attention to the issue of "eye contact" specifically, the informant highlights one of the pitfalls of diversity initiatives, as if by equipping board members with the "cultural rules of eye contact, all players can then proceed from a position of equality" (Razack 1998, 8). The informant rightly questions what happens when Aboriginal offenders do not follow the cultural script expected of them and worries about the possibility that such deviations will be read as indicative of high risk. Here, institutional practices of producing knowledge about Aboriginal peoples treat the complex act of "looking" as a straightforward matter of cultural difference that can be learned by board members and used for decision making. Such ways of "knowing the other" demonstrate the failure of the diversity project because racism is (re)produced in and through knowledge rather than by the absence of it. The "concept of 'educated racism' challenges the assumption that racism is about a lack of education or knowledge, as a form of ignorance or intolerance" (Ahmed et al. 2006, 86). Educated forms of racism may be expressed subtly or politely and in well-meaning ways through practices around knowing the other (90), as the informant astutely observes in the above quote.

Although knowledge of gendered and racialized offenders and different processes for gathering information were seen as important for assessing risk, several informants stressed that risk was still the primary concern. This follows the prescriptive clauses of the *CCRA* around decision making. As one informant noted in relation to women offenders:

> We certainly can't assume because they're women there's no longer risk issues ... [W]e still have to consider are they a risk, at risk to commit another crime ... [W]e can't ignore risk where it exists. (Interview 3)

According to another informant:

> The risk assessment will be the same for Aboriginal as non-Aboriginal or, you know, Vietnamese as non-Vietnamese, or women or men, the assessment of risk will remain the same. It's how we get the information leading to the assessment of risk. (Interview 11)

Issues of gender, race, and culture are to be taken into account, yet the primary focus, as required by law, is the assessment of risk – a concept and practice that is constituted as neutral and ahistorical, yet that scholars have argued is gendered and racialized (see Stanko 1997; Walklate 1997; Hannah-Moffat 1999, 2004a, 2005; Chan and Rigakos 2002; Maurutto and Hannah-Moffat 2006; Hannah-Moffat and O'Malley 2007). The positioning of diversity as secondary to risk has been found in other areas of the criminal justice system that have attempted to respond to difference. For example, in their study of pre-sentence reports in the context of section 718.2(e) of the *Criminal Code* and *Gladue*, Hannah-Moffat and Maurutto (2010, 263) find that the narrow focus on risk supersedes "the type of contextualized analysis of race required by Canadian law." Several PBC documents also reflect the notion that training in cultural awareness and sensitivity does not supplant risk to public safety as the key concern, as required by law. Instead, awareness of, and sensitivity to, other cultures helps board members "to study files better, and to select the information they need to assess an offender's readiness for release" (PBC 2010b, n.pag). As the PBC (2006b, 17) puts it, "being responsive to diversity lends itself to enhanced and improved information collection for quality decision-making." The organization's diversity initiatives (e.g., EAHs, CAHs, sensitivity training, community outreach, etc.) are understood to allow board members to gather better information about others that, in turn, allows them to make better decisions. This focus reinforces organizational concerns around legal compliance and potential litigation as a major institutional driver for change.

Commitment to Diversity

Interviews with informants revealed a range of opinion as to the PBC's commitment to issues of diversity. To some informants, the PBC has welcomed diversity initiatives, while to others there has been significant resistance to change. According to one informant, "the board has been perceived as being the leader in terms of the appointment process [for board members] and in terms of the [sensitivity] training process" (Interview 13). The same informant did not "think there's any [parole] board in the world that gives as much training" as the PBC. Here, the PBC's commitment to cultural and sensitivity training reflects the organization's openness to diverse others.

Several informants noted that there appeared to be limits to the accommodation of diversity initiatives – for instance, the idea of analyzing each policy developed and adopted within the organization against its impact on diversity (i.e., Aboriginal offenders and gender issues) "was difficult to accomplish" and eventually "didn't work" because of a lack of institutional support (Interview 13). Another informant indicated that the work of the Aboriginal and Diversity Initiatives section has been "scaled back" in recent years due to a long stretch of time in which the manager position was vacant and the fact that the unit is "no longer represented on [the] senior management or Executive Committee" (Interview 8). According to another informant, "whether you move ahead [with diversity-related initiatives] or not, is very much at the discretion of the powers that be" (Interview 7). This same informant highlighted the varying levels of will among senior PBC management to support and legitimize the work of the Aboriginal and Diversity Initiatives section. As this person put it, the section was essentially at the "mercy" of senior management. In other words, the informant indicated that work on, and commitment to, diversity at the organization varied according to who was in charge.

Although the PBC may express its commitment to diversity and to being responsive to legislative provisions that require attention to difference, this does not necessarily lead to substantial changes in the culture of the organization. Organizations may demonstrate that they are responding to diversity, but this may be on superficial levels (Brayboy 2003; Ahmed et al. 2006; Wrench 2005). The work of doing diversity within organizations may be met with a lack of support among senior management as well as with the problem of few or no resources and a resulting lack of power to bring forth a diversity agenda. The potential sidelining of diversity initiatives may occur even as an organization outwardly portrays itself as being concerned about, and responsive to, such issues.

One informant pointed to the need to change the organizational culture of the PBC so that issues of diversity are "always in people's mind" and "become part of the culture" (Interview 13). This informant felt that there is a limit to what can be accomplished through policy because "in the end it's a question of individual sensitivity and individual approach." Similar observations were expressed in a discussion paper on Aboriginal issues that points to the need for diversity to be seen as an ongoing project rather than as something that can be "finished":

> The Board must never allow itself to become too comfortable with its accomplishments or it risks becoming stagnant. The [PBC] must continuously reexamine what it is doing to ensure that it continues to grow and develop processes to meet ever changing needs. (PBC 2000a, 11-12)

According to this perspective, "diligence" is required so that the PBC continues "its efforts to improve the way of doing business with Aboriginal peoples, be they offenders, organizations, or communities" (11). Organizational commitment to ongoing attention to Aboriginal and diversity issues is viewed as fundamentally important to bringing about change within the organization.

Conclusions

In this chapter, I examine how the PBC has responded to diversity over time as articulated by informants and within key documents, including the creation of the present-day Aboriginal and Diversity Initiatives section and other initiatives undertaken at the organization to address the problem of difference. I narrow the analytical focus by examining how issues of diversity are recognized, understood, operationalized, and institutionalized by the PBC over time. A key concern is the constitution of diversity within the organization. I illustrate how the institutionalization of diversity reflects a selective understanding and inclusion of difference as well as a lack of clarity around exactly how and when differences matter in the context of conditional release. Diversity ideals and discourses are, for the most part, incorporated in ways that complement existing institutional structures.

I advance our understanding of how the PBC has grappled with issues of difference by considering the various ways that gender and diversity have been institutionalized. Yet, with the general recognition of the need to take differences into account, questions emerge as to how this can occur in practice. My exploration of the creation of the Aboriginal and Diversity Initiatives section, the various forms of diversity work that take place within the organization, and informants' perspectives on how diversity matters to conditional release reveals that the organizational uptake of diversity is by no means a straightforward or simple process. The data presented here illustrate the challenge of accommodating diversity, including which differences are recognized, how they are known, and what sorts of responses can be developed as a result. As Minow (1990, 20, emphasis in original), in what she refers to as the "dilemma of difference," asks:

> When does treating people differently emphasize their differences and stigmatize or hinder them on that basis? and when does treating people the same become insensitive to their difference and likely to stigmatize them on *that* basis?

This quote captures the challenge of accommodating diversity and how best to be responsive to difference. Emphasizing certain differences through processes of othering may subject particular offenders to forms of gendered, racialized, or cultured regulation. These questions speak to the larger themes of *Parole in Canada*, which concern how issues of gender and diversity are seen to matter in the context of punishment. In the next chapter, I build on the discussion of how diversity has been taken up by the PBC by focusing on how issues of diversity are affecting parole and conditional release decision making through training initiatives, the incorporation of the *Gladue* decision, and attempts to meld risk assessment with Aboriginal knowledges.

In Pursuit of "Appropriate" Decisions
Racialized and Gendered Knowledges within Training and Risk Assessment

The Parole Board of Canada's raison d'être is conditional release decision making. As discussed in the previous chapters, attention to diversity has been organizationally identified as a necessary part of quality decision making. In order to make appropriate release decisions, the PBC has recognized that certain differences must be taken into account, as required by section 151(3) of the *Corrections and Conditional Release Act*. The PBC (2010b, n.pag) states that the "actions and decisions of Board members respect the gender, ethnic and linguistic differences of all offenders." This statement of commitment is based on the organization's view that "conditional release decisions need to consider this diversity to be successful" (ibid.). "Appropriate" decisions, then, reflect the organizational goal of being "responsive" and/or "sensitive" to offenders' gender, ethnic, or cultural differences rather than ignoring them. Yet exactly *how* diversity is recognized and seen to matter in the context of decision making is complicated. In the previous two chapters, I argue that how diversity is organizationally defined shapes the types of responses pursued by the PBC. The constitution of diversity as being non-white and female frames how diversity is understood for the purposes of decision making as well as the techniques utilized in the pursuit of appropriate and, hence, accountable decisions. Through this understanding of diversity, non-white and female offenders become the object of knowledge; learning about difference consequently emerges as a key organizational exercise.

In this chapter, I consider organizational knowledge practices that aim to contribute to appropriate conditional release decisions for offenders identified as different according to gender, race, and culture. These knowledge practices are organizational attempts to constitute certain populations and how difference is applicable to issues of risk assessment for release in the context of decision making. I focus on three such practices: diversity training, the interpretation of the *Gladue* decision, and attempts to "Indigenize" risk. The first section, on diversity training, examines how difference is constituted within training manuals and how it reinforces whiteness and maleness as the normative subjectivity of decision makers. The second section, on *Gladue*, illustrates how the Supreme Court's decision and ideas about Aboriginal difference are taken up by the PBC and made applicable to decision making. Finally, the third section, on the PBC's attempts to Indigenize risk, demonstrates the incompatibility of Aboriginal and institutional knowledges of risk. The challenge of ensuring culturally competent and gender-responsive approaches means that decision makers ought to "know" these particular populations, recognize their own personal biases, and ensure that the correct knowledges and sensitivities come together in practice (Zellerer 2003). I argue that the cultural and gendered knowledges of offenders circulated through these practices show the complexities of accommodating difference in the pursuit of appropriate decisions.

Diversity within Training: Constituting Difference and the Imaginary Subject

In addition to training on parole policies and legislation, risk assessment, and decision making, board members receive training in cultural awareness and sensitivity. Cultural awareness and sensitivity training is a key diversity initiative and form of diversity work undertaken by the PBC. Most of this training is directed towards board members, both through orientation and training of new members and through "refreshers" and ongoing training for current members. The awareness and sensitivity training undertaken at the PBC is focused largely on Aboriginal, female, and ethnocultural offenders, with some training directed at "cultural perceptions." According to the PBC (2010b, n.pag), "this training helps [board members] to study files better, and to select the information they need to assess an offender's readiness for release." Awareness and sensitivity are expected to lead to improved decision making.

The PBC's approach to training is focused both on learning about gender and cultural differences and on coming to recognize the various perceptions that shape how one sees the world and makes decisions. Board members are encouraged to look to cultural and/or gendered explanations for understanding female and non-white offenders' behaviours and release plans. Cultural differences are viewed as a cause of misunderstandings or misinterpretations, with the remedy being cultural knowledge to be delivered by various experts and training sessions (van Dongen 2005). The target of change is the individual and her or his biases, not institutional structures or practices (Kalev et al. 2006). Such an approach reduces the likelihood of organizational change and does not encourage critical thinking about dominant paradigms.

Bannerji (2000, 38) argues that "diversity sensitization or training has largely displaced talk about and/or resistance to racism and sexism."[1] Instead, the focus is placed on acquiring knowledge about others and learning to be sensitive to a range of socially produced differences.[2] The PBC's diversity-focused training is largely directed towards decision making in relation to ethnicized, culturalized, and gendered difference. Armed with acquired racial, cultural, and/or gendered knowledge, decision makers are better able to "see" or gaze upon those who are different and to make more responsive decisions. Training is a strategy used by the PBC to disseminate gender and cultural information to board members and staff. The training curriculum is not structured to encourage critical thinking or the questioning of current policies or approaches to decision making. Training occurs within pre-existing organizational structures and is consequently a way of supplementing knowledge of offenders' gender, ethnic, and cultural differences and the (potential) relevance to parole decision making.

The following examines how notions of diversity and difference are constituted and disseminated through the PBC's training initiatives. It begins with an overview of training at the PBC, followed by a consideration of how diversity is constituted within training. I argue that such initiatives work to produce and circulate gendered and racialized knowledges of female and non-white offenders. The training texts are based on an imaginary subject who is white and male, thereby reproducing rather than challenging institutional whiteness or destabilizing masculine norms. Such an approach to training does not work towards cultural integration or a reconsideration of dominant paradigms; rather, it focuses on making exceptions in the case of those constituted as different from the white male norm. Training also addresses organizational concerns around reputational risk where the training of board members to be aware and sensitive can reduce instances of (overtly) biased decision making and thus legal liability (Barlow and Barlow 1993) as well as demonstrate to observers that the organization is committed to diversity. Finally, I argue that the training approach reflects a selective inclusion of issues related to gender, race, and culture – one that fits with the overriding organizational focus on risk as the basis for decision making.

Board Member Training

The responsibility for training is divided between the national office and regional offices (PBC 2008e). In terms of the training of new board members, the national office provides two weeks of foundational orientation training, while the regional offices offer a further three weeks of regional orientation training. Prior to these in-house training sessions, new board members are given an introductory reading package to review and upon which they are assessed (Interview 2). Regional training allows for new board members to learn regional issues, including the offender population demographics (PBC 2008e), problems associated with Aboriginal gangs (Interview 11), and issues that are unique to various ethnocultural communities, such as the "cultural impediments to change" for offenders from communities deemed to "hold values that are in conflict with our law, Canadian law" (Interview 2). The regions largely provide ongoing training for board members, with some training-related presentations occurring nationally at the PBC's annual general meetings (PBC 2008e). According to one informant, ongoing regional training workshops for board members occur several times per year (Interview 13).

As part of the national orientation program, the Aboriginal and Diversity Initiatives section gives a presentation about its work (PBC 2009f). The presentation explains the section's organizational purpose, its legislative and policy relevance, and some of its ongoing projects. It provides information about diversity initiatives but not about *how* these initiatives matter or relate to actual practice. As one informant explained, the presentation was reduced "from three hours to fifteen minutes and at one point it was five minutes" (Interview 7). As a result, "the focus ended up being not on any of the actual issues or any of that, but more, here's Aboriginal and Diversity Initiatives, it's an important area within the Parole Board, despite whether or not that was true at the time." New board members were also given documents in relation to Aboriginal and Diversity Initiatives to read at a later time under the pretence that the PBC was committed to female offenders or the advancement of Aboriginal corrections and parole. The informant's comments draw attention to a potential gap within the organization's stated commitment to Aboriginal and diversity issues and what it actually does in practice via its training program. Notwithstanding the PBC's "official" organizational commitment to diversity, several informants viewed sensitivity training as playing an important role in decision making. For instance, one informant noted that diversity training provides board members with the necessary "tools" to "adequately interpret" offenders' release plans and assess their risk by taking into account differences, such as those related to culture or gender (Interview 5). Another informant commented that training allowed board members to "come to an appreciation that there are different paths to reducing risk and to changing behaviour" (Interview 3). For these informants, diversity training contributed to improved decision making through the consideration of difference and its relevance to rehabilitation and reintegration.

In relation to the content of PBC training, another informant explained that the PBC's training programs are "centred on evidence-based research" and are often developed with the help of "an advisory committee of experts in the field" (Interview 2). This informant also explained that experts were used to help deliver the training content to new board members.[3] In addition, Aboriginal board members provide input into training programs, including making presentations during regional training workshops (Interview 13). Elders are identified as "key contributors" to board member training (on account of their cultural expertise) as well as recipients of "training on parole hearing procedures so they can be effective participants" (PBC 2007c, n.pag).

Regional training initiatives have additional informal components for board members and staff. For instance, the Atlantic Region's contracted elder provides a sweat or "cultural day" at his community for interested staff and board members (Interview 10). The Prairie Region also provides "intensive Aboriginal awareness" that allows new board members to "interact with [PBC-contracted] elders and participate in ceremonies" (Interview 11). These components are framed as learning events for (non-Aboriginal) board members. This informant noted that, due to the large number of different Aboriginal groups and cultures, regional training was focused on raising awareness of some cultural differences and experiences that Aboriginal peoples have lived through, with the understanding that there are many more that cannot be covered in training.

Another informant indicated that the PBC's training was "not as sophisticated as it should be" due to the complexity of addressing "a large number of angles" and doing so in the short period of time allotted for training (Interview 5).[4] These angles include differences based on gender, cultural background, immigrant status, age, and so forth. Difference is viewed as adding complexity: individual aspects of identity that diverge from the normative standard complicate matters. The notion that training is difficult to do well because of the large number of angles relates to how diversity is initially defined.

In Pursuit of "Appropriate" Decisions

As discussed in the previous chapter, diversity is a fluid concept because it includes a jumble of differences linked to race or ethnicity with a simultaneous emptying out of meaning. This framing of diversity reflects training approaches that involve both learning about those who are different and participating in feel good activities.

I made several requests under the *Access to Information Act* to the PBC to see its training materials related to diversity, including those pertaining to female offenders, ethnocultural offenders, Aboriginal offenders, and awareness or sensitivity more generally. I received two main training packages. The first, entitled "Module 1 – Diversity in Offender Population and Other Considerations," has three units devoted to issues of diversity that reflect the constitution of certain differences as targets of knowledge: Aboriginal offenders (Unit 1); gender, ethnic, cultural, and linguistic differences (Unit 2); and female offenders (Unit 3) (PBC n.d.-c). These units are positioned in relation to the PBC's core value of "respect[ing] the inherent potential and dignity of all individuals and the equal rights of all members of society" (215). The second training package is entitled "Aboriginal Perceptions Training." In the remainder of this section, I consider how diversity is constituted and disseminated within these PBC training materials as well as how the organization's approach to training reinforces rather than challenges institutional whiteness and masculinity.

Constituting the Other

My analysis of the training materials that comprise Module 1 suggests that, through a process of "othering," diversity is defined as pertaining to non-white and female offenders (Puwar 2004; Hudson 2008a). Those defined as "other" – those who deviate from the white male norm – are constituted as an "object of knowledge" (Mills 1997, 101). The training materials in Module 1 position Aboriginal, female, and ethnocultural offenders as special groups with different experiences and needs in relation to their offending histories and programming requirements. Cultural sensitivity, then, becomes a matter of turning the gaze on these others and acquiring knowledge about their differences, with the end goal of "enhanced" decision-making practices (PBC n.d.-c, 215). Such an approach risks reinforcing the permanence and immutability of various racial, ethnic, gender, and cultural differences, while reducing these differences into simplified constructs that can be learned through short training sessions (Wrench 2005).

For instance, Unit 1 is a one-day session in which participants are expected to learn about the history of Aboriginal peoples and the various legislative, correctional services, and risk factors related to Aboriginal offenders (PBC n.d.-c). The session aims to build skills for cultural sensitivity so that decision makers will know how to review files, assess readiness for release, and communicate with Aboriginal offenders in their parole hearings. Several exercises work to constitute Aboriginal peoples as the other – for example, through lessons about the various differences between mainstream society (i.e., white society) and Aboriginal peoples, such as the dissimilarity in values and senses of power. Consider the exercise on values, which presents a chart contrasting those of Aboriginal peoples with those of the "mainstream," "non-traditional," "urban" society (162), thereby presenting a false binary between "us" and "them," and fixing Aboriginal peoples in time (i.e., in the past) and space (e.g., on-reserve). Similarly, the exercise on power plots the differences between "powerful" and "powerless" people as a way of charting the disparities facing Aboriginal peoples as a result of the intergenerational impacts of colonization (246).

The dichotomous representations of difference in these exercises present simple, uncomplicated stories about diversity. Participants are expected to learn that "they" are like "this," while "we" are like "that." LaRocque (1997) argues that the operationalization of difference into charts, typologies, and modules is especially problematic. Such an approach to cultural appropriateness for Aboriginal peoples runs the risk of conceptualizing difference in relation to stereotypes that were "founded, justified, and perpetuated by the colonial process" (77). Moreover, "reducing and fitting cultural expressions into charted, boxed-in modules falls prey to simplistic, rigid, formulaic, and doctrinaire 'solutions' to very complex issues and problems" (ibid.). These generalizations, through their representation in official training materials, are presented as objective knowledge for participants to learn (Mills 1997). The reduction of diverse Aboriginal cultures and practices into homogeneous constructs in the training materials reflects the challenge of capturing heterogeneous identities and experiences and translating them into formats that can inform decision making.

Similar to the training unit on Aboriginal offenders, the training on gender differences in Part B of Unit 2 constitutes female offenders as different from the male offender norm. Participants are required to learn about female difference, including issues of stereotyping, communication, and the ways in which gender bias may be present in the justice system and its effects (e.g., the creation of laws or policies that do not reflect the perspectives of women) (PBC n.d.-c). The idea that laws or policies may not reflect women's perspectives appears to be something that participants should be aware of rather than something that should lead to a questioning of the policies that board members, as decision makers, are expected to abide by. Although the manual does not explicitly define the concept of gender, the discussion of gender differences works to code gender as female by focusing on women's difference from men in relation to a range of indicators of inequality. Due to this coding, the manual does not enable a critical consideration of gender as a relational concept that includes both masculinities and femininities, and as a part of identity that intersects with other markers, such as race, class, or sexuality. As a result, the only gender differences viewed as mattering are those related to women's equality, such as reducing gender bias and considering women's perspectives. The unstated male norm remains unrecognized and, by default, is deemed not to matter in the context of conditional release decision making. This framing prevents the consideration of the gendered nature of male offending and its relevance to parole.

Part C also works to constitute diversity within the bodies and experiences of non-white others. This session defines concepts such as "ethnic group," "culture," "race," "racism," and "racialization," and it explains the manifestations of racism and racialization within the criminal justice system (PBC n.d.-c). A "key learning point" involves having participants trying to "understand others" by developing "some sense of their life experiences and the impact of these" on people's actions, reactions, and communication (258). Given the session's focus on ethnic and cultural differences, this exercise involves getting to know the other. This other is defined in relation to ethnic, cultural, and/or racial difference in comparison to an unstated, but implicit, white norm. As with masculinity, whiteness is therefore not considered as mattering to conditional release decision making.

Reproducing Institutional Whiteness

One of the consequences of the way in which diversity is manifested within PBC training is that institutional whiteness is reproduced rather than challenged. To say that institutions are "white" is not to say that they are simply made up of white people; rather, institutional whiteness is constituted through assorted processes of racialization that produce whiteness as a norm against which others are seen to appear different (Ahmed et al. 2006). Whiteness is therefore what is unseen and unmarked (Puwar 2004). The training materials imply that the imagined reader is a white male subject, which further entrenches this norm within the information to be learned and how gendered and racialized offenders are to be known. Through the othering of non-white and female offenders, participants are encouraged to focus on various ethnic, cultural, and gender differences as individualized aspects of identity. Although differences are recognized, whiteness and maleness are reaffirmed as characteristic of the normative position (Webb 1997) and are not problematized as potentially relevant to parole.

Part C of Unit 2 encourages participants to consider the impacts of racial privilege as a way to know the other. As part of the introduction to this section, participants are asked to complete an exercise called "Unpacking the White Knapsack."[5] This exercise involves participants assessing which among twenty-three statements apply to them because of their skin colour (PBC n.d.-c, 174). The statements are supposed to reflect "some of the ways having white skin can make a difference in day-to-day life" (ibid.). The exercise is intended to help participants recognize the impact of invisible white privilege and how the statements reflect the "conditions of daily experience which many Canadians [i.e., *white* Canadians] usually take for granted as neutral, normal, and universally available to everyone" (175). The imagined participant is white as the exercise makes less sense when applied to non-white participants.[6] The focus on white privilege does not go so far as to address the issue of white complicity in racism and colonialism (Alcoff 1998). Furthermore, by requiring participants to focus on skin colour, the exercise approaches race, privilege, and racism as discrete issues rather than as inextricably tied to other facets of identity and power. In this sense, white privilege is shaped by gender, class, sexuality, ability, age, and so forth and is not a monolithic experience or marker of advantage.

Despite this exercise requiring participants to consider the impact of white privilege, whiteness is largely invisible in the text of Part C. The imagined participant appears to be white, given references to "we," such as when "we" are asked to consider the experiences of "others" or if "we" would make similar decisions about "others" as white people (PBC n.d.-c, 261). Bannerji (2000, 42) argues that the way in which diversity is constituted must be contextualized in "the historical context of the creation of Canada, of its growth into an uneasy amalgam of a white settler colony with liberal democracy." For this reason, notions of otherness and difference are produced in relation to the presumed norm of white Canadian, where the definition of Canadian is very much tied to the country's colonial past and present. Processes of othering work to position diversity as peripheral to, or outside, normative board member subjectivity.

The white knapsack exercise is reflective of the way in which difference is institutionally defined as being located in the bodies, cultures, and experiences of others. Even as whiteness is identified and discussed, it is not included in the rubric of diversity. The "very idea that diversity is about those who 'look different' hence keeps whiteness in place" within organizations (Ahmed et al. 2006, 43). As Young (1990, 281) reminds us, attempts to ameliorate racial injustice must first recognize processes of racial differentiation that assign penalty and privilege. Training on racial and ethnic diversity does not appear to address

In Pursuit of "Appropriate" Decisions

forms of systemic discrimination, nor does it raise the possibility that the organization's decision-making criteria can be biased and produce inequitable results. Despite an attempt for (white) participants to consider their own racial privilege, this privilege is linked neither to the institution's historical emergence nor to its structures, policies, or practices.

Narrowing the Scope of Diversity

Although diversity is located in female and non-white identities, experiences, and cultures, it is also represented as relating to individual differences and traits rather than to social power. The dominant articulation of diversity within the training manuals "individuates differences by understanding them as residing in or belonging to individuals rather than produced by social structures" (Ahmed et al. 2006, 11; see also Hyndman 1998). In this way, the scope of diversity is narrowed to a focus on communication styles, individual experiences, and cultural beliefs "rather than [on] differences which relate to social power that in turn produce privilege and inequalities" (Ahmed et al. 2006, 11-12). The organizational focus on increasing awareness and sensitivity by learning about others reflects this narrow understanding of diversity.

In Unit 2's three-hour session, participants are expected to know "how gender, ethnic, cultural and linguistic dynamics impact on communications and risk assessment and risk management of offenders" (PBC n.d.-c, 249). They are also expected to demonstrate awareness in relation to several issues, including cultural and linguistic differences, empathy towards others, and the need for assessments that respect diversity. For example, Part D of Unit 2 focuses on linguistic differences. In this section, participants are expected to learn about communicating with others from different cultures. Communication styles are framed as an aspect of diversity that affects how people interact; participants are encouraged to recognize how "cultural backgrounds strongly influence communication styles" (262). Attention is drawn towards the impacts of accents, vocabulary, body language, and styles of communication on decision making. Participants are expected to "be sensitive to these influences" (ibid.), including how various cultural "filters" shape how messages are both sent and received (178). Knowledge of linguistic differences is seen as supporting appropriate decisions through reductions in miscommunication.

Although Unit 2 reviews some research on racism within the criminal justice system, the training reinforces a narrow vision of diversity through its focus on awareness and sensitivity as solutions to individual biases and ignorance. The narrowed scope works to make the PBC responsible for a more limited range of potential problems related to difference. For instance, by focusing on individual biases and ignorance, the organization's efforts are directed towards reducing the risk that individual board members will display bias or allow insensitive comments to enter into their dialogues with offenders and subsequent decision making. In order to be sensitive to various gender, ethnic, cultural, and linguistic differences, the Part D session expects decision makers to avoid using jargon or making racial jokes and remarks, focusing on the offender's accent, or "being misled or distracted by cultural differences such as body language, lack of eye contact, etc." (PBC n.d.-c, 263). The failure to demonstrate sensitivity along these lines poses risks to institutional reputation.

The "wrap up" session in Part E of Unit 2 reminds participants of the various "concessions" that are expected "in relation to gender, ethnic/cultural, and language," including different interview styles, greater flexibility when considering release options, and critical appraisal of "written materials to offset misperceptions" (PBC n.d.-c, 263). These concessions are based on the notion that fairness and equality are often achieved through different treatment in order to avoid placing certain groups at a disadvantage. Importantly, this reflects a key feminist understanding of substantive equality that does not involve treating women like men (Jhappan 1998; Hudson 2002), and here this logic is also extended to other groups. However, in the context of diversity training, concessions speak less of rights and more of needs; that is, certain groups have special needs that must be accommodated. Diversity is constituted as a need that can be responded to within dominant organizational policies and practices. Terms such as "needs" and "concessions" are much softer than terms such as "rights" because they are not necessarily linked to legislation (as something with which we must comply) but, rather, can be seen as good things the organization is doing in response to diversity (Ahmed 2007a).

Seeing the World "Differently"

As a vacuous concept, diversity has the tendency to neutralize "important histories of antagonism and struggle," with part of its appeal being its ability to offer "a 'happy' vision of society where conflict, differences and inequalities have already been resolved" (Ahmed et al. 2006, 12). In this sense, diversity is unhinged from issues of power and is constituted as a level playing field comprised of various differences that are framed as residing in individuals rather than in social contexts and structures (Razack 1998, 21). This understanding is reflected in PBC training on cultural perceptions, which generally aims to have participants recognize how their worldviews differ from those of others and have an impact upon decision making. Within this training, cultural perceptions

In Pursuit of "Appropriate" Decisions

are presented as value-neutral indicators of diversity, with the implication being that people just see the world differently. The social relations of power that work to constitute difference and to shape worldviews – such as racism, sexism, and colonialism – fade from view so that individuals are simply left with cultural perceptions (Razack 1998; Bannerji 2000).

Several informants spoke about the importance for decision makers of training pertaining to cultural perceptions. One informant explained that it was "counter-productive" to deny how one's worldview shapes the decision-making process (Interview 4). Instead, this informant believed in a type of "reflective objectivity" that enables one to be aware of personal biases: "Just be aware of it and question yourself, what are the lenses you're putting on when you're taking that file, reading the file, then meeting that offender, asking the questions and making that decision." Another informant expressed similar views regarding the need to learn about the various "filters," or lenses, that shape how one sees a person from a different background or gender (Interview 5). These comments highlight the importance of being aware of and sensitive to difference in order to help reduce the likelihood of making biased decisions.

Unit 2 offers critical perspectives on the notions of objectivity and impartiality, with the recognition that individuals "are inevitably partial" because everyone has particular worldviews that shape how events and other people are understood and interpreted (PBC n.d.-c, 262). Participants are encouraged to be responsible for keeping their biases in check by being aware of their own worldviews. According to the module, "unrelenting detachment is not invariably the best way to be objective and impartial, since it leaves the decision-maker only with his or her own perspective on the world" (255). Instead, participants are encouraged to empathize with others as a way to better to understand their perspectives and experiences: "Without the exercise of empathy decisions rest implicitly upon the assumption that the persons affected are like the decision-maker" (ibid.).[7] Consequently, the remedy for differing cultural perceptions is awareness and sensitivity in assessment and decision-making processes. The idea that the very laws and policies to which decision makers must abide are partial or biased does not enter the discussion.

A Limited Understanding of Female Offenders

Following Part B of Unit 2's training on gender differences, Unit 3 focuses specifically on female offenders. This follows from the PBC's understanding of diversity as including women as a special offender population, where gender is code for female. However, at the time of data collection, Unit 3 was incomplete, lacking both a lesson plan and learning objectives.[8] The module's outline tentatively indicates that Unit 3 is to be a two-hour session focused on the following topics: women in conflict with the law, Aboriginal female offenders, and special issues related to female offenders such as risk assessment factors and program considerations (PBC n.d.-c, 265). Based on the results of my requests under the *ATIA*, it appears that the training on women offenders consists of two presentations made to board members by Correctional Service of Canada representatives who specialize in the areas of women offender programs and research (CSC 2010a, 2010b). One presentation focuses on the CSC's reintegration programs for female offenders and explains the organization's approach to this population, including notions of risk, need, and responsivity (CSC 2010a). A section on Aboriginal female offenders explains the CSC's "circle of care" program model, which includes a curriculum consisting "of an integration of Aboriginal cultural models and mainstream skills development approaches" (n.pag). The second presentation explains the federal correctional system for women in Canada, female criminality (including comparisons to male criminality), the profile of federally sentenced women, and the assessment of risk and need for this population (CSC 2010b). These presentations are focused on imparting knowledge about federally sentenced female offenders and the system in which they are incarcerated.

The national training module on female offenders offers new board members a limited understanding of this population. The organization's reliance on the CSC to provide information on female offenders reinforces the CSC's approach to this population and precludes other sources of knowledge and information,[9] which may provide alternative perspectives. This differs from the other training sessions, which are compilations of selected materials. While these selections are likely institutionally self-serving, they do include sources beyond that of the CSC.[10] In addition, the information provided via the training presentations perpetuates a one-dimensional understanding of "woman," with Aboriginality included as the main difference among the population. Other intersecting lines of difference are not considered. These training materials constitute essentialized understandings of *the* female offender and *the* Aboriginal female offender, thereby resulting in simplified, one-dimensional understandings of what is a diverse population. This is not unique to training but, rather, reflects the broader organizational approach to issues of gender, as is discussed in Chapter 6.

Aboriginal Perceptions Training

The second training package utilized by the PBC is Aboriginal Perceptions Training (APT). APT is a recent initiative that has been piloted at the PBC since February 2008 (PBC 2008a, 209). This three-day training program is based on

In Pursuit of "Appropriate" Decisions

the RCMP's APT course, which has been modified by the PBC to meet its particular training needs (PBC 2009c). According to one informant, the PBC worked with Aboriginal consultants to develop this training program (Interview 2). Participants are expected to learn about "Aboriginal perspectives of history, justice, education and healing and mainstream perspectives" in order to "promote Board members'" understanding of how the historical variance between both perspectives may have contributed to the "over-representation of Aboriginal people in the criminal justice system" (PBC 2007d, 3),[11] as though cultural differences – not colonial practices – produced this problem. Such statements reflect an understanding of diversity as a level playing field devoid of historical and contemporary relations of power and privilege.

Several informants linked APT to the *Gladue* decision. For instance, one informant noted that APT was created in response to an identified need to implement the *Gladue* decision as "people needed greater understanding of how Aboriginals may ... find themselves ending up in conflict with the law over generations" (Interview 2). According to another informant, APT ensured that board members received training on the *Gladue* decision (Interview 10). With such knowledge of various background and systemic factors, APT is supposed to "facilitate informed conditional release decision-making in the case of Aboriginal offenders" (PBC 2007d, 3). Another informant felt that APT "get[s] people to think differently about the way they see the world" (Interview 8). The same informant noted that APT "is more or less successful depending on the participant's willingness to open up," although the informant had witnessed "people go through radical transformations in the way they think through that program."

APT has four objectives:

- to build awareness of the systemic elements that have contributed to the over-representation of Aboriginal People in the criminal justice system;
- to understand the unique position of Aboriginal People in Canadian Law;
- to provide a greater understanding of the role of healing in Aboriginal communities and in correctional programs; and
- to provide an overview of the background factors to be considered in decision-making. (PBC 2007d, 3)

The three-day training program is broken down into six sessions that cover such topics as perceptual screens, Aboriginal concepts of law and justice, traditional Aboriginal societies, the causes of overrepresentation, state assimilation practices, the concept of healing, and the implications of *Gladue* on decision making (PBC 2007d, 3-4). In each session, participants must complete individual and group exercises that involve reading and answering questions based on various excerpts, some of which are analyzed below.

Similar to Part C of Unit 2 of the general training program discussed above, the first session of APT focuses on perceptual screens. The aim of this session is to understand the various screens that shape how people view their world and affect how judgments are made, along with attitudes and feelings towards different situations (PBC 2007d, 3). The participant exercises in this session are focused on the different influences on individuals' lives, including early childhood experiences and environmental and social structures as well as culturally based communication patterns. Ostensibly, this two-hour session aspires to raise the idea that there is no "right" way to see the world but, rather, a diversity of viewpoints and frames based on one's upbringing and location. The implication for decision making is that board members and offenders may see the same situation differently. The example scenario used to illustrate this point contrasts (1) the environmental and social contexts of a non-Aboriginal male Torontonian with an Aboriginal male from a remote community in the Northwest Territories and (2) the decision-making practices of federal government officials with those of the chief and council of a remote Aboriginal community (PBC 2007d, 10-11). This exercise reinforces the idea that "they" (Aboriginal offenders) are different from "us" (white board members) and therefore think and do things differently.

One key focus of APT is learning about the assimilationist practices of the Canadian state. The fourth training session focuses on the residential school system and the so-called "60s scoop," involving the "adoption" of Aboriginal children by the Canadian state (PBC 2007d). The excerpt in the *Participant Workbook* on the residential school system presents this history from a largely self-congratulatory government perspective that focuses on the federal government's apology and reconciliation process – the "Aboriginal Action Plan" – and the importance of healing for Aboriginal communities. The emerging story is one about "them," not "us," with the result that "we" are not implicated or recognized as complicit (Razack 1998). Notwithstanding the recognition that Aboriginal peoples continue to be affected by the legacy of the residential school system, the focus of the excerpted information is the past. Participants are provided with a directory of residential schools in Canada that includes their names, locations, and opening and closing dates. An accompanying timeline of residential schools provides a rather sanitized version of history as a progression of events located in time and space but somehow not contextualized in colonization, cultural genocide, and white settlement. In comparison, the excerpt on the 60s' scoop provides a deeper context for the discussion of the removal of Aboriginal children from the 1960s to the mid-1980s. The text situates the theft of Aboriginal children within the colonial process and considers how Aboriginal communities have been, and continue to be, affected by this assimilationist program.

The session on assimilationist practices also includes a list of intergenerational impacts resulting from the residential school system and forced adoption programs. These issues are entirely negative, with no mention of the diverse attributes and resiliencies of Aboriginal peoples and communities. The list presents more as an inventory of Aboriginalized risk factors that board members can be trained to watch for when making decisions about Aboriginal offenders. Constituting Aboriginal peoples and communities in this way suggests a static level of dysfunction throughout their involvement with the penal system, thereby deflecting attention away from the role of correctional and conditional release policies in reinforcing these inequalities (Phillips 2011). As noted above, the use of lists or typologies risks relying on essentialized cultural traits that are based on colonial stereotypes and that dilute complex problems, rendering them seemingly susceptible to straightforward solutions (LaRocque 1997). Aboriginal diversity is selectively simplified into a format that is focused on transmitting information. The remaining challenge concerns how decision makers can use this knowledge to make decisions that are "fairer" and more appropriate for Aboriginal offenders.

The notion of "healing" also emerges as a prominent topic in APT. The session on healing seeks to enable participants to "explore and understand the concept of healing from an Aboriginal Perspective" as well as to "understand *healing as a correctional intervention in the rehabilitation of Aboriginal offenders*" (PBC 2007d, 4, emphasis added). Despite these two aims, the latter emerges most prominently in the *Participant Workbook*. The PBC identifies eight "principles of healing" to help inform participants' understanding of Aboriginal perspectives (76). What is conceptually interesting here is how these principles are subsequently reframed into correctionalist formats for training on "healing as a correctional intervention" – an issue that I explore in greater detail in the next chapter. In this context, an Aboriginal offender's culture is viewed as a correctional resource that leads to self-realization (Dhamoon 2009). Healing is reconstituted as something that can be used in the context of conditional release decision making to assess a person's progress towards rehabilitation and likelihood of successful reintegration.

The reconstitution of healing into correctionalist frames and formats is reflected in APT through several examples of file information that could be included in the documentation provided by the CSC for board member decision making. One example is a review of the offender prepared by an elder during four phases of the correctional process: intake, intervention, reintegration, and post-incarceration (PBC 2007d, 80-81). This report is supposed to identify "where an offender is on his/her healing journey" as well as to "assist the CMT [case management team] in completing their assessments on the offender" (80). The report is also viewed "as a holistic approach that *serves as a baseline from which to measure progress*" (ibid., emphasis added) and reflects the notion of the healing journey. Such an approach implies that board members are being encouraged to use their knowledge of healing as a yardstick to assess Aboriginal offenders. Healing is reframed as a necessary and culturally specific indicator of rehabilitation, as understood within the dominant correctional paradigm.

A second example related to healing is the idea of a healing plan. The elder may prepare this plan as part of the offender's overall correctional plan to ensure that "special attention" will be given to her or his "particular circumstances and background" as an Aboriginal person (PBC 2007d, 80). Nielsen (2003, 77) defines healing plans as holistic and as focused "on giving each individual an opportunity to work under close monitoring on the underlying causes of his behavior." These plans reportedly draw on "Aboriginal culture and practices" (ibid.). The *Participant Workbook* includes a sample of information that could be included in a healing plan, which charts out Aboriginal offenders' plans according to four dimensions – physical, emotional, spiritual, and mental – that are identified as being a constitutive part of human beings as well as necessary for holistic healing (PBC 2007d, 84). Yet the sample reflects an attempt by the institution to quantify healing based on the number and types of interventions (e.g., ceremonies, teachings, and activities) used to address each dimension. A sample healing plan provided in the *Participant Workbook* outlines a series of questions for the elder to complete about the Aboriginal offender, including whether s/he "acknowledge[s] a spiritual name," "understand[s] who he is," "understand[s] the four dimensions of human nature," and understands "the symbolism of the sweat lodge" (105-07). As with the above example of the elder review, the healing plan can be seen as an Aboriginalized correctional plan that attempts to translate Aboriginal knowledge into a format that fits within the dominant correctional framework – one in which change can be tracked and counted.

In keeping with other PBC training materials and approaches, gender is not considered within APT. The imagined Aboriginal offender appearing in the pages of the *Participant Workbook* is largely genderless, except for the fact that all Aboriginal offender scenarios are based on males. As LaRocque (1997,

In Pursuit of "Appropriate" Decisions

89-90) observes, the concern over cultural appropriateness works to "white-wash" gender domination within Aboriginal communities, such that "Aboriginal women's experiences, perspectives, and human rights" are often disregarded. This approach also results in the privileging of culture and ethnicity over gender, thereby preventing an intersectional analysis.

One informant explained that APT is

> a way of seeing the world through a different lens, so it could be applied to Aboriginal or any other culture or women or anything like that. The message of [the training] is going to be [that] ... what you perceive of an incidence is not what everyone is going to perceive and just trying to reinforce that. (Interview 11)

Interestingly, the informant understood the program as be applicable to other groups beyond Aboriginal offenders. The notion of seeing the world differently suggests that there is a "normal" way, such as that of white males, and a "different" way, such as that of Aboriginal and various non-white and/or non-male offenders. This quote illustrates the challenge of responding to difference through an approach that constitutes diversity vis-à-vis white male norms and standards: it limits the chance that normative practices and assumptions (such as the relevance of masculinities to offending and punishment) will be reconsidered, and it ensures that diversity remains an exception to the normal parole process.

Assessing the Implications of *Gladue*

The case of *R. v. Gladue* [1999], as shown in Chapter 2, was an important decision pertaining to Aboriginal offenders, with impacts ranging beyond sentencing to corrections and conditional release practices. The *Gladue* decision was welcomed by one informant, who explained that it allowed for the PBC's decision-making policies to be "more sensitive to the needs of offenders" by requiring board members to "take into account [offenders'] histor[ies], their background[s], their experience in the residential school and all that" (Interview 4). According to another informant, "the *Gladue* decision has asked that our board members take into account where [the] offender has come from and to make decisions based on what they feel would be the most effective rather than simply punitive" (Interview 11). Another indicated that the *Gladue* decision has had "a huge impact" on decision making because board members have to consider the backgrounds of Aboriginal offenders (Interview 10). As these responses suggest, the *Gladue* decision requires decision makers to situate Aboriginal offenders within the context of their communities and to take into consideration their histories and experiences as Aboriginal peoples in Canada.

As noted in the preceding section, the *Gladue* decision was interpreted as supporting the provision of knowledge about Aboriginal offenders and their specific backgrounds to board members through such mechanisms as diversity training. The PBC (n.d.-a, n.pag) contends that the "understanding and consideration of the unique background factors of Aboriginal offenders facilitates the decision-making process for Board members in that this information provides a more holistic and relevant picture of the offender." In order for board members to make release decisions, they must be "provided with adequate and relevant information in terms of who this person is, ties to community and supports, urban, rural, progress in addressing criminogenic factors" (ibid.). Such knowledge about Aboriginal offenders should then be used to assess their readiness for release and whether or not they pose undue risk to their communities. Knowledge about Aboriginal communities is deemed to be particularly important as the PBC "is aware that not all Aboriginal offenders are welcomed back into their communities" and thus "is open to other comprehensive release plans" (ibid.) as part of its being sensitive and responsive to Aboriginal difference. In addition, the organization wants information in cases in which an (Aboriginal) offender is "following traditional ways": "For example, if he/she is working with an Elder, participating in ceremony, living on the Pathways [Healing] range, have connections been made with community resources so that the offender may continue on this path upon release" (ibid.).[12] Such cultural information can then be used towards reaching "appropriate" decisions that take these factors into account.

The PBC (n.d.-a) notes that the information shared by the CSC is "critical" to its release decision making. Although board members have in the past "expressed frustration in the lack of information coming forward in the case of Aboriginal offenders," the PBC indicates that it is "very supportive of CSC's application of the *Gladue* decision" (ibid.). This application requires the social history of individual Aboriginal offenders to be taken into consideration in correctional planning and decision making (CSC 2009a) and included in the information submitted to the PBC for conditional release decision making. Aboriginal "social history" is defined as something that "applies to Aboriginal offenders by birth right" (PBC n.d.-a, n.pag). It includes the following factors:

- effects of residential school system (offender as survivor or intergenerational effects from family's historical experiences);

- family or community history of suicide;
- family or community history of substance abuse;
- family or community history of victimization;
- family or community fragmentation and/or displacement;
- level or lack of formal education;
- level of connectivity with family/community;
- experience in child welfare system;
- experience with poverty;
- loss of or struggle with cultural/spiritual identity;
- exposure or membership to street gangs; [and]
- experience with the young offender system and/or custodial sentencing under the Young Offenders Act. (PBC n.d.-a, n.pag)

The social history approach works to constitute a particular sort of Aboriginal subject in the context of conditional release policies and related documents. These factors reflect certain knowledges about, and representations of, Aboriginal peoples as a group that experiences systemic disadvantage due to "birth right," which presumably refers to a person's racial or cultural status as Aboriginal. However, unlike the *Gladue* decision, these factors do not include the experiences or impacts of racism and assimilation in the context of colonialism; nor is there mention of how gender (and other intersecting aspects of identity) interacts with these factors. Yet these factors are clearly racialized as belonging to Aboriginal offenders as a matter of birth right.

The above list reads as a collection of racialized risk factors through which the Aboriginal offender is constituted and subsequently assessed. This (re)framing presents the above experiences "as the calculable and predictable traits of an Indigenous offender" (Spivakovsky 2009, 222). It also works to shape the range of appropriate interventions to identify and target such traits, much in the same way as other criminogenic factors, such as anti-social attitudes or criminal associates, are identified and targeted (Spivakovsky 2009, 2013). As Spivakovsky (2009, 223) observes, in order to have them fit within the dominant correctional frame, "complex experiences of loss and dispossession" are reduced to the individual deficiencies of the Aboriginal offender and, thereby, disconnected from issues of power and privilege. Research by Hannah-Moffat and Maurutto (2010) also finds that *Gladue* principles are incorporated into the dominant language of criminogenic risk/need, with cultural considerations itemized alongside risk factors because the overarching conceptual framework remains anchored in the assessment of risk and need. They caution that the reframing of *Gladue* principles as risk factors will result in Aboriginal offenders continuing to be labelled as "high risk" and "high need." This, in turn, works against the purpose of incorporating *Gladue* principles into PBC policy, which is to make better-informed decisions regarding Aboriginal offenders.

One of the expected outcomes of the incorporation of *Gladue* principles into correctional policies and practices is the "empowerment of Aboriginal offenders to *enhance their cultural competency and celebrate their heritage*" (PBC n.d.-a, n.pag, emphasis added). Indeed, as Martel and Brassard (2008, 341) contend, it is through the provision of Aboriginal programming and spiritual ceremonies that Aboriginal offenders are said to "'learn' of their cultural distinctiveness" and to construct their own racialized identities. In this context, culture is defined as something Aboriginal offenders possess and can (learn to) express competently, while the notion of heritage is linked to the past as something Aboriginal offenders can celebrate. The concept of cultural competency suggests that there is a right way for the expression of one's culture, which is simultaneously framed as something that is immutable and homogenous. The notion of competency also suggests that it is something that can be measured and assessed as a factor affecting an offender's risk of reoffending.

Producing more culturally competent Aboriginal offenders who know and "celebrate their heritage" is seen to contribute to public safety through the reduction of their risk. Aboriginal identities are believed "to hold the key to rehabilitation from a life of crime" (Martel et al. 2011, 243). In the language of risk, the empowerment that is presumed to come through the adoption of an Aboriginal identity is more closely linked to the notion of protective factors as embracing one's Aboriginality could lower her or his risk of recidivism and prevent future involvement in the criminal justice system (Spivakovsky 2009, 2013; Marie 2010; Martel et al. 2011). It is in this sense that my analysis of the PBC's *Gladue* assessment suggests that it is the removal or loss of Aboriginal offenders' Aboriginality that is constituted as the problem, to which culturally appropriate programming and assessments can be applied.

Yet, as Waldram (1997, 38) argues, the correctional system has "profound difficulties ... in accurately identifying Aboriginal inmates in cultural terms and in understanding the influence that culture has on their prison behaviour." His research illustrates problems with the identification and labelling of Aboriginal offenders as Aboriginal and shows how traditional Aboriginal offenders are perceived and described within documentation by correctional staff. For Waldram, greater "accuracy" is needed if Aboriginal offenders "are to be treated as cultural beings" (34). In contrast, for Martel and colleagues (2011, 243), accuracy may not be the issue. These scholars point to the "troubling fact" that the "discovery" of one's Aboriginality occurs "via a state co-opted definition of

In Pursuit of "Appropriate" Decisions

what is and is not aboriginal culture." Penal institutions are setting the standards and expectations around Aboriginality in an effort to be inclusive. This issue is also relevant to the next section.

Divergent Ideologies: Institutional Attempts to "Indigenize" Risk

In the early 2000s, the PBC entertained the idea of developing a risk assessment framework that was responsive to Aboriginal offenders. The organization contracted with a consultant to "research and conceptualize" its risk assessment process for Aboriginal offenders "through a traditional holistic Creational View" (PBC 2001, 1). The consultant's report sets out a "traditional Aboriginal framework" that was used to analyze the PBC's decision-making policies for Aboriginal offenders, with specific focus on section 2.1 of the Policy Manual and elder-assisted hearings. This framework attempts to incorporate Aboriginal philosophies and worldviews, and recognizes the impacts of colonization on Aboriginal offenders through the disruption of "traditional knowledge systems, and traditional social institutions within Aboriginal communities" (2). According to the PBC (2004a, 8, emphasis added), this "framework was to become a training tool that would help the Board members gain a better understanding of *the Aboriginal worldview*, as well as a better understanding of the offender as an Aboriginal person." Such an exercise reflects a common institutional response to difference whereby "aboriginal culture is taken to be a bounded, unified set of customs, habits, values and beliefs" (Martel et al. 2011, 245). The selection and reproduction of *one* Aboriginal worldview within a training tool ensures that "culture operates as a totalizing idiom" instead of reflecting the multiplicity of Aboriginal worldviews, experiences, and cultural practices (ibid.). The homogeneous characterization of Aboriginality reflects the challenge of institutionalizing diversity. The selective inclusion shows that something is being done to address Aboriginal difference, while at the same time it produces a certain version of Aboriginality that Aboriginal offenders may then be expected to represent (an issue that I address further in the next chapter).

A key finding of the consultant's report is that the assessments used by the Correctional Service of Canada and provided to board members for their decision making do not capture "essential cultural information" that would help them understand "Aboriginal specific risk factors and areas of need" (PBC 2001, 51).[13] The example of employment is used to explain how offenders' files do not reflect Aboriginal understandings of employment, such as value attached to "the activities an individual participates in to sustain and enhance life" (ibid.), which may be particularly relevant for Inuit offenders. To rectify this situation, the consultant recommends the creation of a grid based on the seven stages of life for Aboriginal peoples that can capture "areas of need and risk factors" that are "Aboriginal specific" as well as take into account the impacts of colonization on Aboriginal offenders and their communities (52). In this way, the report recommends holistic assessments that are informed by Aboriginal perspectives on healing in the context of Aboriginal offenders' "development through the seven stages of life" (61). Similar approaches have been considered in Australia (see Day 2003; Day et al. 2003; Spivakovsky 2008, 2013) and New Zealand (see Marie 2010; Spivakovsky 2013) to improve the assessment and treatment of Indigenous offenders.

The consultant's proposition of an Aboriginal assessment tool (i.e., grid system) to measure an Aboriginal offender's progress through the seven stages of life reflects an attempt to translate diverse Aboriginal perspectives and knowledges into a format that can be recognized and utilized by the corrections and conditional release system's dominant frame of risk. The consultant's recommendation is an attempt to make the penal system adapt *its* knowledges and practices regarding Aboriginal offenders rather than have Aboriginal perspectives and knowledges integrated into the dominant penal frame. A reading of the consultant's report illustrates the dissimilarity of Aboriginal and mainstream understandings of concepts like healing and risk assessment. For example, the report is critical of healing or rehabilitation being framed and understood via cognitive behavioural theories because of their incompatibility with the "traditional Aboriginal framework" (PBC 2001, 54). In particular, according to the consultant, cognitive behavioural theories of rehabilitation are based on bringing an offender in line with society's norm, which is not appropriate for Aboriginal offenders as this norm has been imposed through colonial policies of assimilation and cultural destruction. To remain consistent with the ideal of diversity when assessing an Aboriginal offender's healing, the PBC ought to consider information from a traditional Aboriginal perspective (60) and not from within the dominant frame based on cognitive behaviouralism and the risk-need-responsivity model. The failure to utilize culturally appropriate modes of assessment could therefore result in unfair and potentially discriminatory decisions.

The consultant's findings reflect Monture-Angus's (1999, 26) long-standing argument that the logic of risk management, as "one of the foundational ideas of the current correctional philosophy," is incompatible with Aboriginal cultures and traditions. This incompatibility goes beyond "cultural conflict" due to the ways that risk thinking frames relationships, as though individuals can be disassociated from their communities and broader social relations. Risk assessments individualize risk into an assortment of domains that cannot capture the interrelationships between an individual and her or his community. The "individualizing of risk absolutely fails to take into account the impact of colonial oppression on the lives of Aboriginal men and women" (27). As a result, risk assessments do not measure risk but, rather, "one's experiences as part of an oppressed group" (Monture-Angus 1999, 27; see also Marie 2010; Martel et al. 2011). The individualization of risk makes it difficult to account for social context factors, such as discrimination or interdependence, that shape people's lives (Day 2003) – a challenge I discuss earlier in relation to the implementation of *Gladue*.

The consultant's attempt to frame Aboriginal perspectives and knowledges into easily digestible bits for the PBC illustrates the challenge of bringing together divergent worldviews. It also raises questions regarding the degree to which different knowledges and perspectives are embraced and integrated into policies and practices. As noted above, the consultant presents a case for the use of an Aboriginal assessment tool based on traditional Aboriginal knowledges and perspectives; in this sense, the penal system is asked to do things differently. The notion of an Aboriginal assessment tool reflects the dominance of risk thinking and the barriers to bringing about change in relation to how penal institutions deal with Aboriginal offenders. As Day (2003, 7) observes, a key issue relates to making change within "a dominant culture that seeks an evidence basis for interventions, defined by an adherence to a scientific method of knowledge production." Existing methodologies for evaluating interventions for Aboriginal peoples may be culturally biased and inadvertently discount different ways of conceptualizing and assessing the likelihood of reoffending or what an individual needs to address the challenges s/he faces.

The PBC contracted with the same consultant in the 2001-02 fiscal year to "develop a final enhanced training framework for risk assessment in a traditional Aboriginal way" (PBC 2004a, 8).[14] This second contract allowed the consultant to "further research and consult across the country" in order to create an "Aboriginal Risk Assessment Framework" (ibid.). However, the PBC determined that it "was not yet ready at this stage to implement" the framework; instead, the organization "recognize[d] that much work remain[ed] to be done before implementing such a tool and that it should move steadily but cautiously in this direction" (9). Subsequent discussions of the framework in the documents accessed were not evident. Nonetheless, this attempt to Indigenize risk is significant because it shows how the PBC combines two incompatible worldviews (or knowledges) in order to accommodate diversity.

Conclusions

In this chapter, I show how the PBC has incorporated concerns about gender and diversity into its dominant institutional frame. The integration of information about Aboriginal, female, and ethnocultural differences into the PBC is characterized by the selective inclusion of information that is more general in nature, partly because the complexities of these differences do not easily lend themselves to concise policy applications. I examine three different organizational knowledge practices that aim to produce gender-responsive and culturally appropriate parole decisions for offenders identified as different according to gender, race, and culture. Diversity training, the assessment of *Gladue*, and attempts to Indigenize risk are organizational attempts to know certain populations and to make diversity applicable to issues of risk assessment in the context of decision making. Yet the challenge of ensuring culturally competent and gender-responsive approaches means that decision makers ought to know these particular populations, recognize their own personal biases, and ensure that the appropriate knowledges and sensitivities come together in practice.

What can we make of these attempts to include diversity and to be responsive to difference? I demonstrate the difficulties associated with the institutionalization of diversity and the pitfalls of institutional approaches that aim to be inclusive yet that work to produce and to circulate gendered and racialized knowledges of female and non-white others. Such practices of knowing the other reflect the "double-edge sword" (Razack 1998, 58) of inclusion, whereby, although cultural and gendered phenomena are recognized as important to contextualizing marginalized offenders' identities and experiences, these phenomena are included within an institutional setting that packages difference as individual traits disconnected from broader historical and contemporary inequalities. Through these knowledge practices, whiteness and maleness are reinforced as the normative subjectivity of decision makers and of the normative offender. There is no space within these approaches to consider issues of white complicity in systems of racism, colonialism, and sexism and how ideas about race and gender are interwoven into the penal system, producing exclusion, disadvantage, and discrimination. In this institutional context, what Ahmed (2012, 164) calls the "smile of diversity" deflects attention away from the complicated and problematic ways in which difference is governed.

Cultural Ghettos?
Organizational Responses to Aboriginal Peoples

Colonial and (post)colonial policies have had devastating impacts on Aboriginal communities, producing poor social, political, and economic outcomes. One such impact can be seen in the relationship between Aboriginal peoples and the Canadian criminal justice system. As discussed in Chapter 1, Aboriginal offenders are overrepresented within federal corrections – a trend that has remained constant for over forty years and that has recently worsened (see OCI 2014). Additionally, parole and conditional release rates for Aboriginal prisoners are consistently lower than are the rates for non-Aboriginal groups, but the rates of revocation and new offences are higher (PBC 2000a). For these reasons, Aboriginal issues constitute the bulk of the Parole Board of Canada's diversity work. The PBC's emphasis on Aboriginal peoples is reinforced by the pivotal Supreme Court decision in *Gladue*. The PBC is therefore cognizant of the various "pressures and expectations for extensive, effective and integrated action" to address "the needs of Aboriginal peoples" (3). In this chapter, I trace the development of Aboriginal-focused initiatives and unpack how Aboriginality is constituted through these strategies.

The primary diversity initiatives related to Aboriginal peoples developed at the PBC are elder-assisted hearings and community-assisted hearings. Both initiatives are included in policy and are intended to respond to the special needs of Aboriginal offenders and their communities and, increasingly, Aboriginal victims. Elders play a key role in EAHs and CAHs and serve multiple functions: as sources of knowledge about Aboriginality for board members, as "interpreters" of culture, as "bridges" between Aboriginal offenders and board members, and as liaisons between Aboriginal communities and the PBC. However, elders and Aboriginal knowledges are used only selectively to allow for the adaptation of conditional release hearings while dominant decision-making paradigms remain intact.

Despite the fact that EAHs have existed since 1992 and CAHs since 1997, there is a paucity of academic research on these initiatives. In this chapter, I detail the genesis of the PBC's initiatives, address the implications associated with their use, and examine how Aboriginal needs and problems are constituted at these hearings. EAHs and CAHs are two techniques used by the PBC to modify and to Aboriginalize standardized practices (i.e., parole hearings) to accommodate diversity demands. In addition, the PBC's implementation of the *Gladue* decision illustrates how the organization is grappling with issues of Aboriginal difference. I argue that Aboriginal offenders are "ghettoized" in the realm of culture, meaning that culture and cultural difference are constituted as the defining features of Aboriginal offenders and the central focus of the modified hearing approaches. Consequently, EAHs and CAHs are considered to be exceptional and peripheral to the "normal" program of parole. These initiatives also serve important institutional functions by allowing the organization to appear responsive to the needs of Aboriginal peoples, thereby reducing potential risks to reputation through claims of inaction and cultural ignorance.

The emphasis on Aboriginal offenders is justified but has the unintended consequence of making diversity initiatives synonymous with Aboriginality and therefore marginalizing other forms of diversity. In particular, gender, although recognized as distinct, is not specifically mentioned within the institutional discussions of EAHs or CAHs, even though it recognized that female offenders have needs that differ from those of male offenders. As I examine in Chapter 6, gender – along with ethnicity and/or culture more generally – is bracketed within the context of initiatives designed to address the needs of Aboriginal offenders. As a result, the focus of EAHs and CAHs is an implicitly male Aboriginal subject.

Elder-Assisted Hearings and the Role of Elders

EAHs are the main diversity initiative at the PBC.[1] This hearing model was the most common initiative named when informants were asked to identify how the PBC had responded to calls for better approaches to diversity, both pre- and post-*Corrections and Conditional Release Act*. The EAH initiative also has the largest volume of documentation (i.e., policy, background, training, and evaluation) produced internally by the PBC. This is consistent with the interview data that suggest that the special needs of Aboriginal offenders are the paramount focus of the PBC's diversity initiatives. In this section, I trace the creation of the EAH model and consider various issues and tensions associated with its implementation and use, including the key role played by elders. I demonstrate how Aboriginal knowledges and practices were selectively incorporated into an "adapted" hearing format that attempts to be responsive to Aboriginal difference while maintaining dominant decision-making frameworks.

Background

The perceived need for improved approaches to dealing with Aboriginal offenders during the parole process was identified before the enactment of the *CCRA*. A key document – as discussed in Chapter 1 – was the *Final Report of the Task Force on Aboriginal Peoples in Federal Corrections* (Solicitor General 1988a, hereafter the Final Report), which makes a strong case for Aboriginal-specific approaches in both corrections and parole. In relation to the latter, the Final Report recommends the use of elders as assessors to aid the decision-making processes of the PBC. The traditional role of elders is framed as helping to counsel "community members in appropriate behaviour, maintaining peace and harmony among community members and generally acting as grandparent to the community" (37). It was believed that elders could better assess Aboriginal offenders' suitability for parole because of their knowledge of Aboriginal communities, spiritual and cultural correctional programs, and how best to communicate with Aboriginal offenders. Elders' perspectives were viewed as adding "significantly to the understanding of the case and thus [facilitating] a more equitable decision" (38). Accordingly, the Final Report includes the recommendation that, if requested by a prisoner, elders be allowed to submit an assessment to the PBC that would be weighted similarly to other professional assessments.

EAHs originated in the Prairie Region in the 1980s as board members and staff tried to "address issues regarding Aboriginal offenders" and, especially, the "disproportionate number of incarcerated offenders of Aboriginal ancestry" (PBC 2006a, 1). The PBC's (2006a) background paper, "Elder-Assisted Hearings: An Historical Perspective," notes that studies conducted by the Prairie Region in the early 1980s indicated that Aboriginal offenders were more likely to be denied parole and waive their right to a hearing than were non-Aboriginal offenders. In addition, it reports that Aboriginal offenders felt "uncomfortable" and "alone" at parole hearings "without having someone with them [whom] they could rely on for support" (2). In sum, the PBC (2000b, 3) recognized that the "conditional release process failed to take into account the unique needs and circumstances of Aboriginal offenders."

The impetus for a more culturally relevant hearing also came from the perception that "Aboriginal offenders were not opening up in the hearing, [that] they were struggling to communicate," and that "they were one word answering" (Interview 8). As this same informant explained, because of these communication barriers, "board members were not getting the kind of information they needed to make decisions," thereby limiting their ability to make "good decisions." Consequently, the communication barriers between board members and Aboriginal offenders were seen as impinging on the PBC's decision-making abilities.

The PBC (2006a, 2) spent much of the 1991-92 fiscal year consulting with elders, Native brotherhoods, and Native liaison officers in the Prairie Region regarding how the parole hearing process could better respond to the needs of Aboriginal offenders. At a November 1991 meeting, one Aboriginal board member "spoke of a vision for the [PBC] to deal with Aboriginal offenders which would include the involvement of Elders in non-confrontational hearings" (ibid.). This idea was supported and steps were taken to pilot the model. The first EAH subsequently took place on January 22, 1992, at Drumheller Institution in Alberta.

Part of the challenge of the EAH related to finding "the ways and means where [the PBC] can adapt [the] hearing and decision process to be more culturally sensitive to the aboriginal way without adversely affecting the Board's role and mandate to render independent, quality decisions" (PBC 2006a, 3). During this development phase, tensions existed around the various ways in which elders were to be defined and integrated into the process. A report prepared by a consultant in 1992 indicates that, initially, elders were "invited to serve as a resource" to board members during hearings as well as to provide "cultural guidance and spiritual knowledge" and "put the offenders at ease" during parole hearings (ibid.). The use of elders as advisors to the process is reflected in the fact that the PBC contracts with specific individuals to provide this service. Yet a key issue related to determining how much information elders were to receive about offenders prior to EAHs and the nature and extent of information they were expected to provide to board members (PBC 2000b, 17).

A point of controversy in the development of EAH policy and practice related to the elders' "place" during board members' deliberations. To some, the elders' presence violated "the principles of fundamental fairness" (PBC 2006a, 4) because they "could have raised issues to Board members during deliberations to which the offender did not have a chance to respond" (PBC 2000b, 3). To clarify the legality of elders' presence, the PBC sought two legal opinions, one in 1995 and another in 1997. Both opinions recommended that the parole applicant consent to the elders' presence (PBC 2006a, 4-5). In response, the PBC established some procedural safeguards to ensure offenders understood their rights at EAHs. For instance, a consent form was created in 1996 that required offenders to agree to the elders' presence at all times. Information was also provided as to the role of the elders, and applicants were asked to indicate whether they wanted their hearing to open with a prayer (5).[2] This was seen to be the "most appropriate way to allow offenders to choose whether or not they want an Elder assisted hearing while also providing the offender's consent for the Board Elder to remain in the hearing room during deliberations" (PBC 2000b, 15). The debate around the presence of an elder during deliberations raises questions as to her or his place in the hearing process and the extent to which s/he is perceived by the offender as a neutral third party, as an agent of the PBC, and/or as a source of support.

Another issue that arose during the development of the EAH approach concerned who was eligible for these hearings. During the implementation of EAHs in the Prairie Region, "there were concerns being voiced that EAHs should not be imposed on any offender and that the choice to ... [take part] should be theirs" (PBC 2006a, 3-4). Initially, Aboriginal offenders were given first priority in assignments to EAHs, although, in the Prairie Region, many non-Aboriginal offenders also attended these hearings (4). The Pacific Region attempted to accommodate requests for EAHs by establishing an "order of preference": "1. Aboriginal offenders practicing traditional ways; 2. Non-aboriginal offenders practicing traditional ways; 3. Aboriginal offenders not practicing traditional ways; [and] 4. Non-aboriginal offenders not practicing traditional ways" (8). However, such an order of preference was later abandoned, in keeping with the rationale that, although such hearings are meant for Aboriginal offenders, a "non-Aboriginal offender, who is committed to *an Aboriginal way of life*, may also request" an EAH (PBC 2011c, Ch. 9.2.1, 123, emphasis added). As such, access to an EAH was predicated not so much on one's racialized status as Aboriginal as on one's practising "traditional ways" or "an Aboriginal way of life." As one informant explained, "you don't have to be born an Aboriginal, if you have a genuine desire and you engage in programs to discover Aboriginal spirituality you can also have access to this type of hearing" (Interview 5). Ostensibly, "genuine desire" and a record of programming would be demonstrated within the offender's case file to support her or his request for an EAH. The EAH approach therefore allows for a new type of hearing that can accommodate some Aboriginal offenders, while others remain within the regular hearing format and can continue to have a non-Aboriginal experience.

The physical format of EAHs provoked much debate and disagreement, with the table emerging as the paramount source of contention. According to one informant, "the fight about the table deal for the Aboriginal hearings was unreal because board members like to have a table to do what you're doing [writing], and to not have a table really bothered them" (Interview 7). For some, tables were viewed as a barrier to open dialogue among those participating in the hearings, while others were committed to the status quo. The PBC's (2006a, 5) background paper on EAHs notes that it "was some time before Elder-Assisted Hearings were held in a circle without the benefit of a table." It appears that much debate occurred around the organization of the hearing room and whether or not to remove the table or arrange chairs in a circle format. The same informant notes that "one region in particular just raised hell about that [the removal of tables], like no way, ... gotta have a table" (Interview 7).

Another controversial issue concerned women wearing trousers at EAHs in the Prairie Region: "Cultural protocol is such that women attending [the] ceremony (smudge) wear a skirt or place a shawl, or similar item over their hips" (PBC 2006a, 6). Men are encouraged to wear casual clothing instead of suits (PBC n.d.-d). To accommodate women who did not want to follow the cultural protocol, EAHs were divided into two parts: "ceremonial" and "business," with the former part being optional (PBC 2006a, 6). The PBC (2009g, n.pag) indicates that, in the Prairie Region, the skirt protocol is in place as a sign of "respect for the traditional and cultural values of the First Nations people in the Prairies, and as a show of respect for the Elders performing the ceremony." The protocol is based on the following rationale:

Women are asked to wear skirts as validation to the power they hold. Women are the givers of life; they are the nurturers. Because of that nurturing role and the gift of being able to provide life to the unborn child in the womb, they share a sacred and powerful gift with the Creator and Mother Earth. The wearing of the skirt honours that power and that very sacred connection to Mother Earth. (ibid.)

This protocol does not apply to hearings for Inuit offenders. Ostensibly as a measure to accommodate women who are not dressed appropriately, PBC hearing officers are to "have shawls available at the hearings for women who wish to participate in the ceremony" (ibid.).

Although these alternate hearing approaches for Aboriginal offenders developed in the Prairie Region prior to the *CCRA*, one informant indicated that the legislation gave the PBC "a push to basically kind of force the other regions, because they were not as excited about it, to get going" (Interview 13). According to this informant, the willingness to implement EAHs throughout the regions was mixed, with some regions keen on the idea and others fairly resistant. This informant also notes that the impetus for establishing EAHs was strongest in the Prairie Region because

> they were seeing those offenders on a daily basis. They were seeing them
> coming back. They were seeing them not showing up for hearings because
> they [i.e., Aboriginal offenders] thought, we're kaput anyways, so why bother.
> And they were seeing them going back to situations in the community which
> they knew in advance would probably not be of much help.

The push to create EAHs in the region was, according to this same informant, largely led at the time by an Aboriginal board member and regional vice-chairperson who was described as being "a voice in the desert." The PBC's (2006a, 7) background paper on EAHs also suggests that the drive for these hearings in the Pacific Region was led by this same individual. The informant contended that much of the resistance from other regions was due to a numbers issue: that is, "the numbers [of Aboriginal offenders] in the Prairies was huge, but in Ontario and Quebec and the Atlantic Region there were not that many Aboriginal offenders, so the pressure was not sensed as much" (Interview 13). This person went on to say that to bring about changes in policy, all regions need to be on board. However, with EAHs, "when you have one region [Prairie] and a bit in BC [British Columbia] pushing, it doesn't have the same momentum." For the Ontario and Quebec regions, the need "to develop new approaches for Aboriginal offenders... was not an issue, [as] they would see an Aboriginal offender once in a blue moon."

The PBC's (2006a) background paper does not highlight these tensions in the development of EAHs and their implementation across the regions. It details the different experiences of each region as EAHs were put into practice, but it does not indicate that some regions were resistant to the implementation of this approach to parole hearings for Aboriginal offenders. Similar to the informant quoted above, the resistance appears to be related to numbers: the background paper indicates that the numbers of Aboriginal offenders in Quebec was small compared to the number in western Canada. For this reason, the Quebec Region commissioned a study to determine whether or not any changes should be made to hearings to make them more respectful towards Aboriginal offenders (PBC 2006a, 11), which suggests that some regions needed additional "proof" that such specialized hearings were required, thereby necessitating organizational action. As I discuss in Chapter 5, a similar pattern can be seen in relation to the adoption of different approaches for ethnocultural offenders.

The differing experiences of each region also suggest that the development and implementation of EAHs varied because "the replication of existing models was not appropriate," with the result "that each region should establish their own model in consultation with Aboriginal communities, offenders, CSC staff, Native Liaison Officers and Elders" (PBC 2006a, 13). The PBC (2000a, 5) indicates that the requirement for the organization to be "flexible in its approach to assisted hearings" is based on regional consultations with Aboriginal communities. Regional differences include the presence (or absence) of elders during deliberations, the layout of the hearing room and hearing format, and having elders/Aboriginal advisors on contract with the PBC or using the CSC's elders (PBC 2006a). The regions also used different names for EAHs, with the exception of the Pacific and Prairie Regions. For example, these hearings are known as Aboriginal-assisted hearings in the Atlantic Region, adapted hearings for Aboriginal offenders in the Quebec Region, and Aboriginal circle hearings in the Ontario/Nunavut Region (PBC 2006a). Ostensibly, these name variations reflect the preferences of the regional office and/or the Aboriginal communities in the area.

The Executive Committee gave permission to the other regions to "consider implementing" such approaches to parole hearings for Aboriginal offenders in 1995 (PBC 2000b, 5). Such a directive appears to lack persuasion and does not convey a sense of urgency. Nevertheless, EAHs began in the Pacific Region in 1997, followed by the remaining regions in 2000 (PBC 2006a). Starting in the early 2000s,[3] steps were taken to implement "more culturally sensitive hearings" in the Northwest Territories (PBC 2002a), Nunavut, and in other areas, such as Labrador (PBC 2006a). As I discuss next, Inuit offenders were recognized as distinct from other Aboriginal groups and therefore steps were taken to develop a separate EAH model to reflect this difference.

Hearings for Inuit Offenders

Inuit offenders are recognized as a special group in the context of Aboriginality, thereby justifying that PBC policies and practices adopt a more specific approach to Inuit parole hearings. The PBC (2004a, 13) views the EAH model as being "based on First Nations traditions and culture." Despite the fact that the other

Aboriginal offender populations (i.e., Métis and Inuit) are "considerably smaller," the PBC recognizes that "the needs and circumstances" of these populations "are equally as important" (ibid.). However, it appears that hearings for these other Aboriginal populations have lagged behind. Hearings for Inuit offenders developed at different times in the regions. Inuit offenders are seen as a unique Aboriginal group because of their isolation and "connection with their home," and because many of them can speak neither English nor French (PBC 2006b, 3). Inuit offenders from northern Canada experience geographic dislocation during incarceration in southern penitentiaries and may face additional challenges while on conditional release if they are not paroled to home communities.

The first Inuit hearing was held in the Atlantic Region in September 2001 after consultations with Inuit and Innu communities in Labrador (PBC 2006b). An Inuit hearing model was explored in 2004 in the Ontario/Nunavut Region when it contracted with an Inuk consultant to prepare guidelines for Inuit hearings (PBC 2004b). Following the PBC Policy Manual's EAH model, flexibility was allowed to enable the region to provide hearings for Inuit offenders. As with EAHs, it was recommended that Inuit hearings allow Inuit offenders to be assisted by elders and liaison officers and that they provide for ceremonial practices and a circle format (PBC 2004b). For instance, prior to the start of a hearing, time would be allotted for the lighting of the *qulliq* (a crescent-shaped stone lamp typically fuelled by animal fat) and a prayer given by the elder in the offender's chosen language. The guidelines also recommend that Inuit hearings follow a circle format, without a table, in which participants are arranged in a particular order (PBC 2004b).

As with the general EAH model, Inuit hearings are viewed as allowing for board members to gain greater knowledge of Inuit offenders for risk assessment and decision-making purposes. Inuit hearings are also presented as improving board members' "confidence level[s]" as well as enhancing "cooperation from the Inuit offenders" (PBC 2004b, 11). The consultant's report also stresses the role of Inuit cultural awareness training for board members and staff and recommends that the PBC provide funding for some members and staff to travel to Nunavut "to experience the living ways of the Inuit and meet with people who impact the community the most" (6). To further develop its hearings for Inuit offenders, the report encourages the organization to forge partnerships with community organizations in order to enhance its decision-making process for Inuit offenders as well as to create an "ongoing communications strategy" so that the PBC can better share information about its roles and responsibilities (PBC 2004b, 11). The report also recommends a review of the risk assessment used by the PBC to ensure that it is "culturally sensitive to the Inuit lifestyles" (9). As discussed in the previous chapter, attempts to meld risk logics with holistic approaches, such as through hearings for Inuit or Aboriginal offenders, pose conceptual and practical difficulties that are not easily overcome (see Monture-Angus 1999; Hannah-Moffat and Maurutto 2010). For instance, producing a "culturally sensitive" risk assessment approach to parole hearings that considers Inuit lifestyles may result in various cultural considerations being translated into a list of Inuit risk factors. This is because the overarching conceptual framework of risk assessment remains focused on individualized traits associated with the likelihood of recidivism.

Implementation Issues

The inclusion of Aboriginal difference through the EAH model is characterized by institutional disagreement about how best to integrate Aboriginality into the PBC's policies and practices. The implementation of the EAH approach to Aboriginal offenders was monitored by the Performance Measurement Division of the PBC. Requests made under the *ATIA* yielded one evaluation of the EAH model from March 2000. One of the purposes of this evaluation was to determine whether or not the implementation of the EAH policy had "lived up to its original spirit and intent" (PBC 2000b, 9).[4] Several areas of concern in relation to the implementation of EAHs in the Prairie Region are highlighted in the evaluation report. These concerns echo some of the tensions discussed previously around the role of the elder and the degree to which Aboriginality could be safely or appropriately accommodated without undermining the integrity of decision making.

One identified concern related to the failure to remove barriers as most EAHs were being held in regular hearing rooms. The level of participation of elders at EAHs also differed depending on factors such as the elders' and board members' personalities and the type of case under review (PBC 2000b, 9). In addition, there was apparent difficulty on the part of some board members in relating "information on Aboriginal cultural and spiritual traditions to the risk assessment criteria" (ibid.). Such implementation issues hint not only at the difficulty of modifying an existing approach to make it sensitive to culture and other forms of difference but also at the resistance of some staff and board members to the accommodations required by the EAH format.

Another implementation issue pertained to the "conflict between the need for regional flexibility and national consistency" (PBC 2000b, 9). For instance, with the implementation of EAHs in the Pacific Region, there was concern that the process reflected "Prairie Indian traditions, which may not [have been] culturally appropriate to other Aboriginal groups within the region" (11). Here, "regional flexibility" was desired because it would allow the Pacific Region to adapt the EAH approach so as to base it on Coast Salish traditions and, thus, avoid imposing different cultures on offenders. According to the evaluation report, the needs of Métis offenders could be met by the regular EAH model, but Inuit traditions had yet to be addressed (20). The report recommends that the PBC "consider what steps could be taken to accommodate the needs of Inuit offenders within the Elder assisted hearing approach or whether this is appropriate" (39). Interestingly, despite the unique status of Métis peoples in Canada (see, for example, Restoule 2000; Sawchuck 2001), Métis offenders, unlike Inuit offenders, are not given much consideration within the PBC's documents on EAHs. One document notes that Métis offenders were "comfortable" using the EAH model, although they preferred access to Métis elders (PBC 2004a, 14). Perhaps this is because there is an organizational understanding of Métis offenders as different – but not different enough to warrant an approach separate from that offered Aboriginal offenders.

The issue of knowledge emerged as another implementation concern. In particular, questions were raised around PBC-contracted elders' knowledges of "Aboriginal traditions," especially those of nations or groups that are not their own (PBC 2000b, 20). The report explicates that both the Prairie and Pacific Regions attempted "to ensure that their Elders represent[ed] the diversity of the Aboriginal population in the region" (ibid.). However, despite the recognition that "Aboriginal traditions differ from nation to nation," the PBC maintains that "the core values of Respect, Caring, Kindness, Honesty, Sharing, Trust and Honour remain pretty much the same for all" (ibid.). The notion of "core values" reflects a homogenous approach to what are heterogeneous populations. Such an approach is suited to the organizational mandate to be responsive to and accommodating of Aboriginal needs, yet only to the extent that doing so is reasonable, as defined by the institution. One informant indicated that there "was never any claim that" an elder would "have to be of the same background as the offender" for an EAH (Interview 8). The perception was that "an Aboriginal offender who was truly following his path would respect an elder no matter what their culture was."[5] Again, it is left to organization's discretion to select elders' knowledges and the elements that comprise a culturally sensitive hearing format.

The form and structure of EAHs are based on particular conceptions about Aboriginal traditions and vary across the regions. The circle format is one common form used in EAHs in the Pacific Region and, more recently, in the Prairie Region. EAH policy for the use of the circle outlines where each person attending the hearing sits, whether within the main circle or outside of it in a semi-circle (PBC 2000b, 22; PBC 2009g). The policy also explains the direction and order of speech around the main circle (e.g., clockwise, starting with board members) (PBC 2000b, 22). Other traditions reflected in EAHs are prayers and smudging, which are conducted upon the offenders' request. In the Pacific Region, a prayer may be conducted at the start of an EAH "for truth, honesty and good judgement" (23). A smudge of the hearing room may also occur "depending on the traditions of the Board Elder" (ibid.).

Another tradition concerns the use of an eagle feather when speaking. This feather "is used as a symbol of speaking the truth and speaking from the heart" (PBC 2000b, 23). The use of the eagle feather is dependent on whether or not it is part of "the traditions of the Board Elder" (ibid.) and is associated mainly with the Pacific Region. In contrast, in the Prairie Region an eagle feather may be used during a smudge but not as a speaking instrument. The PBC notes that the "use of the Eagle feather has been a somewhat controversial issue in the Prairie region with some Aboriginal people and at least one Board Elder feeling strongly that it should not be used in such a public place as the [correctional] institution" (ibid.) More specifically, there was concern that the feather was "too sacred" to be used in a penitentiary, suggesting that not all symbols or practices are easily portable to penal environments.

In sum, the various ways that the PBC has (selectively) taken up Aboriginal traditions highlight some of the tensions and contradictions associated with creating culturally appropriate hearings in the context of penal institutions, particularly where certain practices are transported into foreign and incompatible contexts. The institutionalization of Aboriginal traditions requires certain decisions to be made concerning which symbols and practices to import and incorporate. For example, although the eagle feather may be a preferred symbol for inclusion within conditional release hearings, its meaning and use within penal spaces are contested. As evidenced by the different approaches taken within the Pacific and Prairie Regions, not all traditions are easily universalized. Tensions also exist around the backgrounds and knowledges of PBC-contracted elders and the degree to which they can assist hearings with Aboriginal offenders from different cultures and/or nations. These findings echo previous research on including certain differences in penal structures, whereby the original meanings and intents underlying diversity initiatives are reframed in ways that are consistent with existing policies and practices (see, for example, Hannah-Moffat 2004a, 2004b; Hannah-Moffat and Maurutto 2010; Martel et al. 2011; Pollack 2011).

The debates around the set-up of the hearing and the incorporation of various traditions are not minor matters. As McMillan (2011, 181) observes, "articulating what are the customary practices and how they are made meaningful today – and who decides – are complex and highly contested."[6] In the context of penal responses that aim to be culturally appropriate and fair, these issues are especially important in how non-Aboriginal institutions come to understand and embrace certain aspects of Aboriginality and not others. The incorporation of tradition raises questions as to whose traditions are included, particularly given the enormous cultural diversity of Aboriginal peoples and the profound impacts of colonization on Aboriginal cultures and traditions, especially in the context of gender relations (LaRocque 1997). For instance, the skirt protocol raises interesting questions regarding the ideas about gender upon which it is based. As LaRocque observes, there may be some "confusion surrounding cultural and traditional values and their applications, particularly as they relate to the oppression of women" (86). As I discuss later in this chapter, institutional understandings of Aboriginal culture and tradition are intertwined with historically derived notions of Indigenous authenticity (see Garroutte 2003; Raibmon 2005), which work to inform institutional expectations of who Aboriginal offenders are and what they need.

The PBC (2000b, 25, emphasis added) indicates that the distinctions in the practices and procedures for EAHs between the Pacific and Prairie Regions were determined to not "be based on differences in the cultural and spiritual beliefs of the Aboriginal populations in the regions" but, rather, to be "more *a result of different management styles* and the way in which the Elder assisted hearing approaches evolved in each region." This quote points to the importance of organizational culture in how diversity initiatives are implemented. The evaluation report suggests that the less structured approach to EAHs taken in the Prairie Region reflects the fact that the approach was developed on an experimental basis to "address the unique needs and circumstances of Aboriginal offenders" within the region (ibid.). This occurred at a time when the Prairie Region management "did not feel that there was much support outside of the region for the development of an Aboriginal specific hearing process" (ibid.). The lack of consultation with the national office on the development of the EAH model was justified on the basis that the regional management thought that the model would never "have gotten started if they had consulted with and waited for support from" the PBC headquarters (26). In contrast, the Pacific Region developed its EAH approach approximately four years after the Prairie Region and "was thus able to draw on many of the lessons learned" while developing detailed policies and procedures in consultation with the national office (ibid.).

Another pertinent implementation issue involves the selection of elders to be contracted by the PBC. The PBC (2000b, 24) contends that choosing elders is a "key part of the success of the Elder assisted hearing approach" and, thus, that the regions "go to great lengths to get Elders that are highly respected in the Aboriginal community." One informant explained that the PBC considered an elder to be "somebody who in his or her community [was] recognized as being an elder," which differed depending upon the Aboriginal group with which s/he was affiliated (Interview 5). The informant noted that being an elder was not dependent on age but, rather, on being recognized by the community for one's wisdom. Yet the PBC looks for certain skills in the elders it hires, especially language skills. For instance, elders are expected to be fluent in English as well as in "an Aboriginal language appropriate to the majority of the incarcerated Aboriginal population" (PBC 2000b, 24). However, in northern Canada, it is preferable for elders to speak more than one dialect of the languages used in the Northwest Territories because "it was recognized that offenders would prefer an elder who spoke their dialect" (PBC 2002a, n.pag). However, due to the number of different dialects, several elders could be put on "'standby' to accommodate the differences among offenders" (ibid.).

The selection process for elders varies between regions. For instance, in the Prairie Region, the PBC selects "Elders that have been given that title out of great respect by their community, who have extensive knowledge of the traditional ways and ceremonies, and who have gained wisdom through many years of living and are therefore generally in their 60's or older" (PBC 2000b, 24). In contrast, the selection process in the Pacific Region was (at least initially) "largely based on the Regional Vice-Chairperson's extensive knowledge of, and connections in, the Aboriginal communities in the region" (ibid.). A noted difference between the Pacific Region's and Prairie Region's approaches was that the former preferred elders who had extensive experience working in the penal system, while the latter preferred elders who did not have such experience. Concerns were expressed that elders in the Pacific Region would often have personal knowledge of, or experience working with, many of the offenders who came before board members, thereby compromising its "independence" and putting it in a "conflict situation" (25). In this sense, tensions exist around the sorts of permissible knowledges that elders possess and are allowed to bring to the EAH format.

Yet, for the PBC (2000b, 29), the "presence of the Elder alone does not create a respectful and comfortable environment." Offenders may not embrace the elder, while others may not agree with the available EAH format. For instance, the evaluation report cites some interviews with offenders from the Prairie Region who felt that the EAH model "was not respectful to them or their Aboriginal traditions" (27). Some offenders considered the elder to play a "token role" in the hearing, either because s/he was not very involved in the process or because s/he was viewed simply as "another Board member" (ibid.). To address these issues, the report recommends that the EAH model show "respect for Aboriginal ceremonial tradition" and ensure that "the Elder has, and is perceived to have, an important role in the hearing" (29). These concerns about the role of the elder and the EAH model raise questions about the space given to elders to work within the confines of organizational structures and practices governing Aboriginal initiatives. More specifically, elders must navigate the spaces and opportunities made possible within the legislation and policies guiding hearings and decision making.

The PBC (n.d.-d, 13) acknowledges "that there are differences among Aboriginal cultures and the teachings that Elders hold." As such, it "recognizes the flexibility, acceptance and respect of these differences among Elders" (ibid.). Yet the PBC maintains that "certain accommodation" is permitted while trying to maintain the "integrity" of EAHs (ibid.). Interestingly, although "flexibility" with regard to cultural "differences" is encouraged, both the Prairie Region's Elder Reference Manual (PBC n.d.-d) and the Elder-Assisted Hearings General Guidelines (PBC 2009h) outline fairly specific EAH protocols around offerings, eagle feathers, smudges and prayer, skirts, the circle, the temporal and spatial ordering of cultural or ceremonial aspects, and the hearing itself (e.g., smudges cannot occur during the hearing but only as part of the ceremony prior to its commencement). Ostensibly, this is to help keep EAHs consistent across the region, or perhaps to prepare non-Aboriginal hearing attendees for a typical EAH process. Yet it does raise questions as to the ability of such hearings to be flexible enough to accommodate the elders' and/or offenders' preferences regarding which aspects of culture they wish to "perform" for board members. As research by Waldram (1997), Martel and Brassard (2008), and Martel et al. (2011) suggests, the cultural heterogeneity of Aboriginal offenders poses problems for the penal system. More specifically, Waldram (1997, 79) contends that the success of culturally oriented programs is "predicated on the ability of Elders and inmates to negotiate meaning and ritual, to establish a common cultural ground and understanding of the symbols to be used." Given the detailed protocols for EAHs, it is unknown how much flexibility is permitted for the accommodation of different cultural and/or spiritual practices.

Waldram's (1997) work is also helpful for thinking about the contradictions and complexities related to the hiring of elders to work in penal institutions. To be successful, elders have to be both knowledgeable and adept at cultural and spiritual services as well as able to fit into the institutional culture in terms of interacting with staff, attending meetings, giving presentations, and doing paperwork. As Waldram argues: "In effect, Elders are expected to behave like the (invariably Euro-Canadian) chaplains and other correctional staff who are involved with offender rehabilitation" (124). Additionally, to gain contract work within corrections, elders must submit bids through the tendering process. "Euro-Canadian" skills, such as proposal writing and advanced education, rather than knowledge of Aboriginal offenders or spirituality, may be more likely to lead to the awarding of contracts. As a result, non-governmental Aboriginal organizations tend to be more successful at gaining contracts than independent elders (Waldram 1997). Martel and colleagues (2011) also observe that elders and other Aboriginal workers are increasingly required to meet the specifications of institutionally accredited programs in order to work in federal penitentiaries. In the correctional context, then, elders are expected to adapt spiritual knowledges and practices to fit the dominant regime, which is, in essence, white and Eurocentric (Waldram 1997; Martel and Brassard 2008; Martel et al. 2011). They must also be willing to follow the institution's rules and practices, which may comprise their independence (Hayman 2006).

It is unknown whether these pressures and preferences around hiring and institutional practice are similar in the context of the PBC. However, several PBC documents obtained via the *ATIA* suggest that some of the concerns raised by Waldram (1997) and Martel et al. (2011) could apply. For instance, the PBC also contracts with elders for the provision of services for hearings and cultural awareness and sensitivity training. As noted above, there are regional preferences as to what type of elder should be contracted to provide services. The Prairie Region, for example, has a "priority listing" for its elders (PBC 2009h, n.pag). This listing organizes elders into "core" and "secondary" (or back-up) groups, where the core elders for each regional penitentiary are given first priority. It is unclear whether the organization of elders by type and priority relate to human resources concerns around seniority and/or whether there are institutional preferences for certain "kinds" of elders who are more willing to work within the dominant correctional box and who do not challenge institutional policies or practices. There is a possibility that the priority listing is a technique of governing elders' knowledges and censoring what goes into culturally sensitive approaches for Aboriginal offenders.

Waldram's (1997) concerns about the need for elders to adapt their knowledges and practices according to institutional structures may also be reflected in the protocols the PBC developed for EAHs and CAHs. The Prairie Region's *Elder Reference Manual* (PBC n.d.-d), for example, is quite specific regarding how these hearings are to be conducted. The manual also explains what is expected by contracted elders, including values and ethics related to public service and confidentiality issues. Elders under contract with the PBC are also expected to participate in meetings and training sessions with board members and staff. Accordingly, part of the job is making non-Aboriginal board members and staff aware of Aboriginal issues through various training exercises. Clearly, the job profile of elders is diverse and requires elders to serve multiple, often conflicting, functions – a point I return to below in the section on the role of elders.

"Mainstreaming" the EAH Approach

Despite the challenges related to the implementation of EAHs for Aboriginal offenders, the PBC took initial steps to "mainstream" the model. According to the PBC's (2006a, 13) background paper, a decision made at the May 1999 Executive Committee meeting led to the creation of a subcommittee of the Aboriginal Circle to review the PBC's policy from "an Aboriginal perspective." This review resulted in "policy pertaining to Aboriginal offenders" being put into the PBC Policy Manual (PBC 2006a, 13; see also PBC 2004a). The rationale for the policy shift was that "what was being stated in relation to hearings for Aboriginal offenders was actually relevant for *all offenders* coming before the Board" (PBC 2006a, 13, emphasis added). As I discuss later, the notion of all offenders became largely operationalized as ethnocultural offenders, albeit with the occasional reference to female offenders. One of the primary drivers for the mainstreaming of the EAH approach was the release of the *Gladue* decision as well as greater attention being paid to the "importance of inclusive measures" (ibid.) for ethnocultural offenders. It also appears the PBC "anticipated that other groups may require cultural hearings" under section 151(3) of the *CCRA* (PBC 2006a, 14).

In 2004, based on the review by the Aboriginal Circle's subcommittee, changes were made to the PBC Policy Manual, most notable of which was "Elder Assisted Hearings" being renamed "Cultural Hearings." A 2004 policy circular explains that the "Cultural Hearing is a clear expression that the Board views people of different ethnic backgrounds as equal and valued members of society" (PBC 2004c, 1). The term "cultural hearing" was considered to better reflect "ethnic pluralism as a fundamental characteristic of Canadian society" and the

PBC's need (i.e., its legal obligation) to be responsive to the groups specified in section 151(3) of the *CCRA* (PBC 2006a, 15). This move towards a more mainstreamed and generic cultural hearing format risked eroding the basis for why EAHs were created in the first place, which was to address the specific needs of Aboriginal offenders. Alternatively, this manoeuvre to accommodate *Gladue* worked to present the organization as one that is responsive to the needs of diverse offenders, not *just* Aboriginal offenders who are often constituted as recipients of "special treatment."

However, the changes to the Policy Manual were more rhetorical than substantive. The altered name and statement of commitment to ethnic pluralism allowed the organization to claim that methods exist to accommodate diversity, even as this alternative hearing format remains largely directed towards Aboriginal offenders. Indeed, despite the name change and expanded scope, cultural hearings remained focused on Aboriginal offenders. The PBC notes that:

> Conducting hearings with an Aboriginal Cultural Advisor reflects, in part, the Board's responsiveness to Aboriginal people. The Board will continue to develop its hearing process to be responsive to other diverse ethnic and cultural groups and to the special needs of women. (PBC 2004c, 1)

The 2004 stated purpose of hearings with Aboriginal cultural advisors was "to create a responsive hearing process for Aboriginal offenders (First Nations, Inuit, and Métis), and one that will facilitate a more accurate understanding of the offender for Board members" (PBC 2004c, 1). The policy for prioritizing which offenders could have hearings with Aboriginal cultural advisors was removed on the following basis: "Whether or not Aboriginal offenders follow an Aboriginal way of life, Aboriginal programming, or Aboriginal spirituality is not relevant; the *fact that they are Aboriginal* means they may choose to request a Cultural Hearing" (PBC 2006a, 14, emphasis added). As such, the "right" to an EAH was once again predicated upon one's racialized status as Aboriginal, whereby identity became more relevant than what one did. The amendments were also intended to ensure that *all* Aboriginal offenders were included as it was thought that the "previous policy alluded more to First Nations' culture rather than reflecting all groups included in the term Aboriginal – Inuit, Métis, and First Nations" (ibid.). Such inclusion provides direction towards "global compliance while allowing for regional specificity" (PBC 2004a, 8).

The 2004 amendments to the Policy Manual also removed references to elders and instead used the term "Aboriginal cultural advisors" on the basis that

Cultural Ghettos?

not all PBC Aboriginal advisors were elders (PBC 2006a, 15). The broadened term not only better reflected the participation of "those individuals knowledgeable of Aboriginal culture and respected in their communities" but also allowed for the participation of advisors from "other cultural groups" once cultural hearings were initiated for these groups (ibid.). As outlined in the policy circular (PBC 2004c, 2), "an Aboriginal Cultural Advisor must be an Elder or another respected and knowledgeable Aboriginal person." Her or his role is "to provide Board members with information about the specific cultures and traditions of the Aboriginal population the offender is affiliated with, and/or Aboriginal cultures, experiences, and traditions in general." It states further that advisors "may also offer wisdom and guidance to the offender and may advise the Board members during the deliberation stage of the hearing to provide insights and comments with respect to cultural and spiritual concerns" (ibid.). Cultural advisors are constituted as "bridges" over "cultural divides" between board members and offenders.

New amendments in 2007 to the Policy Manual resulted in section 9.2.1 being entitled "Hearings for Aboriginal Offenders" (PBC 2011c, Ch. 9.2.1, 123). The term "elder/advisor" replaced the term "Aboriginal cultural advisor," and the definition of who this person is was removed. The amendments also add to the statement of purpose of EAHs that such hearings will adhere to the "established criteria for decision-making" (ibid.). Additionally, the "policy now focuses solely on hearings for Aboriginal Offenders," thereby removing reference to other groups and non-Aboriginal offenders who are following traditional ways (PBC 2011c, Annex A, 206). Interestingly, the 2007 amendments reversed many of the changes made in 2004. Of note is the refocusing of the hearings on Aboriginal offenders and the move away from opening such hearings to other groups of offenders. The 2007 amendments also reasserted the primacy of risk assessment as the key focus of these hearings, even if it is cultural in nature.

Recent amendments to the Policy Manual have renamed and renumbered the section, now 11.1.1, entitled "Elder-Assisted and Community-Assisted Hearings" (PBC 2015, Ch. 11.1.1, 1), and have included once again the option for a "non-Aboriginal offender, who has demonstrated a commitment to an Aboriginal way of life" to "also request an Elder-Assisted and Community-Assisted Hearing." However, this option is qualified by the following statement: "Board members will indicate reasons for accepting or rejecting requests from a non-Aboriginal offender" (ibid.), suggesting that there are restrictions on the availability of these hearings for non-Aboriginals. The term "elder" is specified once again, replacing the "elder/advisor" role previously contained in the 2011 version of the Policy Manual. The Policy Manual also explicitly defines an

EAH as "a hearing traditionally held in a circle, with an Elder performing Aboriginal cultural protocols and spiritual ceremonies, as requested by the offender" (ibid.). As with the 2007 amendments, the most recent Policy Manual maintains the organization's policy direction away from the changes made in 2004, which aimed to open "cultural" hearings to other groups of offenders.

These developments are illustrative of how the organization has grappled with questions of difference and the limits of accommodation as well as of how priorities and actions related to diversity can fluctuate over time. While there was an attempt to broaden the scope of the EAH model by making it more generically cultural rather than Aboriginal-specific, the organization abandoned this approach and returned the focus to Aboriginal offenders. Chapter 5 considers the extension of alternative hearing formats to ethnocultural offenders in more detail.

EAHs in Practice

EAHs are defined as a "hearing format which takes into account the uniqueness of Aboriginal culture and heritage" (PBC 2009g, n.pag). These hearings aim to provide "an environment of trust and respect where the offender can feel comfortable in sharing information related to his/her journey." EAHs also utilize "an interview style respectful of traditional values" (ibid.). For instance, in order to be respectful, the style of questioning used by board members is supposed to be "compassionate and non-confrontational" and focused "on healing and accepting responsibility rather than the offence" (PBC 2000b, 23). This approach aims to "allow the offender to build a sense of comfort in speaking." To build this "sense of comfort," questions may focus on "the offender's Aboriginal heritage or participation in Aboriginal ceremonies" (ibid.). Ostensibly, this is because heritage or ceremonies are comfortable topics of discussion for Aboriginal offenders.

The set-up of hearing rooms for EAHs is also important and differs among the regions. In the Prairie Region, hearings are to be "held in secure and culturally appropriate location[s],"[7] such as rooms that allow for a circle format, with space in the centre of the circle to be allotted to elders to make use of such ceremonial items as the eagle feather and smudge bowl (PBC 2009g). A similar set-up is specified in the Ontario/Nunavut Region's Aboriginal Circle Hearings guidelines (PBC 2010f). A key component of EAHs relates to the removal of "barriers." These barriers may be "physical" (e.g., tables) or "social" (e.g., use of language, style of dress, etc.) (PBC 2000b, 2). In order to best facilitate the "exchange of information," such barriers should be minimized. For example, the Ontario/Nunavut Region guidelines request that, based on tradition, "Board members wear casual clothing when possible" (PBC 2010f, 1). These modifications alter the style and appearance of the hearing in ways that the PBC defines as "culturally appropriate" for Aboriginal offenders.

The offender can select whether s/he would like the hearing to open and/or close with the elder conducting a prayer and/or smudge (PBC 2009g). In the Ontario/Nunavut Region, the Aboriginal advisor, in consultation with board members and the hearing officer, determines the place (e.g., within the circle or outside the hearing room) and timing of any prayer and/or smudge, while taking into account participants' allergies or differing religious beliefs (PBC 2010f, 2). Guidelines also exist around the timing of procedural safeguards and which hearing elements are subject to audio recording. For instance, the Atlantic Region's guidelines for EAHs specify that the elder is to conduct a prayer and smudge after the procedural safeguards are completed but that these are not to be recorded (PBC 2010g). EAHs may also involve the elder "conducting traditional teachings [with the offender] in preparation for a hearing" (PBC n.d.-d, 13). In the Ontario/Nunavut Region, the Aboriginal advisor may give advice to the offender during the hearing (PBC 2010f, 4).

EAHs also differ from regular hearings in relation to persons in attendance. The Policy Manual notes that the PBC "will take into consideration relationship values which may influence the offender's rehabilitation and reintegration, such as the importance of the offender's family, the community, and its leaders and Elders' when determining who may be present" (PBC 2015, Ch. 11.1.1, 2). The term "family" is further explicated in the manual, drawing attention to "Aboriginal understandings" of family that extend beyond blood relations. The Policy Manual also specifies the process for the involvement of the victim, including her or his inclusion in the circle format (3).

Compared to regular hearings, EAHs cost more to conduct due in large part to honoraria for PBC-contracted elders (PBC 2000b, 34). Figures from the 2005-06 fiscal year indicate that the approximate cost of an EAH is C$1,450, while a regular hearing costs around C$850 (PBC 2006c, 11). EAHs also take a "significantly longer" amount of time to conduct, resulting in fewer hearings per day (PBC 2000b, 36). The PBC has estimated that EAHs take an average of 50 percent more time; so if a regular hearing takes an hour, an EAH takes an hour and a half. Consequently, an average of "three EAHs can be conducted per day compared to five regular hearings" (PBC 2004a, 26). In 2009-10, 428 hearings in Canada were elder-assisted, which represents 3 percent of the 16,992 federal and provincial reviews conducted that fiscal year (PBC 2010d). Although the majority (84 percent) of participants were Aboriginal, the proportion varied among the regions, with 100 percent of Aboriginal offenders in the Quebec

Region and 80 percent in the Pacific Region (PBC 2010d). Of the 1,125 panel reviews conducted for Aboriginal offenders in 2009-10, 32 percent were elder-assisted (PBC 2010d). That the majority of Aboriginal offenders are going through the regular hearing format may signal a potential disconnect between the institutionalization of Aboriginal diversity in the EAH model and what Aboriginal offenders prefer for their conditional release hearings.

"Different" Format, "Same" Focus

Despite the challenges and contradictions associated with the implementation and use of the EAH model, interviews with informants show a high level of support for EAHs. Informants generally perceived these hearings as more fair, culturally sensitive, and respectful for Aboriginal offenders. According to one informant: "What we discovered in doing [EAHs] is it doesn't maybe change the decision, but at least there's a fair chance" because "Aboriginal offenders feel more respected, their circumstances are really more taken into account and they open [up] more" (Interview 4). Several informants indicated that improved communication between Aboriginal offenders and board members led to better decisions because offenders would have had a "fair chance to tell their story and to say what are the supports that they will have in the community" (ibid.).

Although EAHs have different formats from regular hearings, the PBC is clear that the hearing process itself does not change board members' decision making (PBC 2003a, 5). According to the PBC (2009g, n.pag), "risk assessment is the same for Aboriginals as it is for non-Aboriginals." Several informants also stressed that EAHs did not change either the criteria board members have to consider for release (i.e., the protection of the public) or their analysis of risk but that "the process itself [was] more culturally sensitive" (Interview 2). In terms of bringing about actual change to the release of Aboriginal offenders, it appears that EAHs serve a largely symbolic function as long as the decision-making criteria remain the same. Put differently, board members' policy compliance in the context of EAHs will not produce different outcomes if the criteria themselves are discriminatory (Hudson 1993). These criteria are set by the *CCRA*, thereby limiting what the PBC can do in this regard.

In an attempt to be culturally appropriate, the organization has indicated that "the word risk is not a meaningful term for Aboriginal people" (PBC 2006a, 15). Yet, rather than do things differently for Aboriginal offenders, the PBC opted to amend its Policy Manual to remove references to terms like "risk assessment" to reflect this idea, using instead the language in Part II of the *CCRA*, which requires board members to review cases and make decisions as to whether offenders present "undue risks" to society. The PBC is clear that the "absence of such terms as 'risk assessment' from policy did not signify that the Board does not continue to do a thorough assessment of the offender" but, rather, that the *language* in policy should change (ibid.). Notions of what is culturally appropriate also come into play in such assessments. Indeed, board members are to assess Aboriginal offenders on their healing and participation in Aboriginal programs and in ceremonies that incorporate Aboriginal teachings as factors that influence risk (PBC 2000b, 2). Unfortunately, previous research has shown how decision makers' attempts to be appropriate to a variety of socially produced differences (e.g., gender, culture, race, etc.) can actually reproduce stereotypes and illicit unintended consequences (see, for example, Nightingale 1991; Chiu 1994; Volpp 1994; Lawrence 2001; Fournier 2002; Hannah-Moffat 2004a; Silverstein 2005).

One informant explained that the EAH approach provides a more "efficient" interview format and a method of gathering information that is "different" and "dynamic" (Interview 13). In a regular hearing, according to this person, "the interviews are somewhat confrontational with the offender, whereas in the elder-assisted hearings it's much more like a talk, a discussion." EAHs were described as enabling Aboriginal offenders "to share more freely and honestly with the board members so the board members can make the best possible decision" (Interview 11). The format of the EAH was thought to be "more familiar" to many Aboriginal offenders who would have had opportunities to engage in circles while incarcerated. This same informant contrasted this to the regular hearing model, which was viewed as prohibiting the information gathering process for board members: "Walking into a boardroom with a bunch of people who are in suits, who are firing questions at them [Aboriginal offenders], will not assist them in saying what they need to say" to board members. By improving communication, EAHs are viewed as enabling board members to better gather and assess risk information and so reach the right decision (PBC 2004a).

Despite producing a different format through the arrangement of the hearing room, the availability of ceremony, and the assistance of an elder, the focus remains the same: the assessment of risk – or, as the PBC (2007c, n.pag) puts it: "The risk an offender poses is a first consideration in seeking harmony, peace, and balance in the successful integration of offenders from confinement to the community." Couched in a restorative justice discourse, this odd statement reflects the attempted melding of risk thinking, as required by law, with discourses of Aboriginality. One implication of the ascendancy of risk thinking is that the EAH format may be more symbolic than substantive in effect. A parallel can be drawn here between EAHs and healing lodges for Aboriginal offenders. According to Monture-Angus (1999, 25), healing lodges "are institutions no matter how much Aboriginal culture and tradition inspires their contour, shape, and form." In this sense, although the EAH may look different, it is still a conditional release hearing that is based on the letter of the law and focused on the assessment of risk – a practice that is said to be "incompatible with Aboriginal cultures, law, and tradition" (26). The process was adapted rather than fundamentally changed. The creation of EAHs reflects "the adaptation of an approach, without rethinking the epistemological issues of whose knowledge" or approaches prevail (Hyndman 1998, 251). Decision makers are therefore called upon to be sensitive to Aboriginal cultures and traditions, as reflected in the reoriented hearing space and use of ceremony, while applying decision-making criteria that were developed based on non-Aboriginal norms.

The Role of the Elder

As the preceding discussion suggests, elders play a key role in EAHs and provide a variety of services for both board members and Aboriginal offenders. Elders are relied upon for their expertise in Aboriginal matters, including issues of tradition, culture, and spirituality. They are variously constituted as "interpreters" of culture and "bridges" between Aboriginal offenders and board members. At the same time, elders are supposed to support Aboriginal offenders by creating culturally appropriate environments for their conditional release hearings. In this way, elders are called upon to serve an important, yet complicated function within an institutional context that selectively incorporates Aboriginal knowledges and practices and confines their expertise to specific matters. The following discussion explores the role of the elder in more detail. I argue that, despite the best of intentions, the organization has a difficult time "hearing" other voices in ways that do not reproduce "long-standing, and much criticized, dichotomies" (Puwar 2004, 70). There is a straight-jacketing effect whereby elders' voices tend to be locked into their marked identity as Aboriginal, therefore being kept outside the realm of normative conditional release processes.

The current definition of the elder's role is the same as that outlined in the 2004 Policy Circular (see PBC 2004c), which is to supply board members with information pertaining to Aboriginal "cultures, experiences, and traditions"; this information may be "general" in nature (i.e., applicable to all Aboriginal peoples in Canada) or specific to the "cultures and traditions of the Aboriginal population the offender is affiliated with" (PBC n.d.-d, 13). The Policy Manual specifies that elders "may be active participant[s] in the hearing and

Cultural Ghettos?

may ask about the offender's understanding of Aboriginal traditions and spirituality, progress towards healing and rehabilitation, and readiness of the community to receive the offender if return to the community is part of the release plan" (PBC 2015, Ch. 11.1.1, 2). During EAHs, elders may converse with offenders in "an Aboriginal language to gain a better understanding of the offender, and to assist the Board members with gaining further information helpful to achieving a quality decision" (ibid.). Elders summarize these discussions for board members and other hearing participants prior to decisions being made.

The PBC considers the elder to be "an independent advisor to the Board" who "can ask the offender questions which *test* the offender's understanding of Aboriginal teachings" (PBC 2000b, 27, emphasis added).[8] Board members may also rely on the elder to answer various questions during the deliberation process. Such questions may "relate to specific Aboriginal beliefs or traditions that were discussed during a hearing or be more general to get the Elder's perspective on the offender's openness and honesty during the hearing or the offender's understanding of Aboriginal cultural and spiritual traditions" (28). The PBC states that this "aids the decision-making process because it provides Board members with a better understanding of the offender and the offender's risk factors" (27). So, although elders are not to provide direct opinions on decisions to grant or deny release (29), they are called upon to be cultural and spiritual "translators" for board members who are implicitly constituted as non-Aboriginal. They are entitled to speak to certain issues (i.e., matters of culture, spirituality, and tradition) and not others.

Elders are also called upon to "maintain the fluidity of the circle process" (PBC 2009g, n.pag). The elder is described as "someone who creates an interview environment which facilitates a culturally-sensitive hearing process" (PBC 1996, 4). This allows the offender to have a "fair opportunity" to make her or his case and the board members to ascertain the relevant information required to make a decision. As one informant put it, the elder's "job is to make sure that the communications flow between parole board members and the offender goes well" (Interview 5). Elders, this informant continued, are expected to facilitate the dialogue in a more culturally appropriate, non-confrontational manner and ensure that "what the offender is trying to explain to the board goes through or is conveyed clear in a way that board members can understand." The PBC (2004a, 14) notes that elders, in conjunction with the circle format, help produce a "calming atmosphere" that makes offenders "feel more at ease and keep[s] them honest and open as they speak from the heart." The organization also contends that "the insights the Elders provide into the offender's progress in healing and potential for growth in the future ... help [board members] make better decisions" (PBC 2000b, 27).

The elder is also framed as assisting by creating "a bridge between the offender and parole board members" (Interview 5) and by providing board members "guidance related to culture" (Interview 8). The elder is viewed as a support for board members, providing them with cultural awareness and information if they have questions during hearings (Interview 10). For instance, s/he could aid board members in their understanding of what "an offender was talking about [when referring to] being on his healing journey" (Interview 8). The elder is constituted as an authoritative knower of all things Aboriginal and is positioned as key to translating this knowledge to (non-Aboriginal) board members. Indeed, a number of informants viewed the elder as a "cultural interpreter." As one informant explained, "The elder does not interpret language, [s/]he interprets culture" for board members (Interview 5). As a cultural interpreter, PBC-contracted elders do not shape decisions but, rather, help in matters of culture. In this sense, elders must translate Aboriginal otherness into the normative framework of the hearing and into formats that (non-Aboriginal) board members can understand. The narrowing of elders' responsibilities to matters of cultural interpretation and the performance of ceremony in hearings suggests that their expertise is limited to that of culture and spirituality. The focus on culture also steers the discussion away from other topics, such as the impact of racism on Aboriginal offenders' behaviours, both prior to and during incarceration.

One informant indicated that there has been a move to have elders (and/or their assistants) provide assessments to board members that can be "considered as the same as ... a community assessment or a psychological assessment" (Interview 8). Elders' opinions may be considered along with that of other professionals, such as judges or police officers (PBC 2007c). This approach places elders among other experts that provide reports to the PBC in preparation for hearings. Yet, at the same time, such an approach runs the risk of compartmentalizing elders' expertise, which would run counter to a more holistic approach to hearing processes for Aboriginal offenders.

Community-Assisted Hearings

The above discussion details the genesis of the EAH model and highlights some of the contradictions and challenges associated with its development and implementation as a culturally appropriate initiative for Aboriginal offenders. CAHs comprise another key PBC initiative for Aboriginal offenders. Like EAHs, CAHs provide a venue for the organization to learn about Aboriginal offenders and their communities by using the assistance of elders to help it make more appropriate decisions. However, compared to EAHs, CAHs are conducted infrequently and are much more costly and intensive undertakings. CAHs are rationalized as a restorative justice initiative for Aboriginal offenders that brings parole hearings to the community and includes, where possible, the participation of victims. In this section, I trace the creation of CAHs and discuss some of the implications associated with their use. I suggest that, for board members, CAHs function to produce knowledge of the Aboriginal offender and her or his community. At the same time, knowledge is produced about the offender for the benefit of the community, enabling it to take responsibility for the care and supervision of the offender.

Background

As with EAHs, the idea for CAHs may be traced back to *Final Report: Task Force on Aboriginal Peoples in Federal Corrections* (Solicitor General 1988a). The report recommended greater participation of Aboriginal communities with the corrections and conditional release process through the expansion of services to Aboriginal organizations and their greater authority in decision-making processes. Although it does not specifically mention CAHs, the Final Report's recommendations call for mechanisms to ensure that Aboriginal communities are consulted when decisions are made about releasing Aboriginal offenders back into these communities. Furthermore, it recommends allowing the community's leadership to propose special conditions to be attached to conditional release orders. This position was reflected in the Correctional Law Review's working paper on Aboriginal offenders, which proposed a provision for Aboriginal community involvement "on a local, specific level" in cases in which Aboriginal offenders wanted to be released back to their reserves (Solicitor General 1988b, 379).

Given the similarities in wording, the CLR's proposed provision appears to have formed the basis for section 84 of the *CCRA*, which states:

> Where an inmate who is applying for parole has expressed an interest in being released to an aboriginal community, the [Correctional] Service [Canada] shall, if the inmate consents, give the aboriginal community (a) adequate notice of the inmate's parole application; and (b) an opportunity to propose a plan for the inmate's release to, and integration into, the aboriginal community.

Section 79 of the *CCRA* defines an "Aboriginal community" as "a first nation, tribal council, band, community, organization or other group with a predominantly aboriginal leadership." The PBC (2007e, 1) has gone further to operationalize this definition for CAHs, specifying that "the community must be reasonably well defined by reason of racial origin of its members, culture or by geography or some other feature which distinguishes it from other communities."[9] Such a definition reflects the "conceptual practice of spatial segmentation" of "peoples and cultures" (Malkki 1992, 28). There is a tendency "to tie people to places through ascriptions of native status: 'natives are not only persons who are from certain places, and belong to those places, but they are also those who are somehow incarcerated, or confined, in those places'" (Appadurai 1988, 37, cited in Malkki 1992, 29). The reserve is a key example of a spatialized practice that segments people defined as Indigenous to particular spaces. The notion of an Aboriginal community reflects the assumption that Aboriginal communities are spatially distinct from other groups. This raises questions about notions of community in the context of urban settings – an important issue addressed by *Gladue*.

The PBC (2002b, 2) indicates that CAHs were created in response to section 84 of the *CCRA* and are "based on restorative justice principles of returning balance to the community." The PBC's self-identified "role is that of an advocate for their promotion and use" (PBC 2000a, 9). The PBC's 2002 evaluation of CAHs positions this hearing format as an "innovative" response that helps address the "distinctive needs and interests of Aboriginal offenders," which "is of vital importance" for the organization (PBC 2002b, 2). The aims of these hearings include "bridging differences," "healing," and "reconciling parties" through the restoration of relationships (PBC 2006a, 7). CAHs are framed as a culturally appropriate mechanism for bringing together Aboriginal offenders and their communities in the pursuit of a restorative process of reintegration.

As one informant explained, the Aboriginal Circle helped come up with the idea of using CAHs as a way of enabling the PBC to support section 84 (Interview 7). With the PBC's narrow mandate (i.e., making release decisions) in mind, including the fact that this section falls under the CSC's part of the *CCRA*, it was determined that what the PBC could do

> was not ever be a barrier to community involvement. And so if a community was so engaged in the return of an individual to their community that they wanted to have a say in how that release was going to work and what they wanted in that release ... so we decided okay then, it's easier for us to go to your community than for all of you to come to an institution where you may or may not get security clearance. (Interview 7)

CAHs therefore provide a mechanism that enables interested communities to be involved in the hearing process (Interview 7) and to play a greater role in release planning (PBC 2009g). And, as the above quote attests, by locating hearings within the community, one potential barrier to participation (i.e., the need for security clearance) is reduced. The quote also reflects the language of equality of opportunity, not outcome (Phillips 2007, 85). In other words, the PBC can try to create opportunities to increase the "fairness" of the process by including the community; however, not being a barrier does not say much about the outcome – such as the making of "culturally appropriate" decisions. Although CAH participants provide important input, the PBC is clear that the final decision rests with board members, as per the *CCRA* (PBC 2002b).

It is also notable that section 84 of the *CCRA* – the basis of the CAH – does not enable Aboriginal self-determination over correctional matters affecting Aboriginal peoples. As Dyck (1991, 40) cautions, it is important to consider how "the 'politics of aboriginality' may, under certain circumstances, serve to maintain rather than to eliminate the practice of tutelage." In other words, although the institutional discourse surrounding CAHs may appeal to notions of Aboriginality and restorative justice, it may reflect more symbolic than substantive shifts in ownership of corrections and conditional release processes rather than a decolonizing of the relationship between Aboriginal peoples and the penal system (Cunneen 2009). The PBC effectively retains its authority to include or exclude Aboriginal knowledges and to decide if and when certain practices will be altered.

CAHs in Practice

The first CAH took place on April 30, 1997, in the Prairie Region in the Peigan Nation in Brocket, Alberta, followed by six more held between August 1997 and April 2000 in First Nations communities (five in Alberta and one in Saskatchewan) (PBC 2006a, 6).[10] The arrangement of CAHs is more complicated than is that of EAHs. Several factors are considered before a CAH is approved, including "public safety, the seriousness of the offence, the assessment by CSC as to the readiness of the community and the offender for this type of hearing, the potential for re-victimization if the hearing takes place in the community and costs" (PBC n.d.-d, 14). Given these factors, it appears that there is a high threshold that must be passed before a CAH will be approved.

In terms of process, an Aboriginal offender must initiate a CAH and her or his community must be willing to participate in the parole hearing (PBC 2002b). Moreover, the CSC must give a positive recommendation for the offender's release before the CAH process is initiated. This process is justified on the basis that CAHs are labour-intensive undertakings and require significant preparatory work by both the CSC and the PBC (PBC 2006a, 6). Before a CAH takes place, the offender must spend time in her or his community (typically through an escorted temporary absence) and "participate in a circle with community members" as a way of "becom[ing] reacquainted with family and community members" (PBC 2002b, 3). Such requirements reflect the restorative justice focus of this initiative. This preparatory work also helps ensure community buy-in for the CAH process and the potential return of the offender.

To request a CAH in the Prairie Region, an offender must submit a form to the PBC two months prior to the hearing date. The potential for holding a CAH for the offender is then assessed by the regional director, the regional manager of the Aboriginal and Diversity Unit, and the regional vice-chairperson (PBC 2009g). Staff from the CSC and the PBC consult with the community and hold a meeting prior to the hearing to explain the legislation and the responsibilities of each party (including financial responsibilities), and, in conjunction with community and PBC-contracted elders, to decide on the hearing format and protocol. The PBC (2009g, n.pag) notes that this meeting also provides an opportunity to "build a relationship between the community," the CSC, and the PBC as well as to "define the expectations of community responsibility" both in relation to the actual hearing and in relation to supervision issues if the offender is granted conditional release.

Guidelines for the Prairie Region indicate that a CAH "is to be held in a safe, neutral, culturally appropriate location (e.g. community facility rather than a police station)" (PBC 2007e, 4). These guidelines outline the protocols for CAHs, including when ceremonial elements (e.g., prayer, smudge, etc.) take place, the use of a circle format, who can speak and when, and so forth. For instance, the circle must "respect local cultural practices and traditions," and CAH participants "are encouraged to respect ceremonial guidelines such as the wearing of a skirt for women" (5). Despite its intent to be a "responsive hearing process" for Aboriginal offenders and their communities, the PBC prefers CAHs to be held in English, although simultaneous translation services could be made available, albeit at a significant cost to the organization. Arguably, this language preference seems to work against attempts to be responsive as it fails to consider how asking Aboriginal peoples to communicate in English is situated within a legacy of colonialism and assimilation (Waldram 1997). Consequently, the CAH is reoriented towards the preferences and standard operating procedure of the institution.

The PBC (2006a, 7) views CAHs as a "natural progression or extension" of EAHs that allows the affected community to be involved in the parole decision-making process. As with EAHs, elders facilitate CAHs. However, CAHs – at least in their initial articulation[11] – differ from EAHs as they are longer (i.e., tend to take up an entire day), more ceremonial, often include a feast upon the completion of the hearing, and involve more people (i.e., interested community members). According to one informant, a CAH "doesn't change the role of the board member, they have to make a decision," but it "changes the setting ... it involves the whole community, it's quite [a] powerful set-up" (Interview 4). This set-up is seen to enable the offender and community to have a "voice" in determining the conditions attached to the offender's parole release, which may result in the imposition of some unique conditions. In addition, victim involvement is much greater under CAHs than it is under regular parole hearings (PBC 2002b). The PBC sees victims as "full participants": "they have the same right to speak as freely as the offender or other participants" (4). The inclusion of victims is said to reflect the restorative justice frame of CAHs.

Elders also play an important role in CAHs. During the planning stage, elders may act as cultural liaisons between the PBC and Aboriginal communities; for instance, they may work with community elders to determine the format and protocol of the CAH (PBC 2009g). As one informant explained, the regional elder "always goes out before us [the PBC] and, you know, meets with the band and council" to do outreach in preparation for CAHs (Interview 10). Elders bring "knowledge and expertise than can foster the healing process between the community and the offender" (PBC 2007c, n.pag). During the hearing, the elder is called upon to "maintain the order and fluidity of the circle" (PBC 2007e, 4) and help "ensure that other agendas do not overrun the circle" (5). Elders also provide the "guidance [that] is needed to reach culturally appropriate ways of restoring a just relationship between the offender and the community where harmony, peace, and balance can be restored" (PBC 2007c, n.pag).

Implementation Issues
Based on several interviews and analyses of institutional documents, CAHs emerge as a popular initiative, yet as one that has encountered several implementation difficulties. According to one informant, "the success rate [with CAHs] is very, very high" (Interview 7). However, another informant observed that CAHs are "something that communities are not very willing to become involved in for some reason" (Interview 11). The informant explained that not all Aboriginal communities wanted to accept offenders and the associated responsibilities of supervision. Another informant highlighted the challenge for Aboriginal offenders returning to home communities that are poor and lacking employment or other options (Interview 13). The 2002 evaluation of CAHs also

notes that "not all Board members are comfortable with the circle format and 'stepping outside' the traditional PBC roles" (PBC 2002b, 5). Without the support from board members and Aboriginal communities, the CAH model may be difficult to institutionalize as a diversity initiative for Aboriginal offenders.

The PBC (2004a, 17) has indicated that "the lack of funding makes it a difficult approach to implement." As noted above, cost is one of the factors considered prior to the approval of a CAH. However, it is unknown how fiscal restraint works to shape access to CAHs. Another issue is that section 84 is the CSC's responsibility under the *CCRA*: it is up to the CSC to get the process started. Two reports released in 2003 are critical of the lack of use of section 84, particularly with regard to the reintegration of Aboriginal women offenders. For instance, the Auditor General of Canada (2003) indicates that section 84 releases were not typically discussed with Aboriginal women offenders during the intake process. Likewise, the Canadian Human Rights Commission (CHRC) notes that "little use" was made of section 84 for Aboriginal women offenders, with a total of thirteen agreements between April 2001 and September 2003 (CHRC 2003, 57). Both the Auditor General and the CHRC recommend that the CSC review its approach to section 84 to help increase the use of this legislative provision. Similarly, the 2005-06 and 2008-09 annual reports of the Office of the Correctional Investigator of Canada recommend greater use of section 84 (OCI 2006, 2009a, 2009b). These recommendations suggest that there are institutional impediments to the use of CAH as an alternative hearing format for Aboriginal offenders.

CAHs as Restorative Justice

CAHs are framed as a restorative justice initiative under section 84 of the *CCRA* (PBC 2000c). As indicated above, the intent of CAHs is to "provide the opportunity for restoration to take place between the offender, the community and possibly the victim" (PBC 2006b, 18). CAHs are framed by the PBC as "an innovative decision process which recognizes the value of restorative approaches to conditional release decision-making" (ibid.) and are noted as being "very successful" in terms of "healing, restoring balance, reconciling parties, bridging differences and involving the community in the decision-making process" (PBC 2002b, 8).

Pavlich's (1996a, 1996b, 2005) work on restorative justice – or what he refers to as "restorative governmentalities" – is especially helpful for thinking about how power works through such practices as CAHs and for unpacking taken-for-granted concepts such as healing, the victim, and the community. Drawing on Foucault's notion of governmentality, Pavlich shows how restorative approaches constitute particular subjects (e.g., the victim, community, and offender) as targets of governance. As partners in the "timely reintegration of [Aboriginal] offenders" (PBC 2000c, 10), these subjects are given certain roles to play in the context of CAHs. Yet not all partners are willing to partake of this restorative process (e.g., cases in which communities do not want a particular offender to return or do not have the appropriate resources to ensure that s/he can be supervised).

One area of difficulty and a barrier to the success of CAHs, as raised by the PBC (2002b), is victim participation. Victim participation poses a key problem for CAHs as restorative justice, given that it is championed as a defining feature of the latter (Pavlich 2005). For the PBC (2004a, 16), "victim participation is one of the most sensitive aspects" of the CAH approach. Part of the difficulty relates to involving victims in "meaningful ways" while ensuring that they are "informed of the nature of the process and provided with a safe method of participating" (ibid.). Restoration is viewed as best achieved when victims participate in CAHs. However, the CAH initiative has suffered from a low rate of victim participation (PBC 2002b). The PBC notes that victims may not want to participate due to a lack of comfort with the circle format or due to there being divisions within their communities regarding the offence. Victims' refusal to participate is constituted as a problem by the PBC because victims are seen as assisting Aboriginal offenders' healing journeys and the CAH process more generally (10). Consequently, without the participation of victims – a key constitutive element of restorative justice (Pavlich 2005) – the potential for restoration decreases.

Producing Knowledge, Building Reputation

As with EAHs, CAHs also "promote better understanding of Aboriginal communities and their citizens" (PBC 2007c, n.pag) for board members. As the PBC (n.d.-d, 14) explains, this is a more "responsive hearing process for Aboriginal offenders" because it "facilitate[s] a more accurate understanding of who the offender is as an individual in his/her community." CAHs are said to contribute to "quality decisions because of the honesty, openness and respect in the process" (PBC 2002b, 6). CAHs are framed as more "effective" mechanisms for gaining information about the offender and his or her community: "By bringing the offender and community together in hearings, there is better understanding of how the offender can return to the daily, shared experiences of the members of the community" (PBC 2007c, n.pag). Community participation is therefore constituted as an important mechanism for producing knowledge about the offender in the context of her or his community and works to improve board members' decision-making abilities (PBC 2006b, 18). The production of knowledge about the offender and community may, in turn, lead to more innovative and "fair" techniques of governance (Hannah-Moffat and Maurutto 2010).

CAHs are also represented as beneficial for Aboriginal communities as mechanisms for getting a better glimpse of the "soul" of the offender: these hearings enable communities to "judge for themselves the sincerity of the offender's commitment to change, his acceptance of traditional ways and his ability to manage himself in the community" (PBC 2002b, 6). The PBC contends that CAHs contribute to the protection of society (the paramount principle of the *CCRA*) by preparing Aboriginal communities through the provision of knowledge about returning offenders. Through a CAH, an Aboriginal community "is better prepared to accept and support the offender because it has more information about the offence, the steps the offender has taken, the barriers the offender needs to overcome and ways in which they [the community] can assist him" (11). The community is then "prepared to welcome the offender back into the community with *full knowledge of the issues*" (ibid., emphasis added). Of course, the offender's issues are institutionally defined and reflect the penal system's dominant paradigm of rehabilitation and reintegration. CAHs produce knowledge about the offender that fits within the overarching mandate of the organization.

CAHs are also framed as beneficial for Aboriginal communities by enabling them to better understand the parole system, thereby providing more information to the PBC about offenders and their communities (PBC 200b2, 6). The PBC notes that "one unexpected benefit of holding the [community assisted] hearings in Aboriginal communities is the restoration (or, perhaps more correctly, creation) of respect for the [PBC] and CSC" (9). The PBC's involvement in the community through the outreach necessary to hold CAHs therefore helps the institution build its reputation by providing information about the parole system to Aboriginal community members; in turn, community members "gain respect" for the organization. The PBC (2004a, 18) contends that its outreach activities have been perceived positively by Aboriginal community members, in contrast to "past experiences with government [that] have often been negative in that [Aboriginal people] felt that they were not being listened to." Through the CAH format, the PBC can show that it is being responsive to Aboriginal communities and thus bolster its reputation as an organization that listens to diverse communities.

"Responsible" Aboriginal Communities

One implication of CAHs as a technique of governance relates to the potential for Aboriginal communities to be responsibilized for the supervision of

Aboriginal offenders on parole. As Martel and colleagues (2011, 246) observe, the community has become a key "programmatic locale" for the shaping of Aboriginal subjectivities and the governance of risk. Aboriginal communities are identified by correctional institutions as important sites for responsibilization through both "community and individual empowerment" (ibid.) and as "better equipped to manage the risk of Aboriginal parolees" (Silverstein 2005, 347; see also Kramar and Sealy 2006). Notions of tradition help constitute peaceful individuals and responsible communities (Andersen 1999) as desirable elements of CAHs. Neoliberal criminal justice discourses of partnership and capacity building combine with culturally appropriate practices to target Aboriginal communities as vital conduits for the risk management of Aboriginal offenders on parole.

Within official documents, CAHs are framed as establishing partnerships with Aboriginal communities that "promote[s] their active role in the reintegration of offenders" (PBC 2004a, 24). The PBC (2007c, n.pag) contends that CAHs "respect and contribute to the traditional sense of responsibility felt by every community member for each other and for the creatures and forces that sustain all human life." This quote is illustrative of the incorporation of Aboriginal discourses into conditional release policy. Yet it is unclear how the "traditional sense of responsibility" is operationalized on practical levels or what the implications of this might be for Aboriginal communities. Martel and colleagues (2011, 247) argue that "at the heart of such responsibilization of Indigenous communities lay several myths about the community being a zone of ensured healing." The institutional framing of Aboriginal communities as spaces of tradition and healing reconstitutes these communities as the appropriate risk-reducing locales for Aboriginal offenders. Yet the portrayal of Aboriginal communities as having a "traditional sense of responsibility" that is "felt by every community member" suggests that there are "good" Aboriginal communities that will take offenders back into the fold and participate in healing and in the restoration of peace and harmony. The logic of such responsibilization reflects the idea that Aboriginal communities will help guide and shape Aboriginal offenders into responsible subjects in ways that correspond with the objectives of the community (Pavlich 1996b) and the broader penal apparatus.

The responsibilization of Aboriginal communities through CAHs also requires that the community be enmeshed within the dominant institutional paradigm of community supervision. As the PBC (2002b, 5) notes, if a CAH results in parole being granted, the Aboriginal community "has a great deal of work to do."[12] To transfer responsibility for parole supervision to an Aboriginal community, community members must be mobilized with knowledge of what is "proper, informed community supervision" so that they can recognize the "danger signs" leading to relapse, such as alcohol use (ibid.). Through such knowledge, community members can be responsibilized for intervening when the offender is "slipping back into old habits" and putting her or him "back on the right track" (ibid.). Despite the apparent cultural appropriateness of the CAH and the release decision, the community must follow the institutionally prescribed practices of proper and informed supervision.

This shifting of responsibility for supervision is rationalized as a culturally sensitive approach to restorative justice for Aboriginal offenders and their communities. According to the PBC (2002b, 7), CAHs represent a "return to the old ways" by "returning the process to the community where it used to belong." Ostensibly, this nostalgic statement references the presumed primordial state of Aboriginal communities prior to the devastation wrought by white settlement and colonization. Various features of CAHs – the circle format, the inclusion of ceremony and prayer, and so on – are based on notions of traditional practices for resolving disputes in Aboriginal communities (PBC 2002b). Such institutional discourses construct Aboriginal communities as being made up of "people of consensual culture rather than dissenting politics" (Raibmon 2005, 12). The constitution of Aboriginal communities as bastions of tradition and consensus reflects contemporary popular discourses that romanticize Aboriginal peoples and essentialize cultural difference (Buchanan and Darian-Smith 2011). Such discourses do not acknowledge the impacts of colonialism on Aboriginal communities and governing structures (Monture-Angus 1999). Many communities lack the financial and other resources to participate in the supervision of returning offenders or embrace the so-called "traditional sense of responsibility" that is expected of them (Dyck 1991; LaPrairie 1996; Martel et al. 2011). The shifting of responsibility for supervision through CAHs helps absolve the state of responsibility while simultaneously portraying the PBC and the CAH initiative as being culturally responsive.

Presenting an "Authentic" Aboriginal Self

The discursive constitution of both EAHs and CAHs as enabling more open and honest communication between the offender, the PBC, and, in some cases, the victim's and/or the offender's community relies on the offender's presentation of an "authentic" Aboriginal self, one in which s/he must demonstrate genuine commitment to her or his "cultural and spiritual traditions" (PBC 2002b, 7). This has important implications, especially if Aboriginal prisoners' participation in Aboriginal programs or practices is linked to their release (Silverstein 2005; Martel and Brassard 2008; Martel et al. 2011). The focus on spirituality and culture in relation to Aboriginal offenders may also enable the sidestepping of other important issues, such as racism and the systemic effects of colonialism. As Cowlishaw (2003, 109) shows, appeals to cultural difference tend not to reflect an "understanding that culture and history are intertwined." As a result, the "kind of culture that receives automatic respect is *old* culture, culture without history" (112-13, emphasis in original; see also Razack 1998). In this sense, the separation of culture from history tends to remove references to how colonial practices have affected Aboriginal peoples and communities and (re)shaped cultural practices, traditions, knowledges, gender relations, and so forth. Appeals to cultural difference, then, may work to generate particular expectations for Aboriginal peoples and communities without an understanding of how the contexts have changed (Andersen 1999).

In a similar vein, LaRocque (1997, 88) suggests that criminal justice attempts to be culturally appropriate have had the effect of constituting particular identities for Aboriginal peoples, including the idea of spirituality as a "precondition of being accepted" as Aboriginal. Various notions of Aboriginal authenticity underpin penal discourses and the production of culturally appropriate practices. Yet, as Raibmon (2005, 3) notes, such notions have "achieved a common-sense status that obscure[s] their historical roots." In other words, institutional expectations about who authentic Aboriginal offenders are, what they need, or how they behave are entrenched in a long history of Canadian colonialism and its contemporary manifestations. It is therefore important to consider the role of penal discourses in producing ideas about Aboriginality and how the authentic Aboriginal offender is constituted.

For instance, the notion of the traditional path works to produce an authentic Aboriginal subject to which Aboriginal offenders are compared. In the context of EAHs and CAHs, Aboriginal offenders are encouraged to "emphasize certain aspects of their *selves* congruent with the larger objectives of the programme principles" (Andersen 1999, 310, emphasis in original). Put differently, decision-making policies that stress the assessment (or testing) of an Aboriginal offender's commitment to cultural or spiritual traditions necessitates the presentation of certain aspects of self and identity that conform to popular notions of Aboriginality that are inscribed within PBC policies. If "good" (and thus authentic) Aboriginal offenders are those who follow a traditional path and have embraced their Aboriginal spirituality, then the hearing provides a space for the presentation of particular aspects of the self that reflect these desired attributes. In this context, culture is envisioned "as a rather straightforward *performance*" that demonstrates an Aboriginal offender's reduced level of risk (Martel et al. 2011, 246, emphasis in original).

EAH and CAH policies reflect the incorporation of Aboriginal knowledges and traditions into the dominant correctional agenda, whereby complex histories, current realities, and diverse identities are simplified for practical application. Indeed, as Andersen (1999, 318, emphasis in original) points out, only "*selected* notions of Aboriginality are put into practice" and there is a tendency for these to be valourized rather than thoughtfully contextualized in terms of their traditional usage and meaning (see also LaRocque 1997; Raibmon 2005). For Martel and Brassard (2008, 342), there has been an increasing "Aboriginalization" of Canadian prisons, meaning that particular constructions of Aboriginal identity are reflected and perpetuated within correctional institutions and discourses, and this can be viewed as a technique of contemporary colonialism. Such Aboriginalization is reflective of symbolic adaptations rather than as meaningful change or the creation of separate justice processes (Haslip 2002).

Martel and Brassard (2008, 344) argue that the Canadian penal system has created an "authoritative Aboriginality [that] is built upon the identity criteria of the Canadian government – under the impetus of Aboriginal lobbies – and is a clear racialized construction of the otherness of Aboriginal peoples." Aboriginal prisoners are confronted with this institutionally imposed Aboriginality and a range of culturally appropriate options, including programming and spiritual practices, that reflect a homogenous, "oversimplified, [and] over-generalized version of Aboriginal identity" (ibid.). According to Martel and Brassard, the prison system draws upon and incorporates certain traditional markers and symbols of Aboriginal cultures (e.g., sweat lodges and smudging) that help constitute a hegemonic Aboriginality, thereby subordinating and delegitimizing "alternative representations of Aboriginality." In this sense, penal policies and practices help mould the category of the authentic Aboriginal subject (Buchanan and Darian-Smith 2011, 119).

The constitution of this penal subject through institutionally promoted discourses on Aboriginality "can be constrictive and colonizing, especially when Aboriginal identity assumes a permanence and rigidity that is co-opted by [penal] institutions" (Martel and Brassard 2008, 347; see also Restoule 2000). The process of establishing EAH and CAH policies tends to essentialize various customs and practices "as being necessarily traditional and timeless" (Buchanan and Darian-Smith 2011, 121). Similarly, the tendency to act as if there is a singular Aboriginal culture – despite the recognition that there are many diverse Aboriginal cultures – holds Aboriginal offenders to difficult standards of "cultural purity" (Raibmon 2005, 9). In writing about the role of law more generally in essentializing cultural difference, Buchanan and Darian-Smith (2011, 121) argue that "change over time, and cultural variegation at any given moment, is occluded as law creates and invokes flattened images of what Native people do and do not do." This essentialization also tends to draw clear demarcations between Aboriginals and non-Aboriginals in determinations of what is authentic, thereby working to solidify the former's presumed otherness.

An important implication of the notion of an authentic Aboriginal self relates to cases in which an Aboriginal offender appears not to have much connection to her or his traditional culture or heritage.[13] As Justice Murray Sinclair asks: "When confronted with an aboriginal accused [or offender] who has no identity with his aboriginal identity, what does one do?" (Waldram 1997, 27). He notes that, in the context of sentencing, the tendency is to assume that, if an Aboriginal accused "has no connection to his aboriginal culture, then it is no longer a factor to take into consideration" (ibid.; see also *R. v. Gladue* [1999]).[14] Justice Sinclair's observations are also relevant to the correctional and parole contexts as policies call upon staff and decision makers to assess Aboriginal offenders' progress in embracing their culture and tradition, including their participation in Aboriginal-specific correctional programming.

There exists, then, a potential "lack of fit between the institutional construction of a hegemonic Aboriginality and individual self-identifications as Aboriginal" (Martel and Brassard 2008, 357). Notions of Aboriginal authenticity thereby present potential challenges for those offenders who deviate from the institutionally produced Aboriginality. Yet, as Buchanan and Darian-Smith (2011, 122) suggest, "conceptualizations of authentic indigeneity are always emergent, taking definition through comparison and contrast across a range of temporalities and contexts." In this sense, authenticities change over time and in different contexts and with push-back from Aboriginal peoples who may work to contest and alter dominant institutional understandings of Aboriginality.

Exceptions to the Rule: EAHs and CAHs as "Alternative" Models

Both EAHs and CAHs are defined as "alternative" models of parole hearings used to "meet the needs of Aboriginal offenders" (PBC 2003a, 1). These hearings are considered to be alternative as they differ from the "regular" hearing model in style and allow for "a better and more thorough Board review" (ibid.). The PBC characterizes these alternative hearings as being respectful, engaging, restorative, dialogue friendly, representative and diversified, meaningful, inclusive, occurring in an open setting with fewer physical barriers, less foreboding and demeaning than regular hearings, and honest. Although the EAH and CAH models differ, both are said to reflect alternative approaches associated with restorative justice that attempt to remove barriers, to facilitate dialogue, and to improve information gathering (7). In this sense, EAHs and CAHs are exceptions to the rule rather than "regular" hearings.

Given the stated characteristics of alternative hearing models, we must ask why all parole hearings are not conducted in this way. One answer is that the maintenance of EAHs and CAHs as exceptions reflects the constitution of diversity within the organization. That is, through a process of othering, Aboriginality is positioned as outside the norm, thereby shaping the organizational focus on adapted hearing formats rather than on a rethinking and/or changing of normative conditional release decision-making processes. For example, a discussion paper prepared by the Prairie Region (PBC 2003a, 7) on alternative models and possible modifications to the PBC's regular hearings notes that any modification must be considered in relation to "several realities," including the notion that "Caucasian offenders comprise the majority of the federal offender population nationally." Unfortunately, the paper does not elaborate on this statement. It is therefore unclear whether this means that the regular hearing format should not be modified because most offenders are white, the assumption being that white offenders would not benefit from a different hearing model, or that the federal offender population is not yet racially diverse enough to warrant alteration to the regular format. Nevertheless, this statement reflects the constitution of diversity within non-white (and female) bodies and its location outside the norm.

It appears that with the PBC's reading of the *Gladue* decision consideration was given to extending the EAH and CAH formats to other groups of offenders. In particular, the organization recognizes that female offenders "feel intimidated" by the regular hearing process and recommends the exploration of conducting alternative hearings for offenders from diverse communities (PBC 2003a, 7). Yet, according to one informant, the PBC's senior management did not support the idea that *all* offenders, regardless of their gender and racial, ethnic, or cultural backgrounds, could benefit from the format of EAHs (Interview 7). The informant noted that most aspects of EAHs, with the exception of the elder and ceremonies, were applicable to all hearings:

The respectful environment, the removal of barriers to facilitate dialogue, you know, more simplistic language, you know, more patience, and so, allowing if there's people from the community there, let them talk if they've got something to add in terms of support upon release or whatever, you know, being more inclusive.

This informant suggested that such a hearing format would be useful for all offenders given the offender profile, which includes low literacy levels and learning disabilities, among other factors. That the PBC did not support the extension of the EAH format to all offenders is not especially surprising. In practical terms, such a reconfiguration would be costly and require access to additional human and operational resources. More conceptually, the extension of the EAH model to all offenders would require dissolution of the normative model and entrenched ways of doing things that have been built up since the creation of the organization in 1959. Such a change would also require the organization to "see" diversity in ways that preclude constituting and regulating difference as other than the white, male norm (Puwar 2004). As I discuss in Chapter 5, the PBC has explored alternative hearing models with African Canadian offenders and communities in the Atlantic Region (PBC 2003a), arguably because this fits with the dominant organizational practice of responding to the needs of a constituted other.

Interpreting and Institutionalizing the *Gladue* Decision

Although EAHs and CAHs – as the PBC's primary diversity initiatives for Aboriginal offenders – predate the Supreme Court's decision in *Gladue*, this decision has affected the organization's decision-making policies and cultural sensitivity training for board members and staff, as is shown in Chapter 3. Despite its focus on sentencing, the PBC (2000a, 6) interpreted *Gladue* as having "an impact on every aspect of the criminal justice system" and serving "as the impetus for action consistent with the Board's Vision." Additionally, *Gladue* "helps to crystallize the need for the [PBC] to consider the unique circumstances of Aboriginal offenders in risk assessment and risk management" (ibid.). The PBC (n.d.-a) also points to section 151(3) of the *CCRA* as confirming the need for action on the part of Aboriginal offenders. Both the *CCRA* and *Gladue* help drive action (i.e., policy change) by the PBC in this regard.

In its assessment of *Gladue*, the PBC (n.d.-a, n.pag) states that "it is not nearly enough" for background and systemic factors to only be considered at sentencing; rather, factors that are "associated with Aboriginal offenders" should be referenced in PBC policy (PBC 2000a, 6). The PBC identifies the CSC as having a responsibility "to incorporate similar standards and practices when managing the sentences of offenders, particularly Aboriginal offenders" (PBC n.d.-a, n.pag). More specifically, the systemic and background factors identified by the Supreme Court in its decision "must be taken into account when constructing and implementing sentence planning, correctional program planning, risk assessment, release planning and community reintegration planning and monitoring" (ibid.). The PBC stresses that *Gladue* principles ought to be integrated at every phase of the correctional process in order to provide Aboriginal prisoners with "a culturally relevant continuum of care" as a means of ensuring their successful rehabilitation and reintegration (ibid.). The PBC's recognition of the CSC's responsibilities to implement *Gladue* principles reflects an organizational understanding that the PBC cannot act alone in trying to make the conditional release process more "appropriate" for Aboriginal offenders.

The PBC (n.d.-a, n.pag) indicates that in "March 2000 the Executive Committee directed the incorporation of the *Gladue* principles in the Board's policies relating to the assessment of risk." The PBC determined that the *Gladue* decision supported the initiatives it already had under way, including EAHs, CAHs, and cultural sensitivity training. *Gladue* was also seen to be relevant to the CSC's case preparations and submissions to the PBC for parole hearings. However, the PBC indicates that the consideration and application of *Gladue* principles within the correctional sphere "may not always translate to an earlier release or support for discretionary releases" (ibid.).[15] Rather, the important issue is that "*all of the relevant information is taken into consideration* during correctional planning, release planning, support or non-support of discretionary releases, institutional and community monitoring, etc." (ibid., emphasis added). As I discuss below, the potential for improved information collection is one of the PBC's key anticipated outcomes for the incorporation of *Gladue* concepts and principles. Moreover, the organization's inclusion of the decision makes organizational sense as it supports priorities and practices that were already in place, such as EAHs and CAHs, which are directed towards gathering knowledge about Aboriginal offenders in order to make appropriate decisions.

The PBC's assessment of *Gladue* resulted in the finding that "factors such as racism and ties to community were also relevant to other offenders" (PBC n.d.-a, n.pag). This being the case, incorporating *Gladue* principles into the Policy Manual would require board members "to consider such factors in their assessment of risk for *all offenders* and not solely in decision-making for Aboriginal offenders" (ibid., emphasis added). The extension of the *Gladue* decision to other offenders is linked to subsequent court decisions, such as *R. v. Borde* [2003] and *R. v. Hamilton* [2003], that involved the application of

"*Gladue*-like interpretation[s] of section 718.2(e) to African Canadians" (Kramar and Sealy 2006, 124; see also Murdocca 2013). As one informant explained, the *Hamilton* decision "said the *Gladue* principles should apply to other [groups], like the black community" (Interview 4).

The decision to extend *Gladue* principles to all offenders can be understood as an attempt to mainstream the consideration of systemic and background factors, shifting the original focus from Aboriginal offenders – who, as a group, are uniquely situated given Canada's colonial histories and presents – to all offenders.[16] Ostensibly, the assessment of risk for each offender requires board members to consider how a number of structural factors have affected the individual and shaped her or his conflict with the law. What is not clear, however, is the degree to which all offenders become, in practice, non-white offenders, particularly in the context in which *Gladue* is discussed within the PBC's assessment paper (PBC n.d.-a, n.pag). There is no mention of whiteness or any indication as to whether or not such principles have any applicability to white offenders. By framing "racism and ties to community" as relevant to "other offenders," these factors are seen to only apply to non-white offenders.

The mainstreaming (or generalizing) of *Gladue* principles also raises questions regarding whether this results in a weakening of the original intent of the decision when it is extended to all offenders. Section 718.2(e) of the *Criminal Code* was developed specifically for Aboriginal offenders because of their unique position within Canada's colonial legacy. This provision seems to recognize "that there is a particular structural relationship between Indigenous peoples and criminal justice systems which is quite different from other groups" (Cunneen 2009, 211). Generalized *Gladue* principles are reflected in section 2.1 of the PBC's Policy Manual, which requires board members, when assessing the criminal, social, and conditional release histories of offenders, to examine any "systemic or background factors" such as "the effects of substance abuse, systemic discrimination, racism, family or community breakdown, unemployment, poverty, a lack of education and employment opportunities, dislocation from their community, community fragmentation, dysfunctional adoption and foster care, and residential school experience" (PBC 2015, Ch. 2.1, 2). Although presented without reference to Aboriginal offenders, many of these "factors" clearly reflect the colonial legacy affecting Aboriginal peoples, yet they are relevant to most offenders as well. Exactly *how* these factors are brought into the decision-making process is unknown,[17] especially as these "systemic or background factors" are among thirteen factors to be considered by board members when assessing an offender's criminal, social, and conditional release history.

Conclusions: Producing Cultural Ghettos?

In this chapter, I examine initiatives directed at the special needs of Aboriginal offenders. The PBC has developed EAHs and CAHs to make conditional release hearings more responsive to issues of culture and spirituality. I argue that these initiatives reflect the institution's attempts to Aboriginalize its hearing processes and decision-making policies. With the *Gladue* decision, steps were taken to transfer the key findings into the context of parole decision making (e.g., through the recognition of systemic or background factors as part of board members' assessment of risk). These reforms are rationalized in several ways, including helping to reduce risk through culturally appropriate conditional release decision making, ensuring a more fair and effective parole system, and contributing to the penal goal of reduced numbers of Aboriginal prisoners. These initiatives also serve important institutional functions. They make the PBC appear responsive to Aboriginal peoples' needs, thereby reducing potential risks to reputation through claims of inaction and cultural ignorance.

I offer two key findings. The first relates to the tensions and contradictions associated with creating culturally appropriate hearings in the context of penal institutions, particularly where certain practices are transported into foreign and incompatible contexts. The institutionalization of Aboriginal traditions requires certain decisions to be made around which symbols and practices to import and incorporate. As evidenced by the different approaches taken within the Pacific and Prairie Regions, not all traditions are easily universalized. Tensions also exist around the backgrounds and knowledges of PBC-contracted elders and the degree to which they can assist hearings with Aboriginal offenders from different cultures and/or nations. The second key finding involves the issue of Aboriginal culture. I show that Aboriginal offenders are ghettoized in the realm of culture, with EAHs and CAHs remaining exceptional and peripheral to the "normal" program of parole. EAH and CAH policies reflect the selective incorporation of Aboriginal knowledges and traditions into the dominant correctional agenda, whereby complex histories, current realities, and diverse identities are simplified for practical application, and the dominant focal point is culture.

The ghettoization or confinement of Aboriginal offenders to the realm of culture may work to depoliticize penal practices, thereby downplaying power relations and the ongoing colonial relationship among Aboriginal peoples and the Canadian state (Bannerji 2000). The incorporation of elements of Aboriginal culture and spirituality into parole processes allows for the modification of standard practices without a fundamental reconsideration of the status quo. In other words, these approaches may encourage "culturalist response[s] to structural oppressions" (Kramar and Sealy 2006, 144). A second implication of the focus on culture is that Aboriginal offenders may be over-determined by culture, such that institutional attempts to be culturally sensitive ironically produce a type of cultural straightjacket that captures and constrains Aboriginal offenders within this realm. Such an approach makes an intersectional analysis particularly challenging. Indeed, as noted at the outset of this chapter, gender or female offenders are not specifically mentioned within the institutional discussions of EAHs or CAHs. Given the PBC's efforts to create culturally appropriate and fair practices, these issues are especially important because they show how non-Aboriginal institutions come to understand and embrace certain aspects of Aboriginality and not others. In the next chapter, I consider the selective inclusion of diversity in more detail and examine diversity work targeting offenders defined as "ethnocultural."

Discourses of Difference
Constituting the Ethnocultural Offender

In recent years, the increasing diversity of the federal offender population, in terms of its racial and ethnic composition, has been noted as a challenge by both the Parole Board of Canada (2010c) and the Correctional Service of Canada (2009b). The growing numbers of non-white and non-Aboriginal offenders have created pressure on the penal system to be responsive to additional groups marked by their racial, ethnic, and/or cultural identities. At the PBC, offenders defined as "ethnocultural" are constituted as targets of diversity initiatives that are separate from those developed for Aboriginal offenders. Compared to Aboriginal and female offenders, organizational responses to this population occurred much later and were linked by several informants to the increasing diversification of the Canadian population brought about through immigration. The development of initiatives for ethnocultural offenders can be contextualized within institutionalized multiculturalism and larger debates around the limits of tolerance and accommodation. These reforms occur in a milieu in which the liberal nation-state "is being embarrassed by heterodoxy" as various groups designated as racially or ethnically different from the white, Canadian norm are demanding "respect, recognition, room for self-expression, [and] entitlement" (Comaroff and Comaroff 2004, 188). Within federal penal institutions, the offender population is increasingly shifting from the "usual" to the "unusual" (Bannerji 2000), thereby necessitating institutional adjustment to accommodate these differences.

In this chapter, I explore how the PBC has grappled with the inclusion of difference as represented by the ethnocultural other. I analyze the various documents that define and rationalize this population as targets of ethnicized parole policies and practices. The institution's attempts to accommodate ethnocultural offenders are also examined, including the adaptation of hearing models originally designed for Aboriginal offenders and refocused efforts on interpretation services for offenders who do not speak English or French. Finally, I explore some of the initiatives developed to respond to the needs of ethnocultural offenders, the main initiative being the African Canadian Liaison Project. As with PBC initiatives established for Aboriginal offenders, gender is not considered in the production of knowledge about, and practices for, those offenders constituted as ethnocultural. I argue that ethnocultural difference poses a more challenging set of diversities to be negotiated into parole policies and practices. Unlike the notion of Aboriginality, which can be more easily simplified for inclusion in policy and practice, ethnocultural difference is more nebulous and tougher to conceptualize in concise terms. The construct of ethnocultural may include a variety of different racial, ethnic, and/or cultural minority groups that do not share common histories, traditions, or cultural practices. These diversities represent a greater complication to inclusion and accommodation because penal institutions must select particular offender identities (e.g., African Canadian) in order to rationalize and develop diversity initiatives. If, as argued in previous chapters, the institutionalization of diversity is about making exceptions to dominant practices, such as through modified parole hearings (e.g., elder-assisted hearings), the challenge posed by ethnocultural offenders is determining which and how many exceptions to make.

Institutionalized Multiculturalism

The development of diversity initiatives for ethnocultural offenders may be situated within the broader context of institutionalized multiculturalism.[1] As a federal institution, the PBC is responsible for implementing the *Canadian Multiculturalism Act* within its larger mandate.[2] This legislation, like the *CCRA*, ensures accountability by requiring the PBC to respond to diversity, while at the same time producing reputational risks to be managed vis-à-vis failures to act accordingly. The PBC (2010c, n.pag) frames and justifies its diversity initiatives for ethnocultural offenders as a response to multiculturalism and simultaneously recognizes the "growing ethnocultural diversity within Canada's federal offender population" and the "increasingly diverse communities to which these offenders" return. The concept of ethnocultural offender reflects liberal multicultural discourse, which defines and locates difference in non-white others based on the white English and French "core" (Bannerji 2000; Dhamoon 2009). The category of ethnocultural aggregates different racialized minority groups, thereby erasing the heterogeneity of these populations and their differential treatment by the justice system (Hudson and Bramhall 2005; Bramhall and Hudson 2007). For instance, offenders identified as "black" are overrepresented within the federal penal system based on their proportions in the Canadian population (PBC 2009e, 41; OCI 2014), yet they are not constituted as a special offender group (as are Aboriginal offenders).

The organizational response to ethnocultural difference is outlined in a document entitled "The *Canadian Multiculturalism Act*" (PBC 2010h). This document presents the PBC as an organization that is responding to issues of ethnic and cultural difference through a number of initiatives, including the PBC's participation on regionally and nationally based ethnocultural advisory committees in conjunction with the CSC; the "periodic" organization of "information forums" involving ethnocultural community agencies and groups; the use of "experts from a variety of ethnocultural and ethnoracial backgrounds" for sensitivity and awareness training; the Employment Equity Plan, which aims to help increase the employment (and thus representation) of "equity group members"; and the celebration of events that "promote awareness and understanding of the diversity of Canadian society and to increase respect and inclusiveness" (n.pag). As argued in Chapter 2, these forms of diversity work are based on an understanding of diversity as located in non-white individuals, experiences, and cultures.

This document identifies two provisions of the *Canadian Multiculturalism Act* upon which organizational commitment is based: first, that "all citizens are equal and have the freedom to preserve, enhance, and share their cultural heritage"; and, second, that "multiculturalism promotes the full and equitable participation of individuals and communities of all origins in all aspects of Canadian society" (PBC 2010h, n.pag). The PBC indicates that its executive director has been appointed the multiculturalism champion who "supports, encourages, promotes and endorses activities and initiatives" related to the implementation of multiculturalism within the organization. Such activities and initiatives include ensuring equal opportunity to gain employment at the PBC; enhancing contributions to "the continuing evolution of Canada" by individuals and communities of "all origins"; improving understanding of and respect for diversity; increasing sensitivity and responding to "the multicultural reality of Canada"; and utilizing the language skills and cultural understanding of various individuals (ibid.). According to the PBC, these activities and initiatives are also supported by the organization's legislative basis (i.e., section 151(3) of the *CCRA*), policy manual, core values, and strategic vision.

The organizational commitment to and "investment in multiculturalism is predicated on forgetting [a] range of complicated colonial legacies and racial struggles"; this includes the naturalization of white settlement as Aboriginal nations were displaced and decimated, and the establishment of "intense racialized hierarchies ... between European settlers, Native Nations, Black, Chinese and Asian settlers, and other more recent patterns of immigration" (O'Connell 2010, 538). Organizational discussions of multiculturalism fail to consider whiteness "in its multiple forms and expressions" (ibid.). Institutional understandings of ethnicity do not consider whiteness despite historical patterns of ethnicizing Italian and Irish Canadians. In dominant multicultural discourses, ethnicity is linked to cultural difference and separated from white, Canadian norms.

The critical literature on Canadian multiculturalism can be used to contextualize the PBC's approach to ethnocultural offenders and the discourses of difference that permeate institutionally produced documents about this offender population. This literature is also useful for studying how such discourses of difference tend to preserve, rather than upset, institutional whiteness. Multiculturalism is as a governing discourse that organizes and manages difference. More specifically, Bannerji (2000, 78) argues that multiculturalism is a "vehicle for racialization" because it selectively ethnicizes some groups and not others:

> It establishes anglo-Canadian cultural as the ethnic core culture while "tolerating" and hierarchically arranging others around its "multiculture." The ethics and aesthetics of "whiteness," with its colonial imperialist/racist ranking of criteria, define and construct the "multi" culture of Canada's "others."

The establishment of "the British and French as competing yet 'founding' nations" within multiculturalism policy and the positioning of Aboriginal peoples and racialized immigrants as "external to the nation" helped provide "the basis on which 'race' and ethnicity came to be codified through culture" (O'Connell 2010, 539). For O'Connell, "liberal whiteness is accomplished not through the rejection of diversity, but through its institutionalization in broader cultural and political practices and policies" (538). She argues that the "respect for difference presupposes a white rational liberal subject who defines, measures, and allows for *allowable* differences" (540, emphasis in original). The notion of allowable differences is important because not all differences among the various (non-English, non-French) cultures are legitimated by discourses of multiculturalism: "Ethnic foods, dress, cultural celebrations, and diversity are welcomed and encouraged in the public realm until supposed ethnic enclaves are identified or Native groups initiate land claims on territories they deem have been illegally occupied" (ibid.). Significantly, respect and tolerance are granted as long as multicultural difference is confined to a celebration of diversity, without challenging the current order of things (Hyndman 1998; O'Connell 2010). This, according to O'Connell, maintains hegemonic whiteness in Canada. In the following section, I analyze this tendency in the discursive constitution of ethnocultural offenders in PBC texts.

Constituting the Ethnocultural Offender

The documents I analyze in this chapter illustrate how institutional discourses of difference constitute the ethnocultural offender as a distinct target for special penal practices. The construct of the ethnocultural offender provides an opportunity to consider how "the deployment of diversity reduces to and manages difference as ethnic cultural issues" (Bannerji 2000, 51) in the context of parole. Knowledges of difference emerge in institutionally produced documents to signify non-white and (non-Aboriginal) offenders as both carriers of diversity and targets for diversity initiatives. Through this process, ethnicity and culture are racialized as characteristics or traits of the ethnocultural offender, and whiteness remains the unacknowledged and unmarked point of comparison against which this difference is produced. The constitution of ethnocultural offenders as bearers of culture simultaneously represents board members as having no culture or as putting aside their culture when acting in a professional capacity (van Dongen 2005, 184). It is therefore important to consider how ethnocultural offenders are "made up" within institutional discourses and penal policies.

I made several requests under the *Access to Information Act* for PBC documents relating to ethnocultural offenders and issues of diversity more generally. The documents I received illustrate how the PBC is grappling with an increasingly diversified federal offender population as well as with more heterogeneous communities and victims of crime. More specifically, and with one exception, these texts reflect the production of racialized knowledge about particular groups of offenders and various strategies designed to understand and address difference. In this section, I examine how the PBC has attempted to "know" and respond to ethnocultural difference. Key institutional mechanisms for producing knowledge about this population are research reports, community consultations, and diversity committees. I show that ethnocultural difference poses a more challenging set of diversities to be negotiated into conditional release policies and practices than does Aboriginality or gender.

Producing and Knowing the Ethnocultural Offender through Research

One institutional approach to coming to know the ethnocultural other involves the production of research reports about this group of offenders. My requests under the *ATIA* located three reports, one from the Quebec Region (PBC 2005c), one from the Pacific Region (PBC 2005e), and one from the national office (PBC 2009i). The first two reports focus primarily on the profile and needs of offenders defined as ethnocultural in order to better know them and determine whether the parole process could be altered to address their needs. In contrast, the third report takes a more critical look at how ethnocultural offenders are defined and the implications of these definitions for organizational processes. In addition to being knowledge products, these reports may be seen as techniques of managing reputation and demonstrating that the organization is being responsive to diversity issues. The existence of these reports further illustrates how separate branches of the PBC (e.g., the two regional offices versus the national office) may take varying approaches to the problem that difference poses to dominant frameworks and practices, including how diversity is defined and accommodated.

For the Quebec Region, knowledge of the other was required before it undertook steps to alter its practices. In the 2004-05 fiscal year, a consultant was hired to "conduct a needs analysis among the major stakeholders involved and offenders from various ethnic origins." This was a "first step" for the region "before determining the way it wanted to address the issue of cultural diversity" (PBC 2005c, 3). The consultant's mandate was to determine "whether improvements could be made to the hearing process so that the National Parole Board's decision-making process would be tailored to meet the needs of *offenders of diverse cultural origins*" (4, emphasis added). Although not explicitly defined, a read of the report indicates that "offenders of diverse cultural origins" are non-white ethnic minorities, excluding Aboriginal peoples,[3] and the focus is on male offenders within this population. The use of language and the framing of issues within the report suggest that the imagined reader is white; indeed, whiteness is the implicit norm against which others are constituted. The report highlights the differences exhibited by these ethnocultural others, such as their different perceptions of justice and the experiences of (white) stakeholders in dealing with this offender population. In relation to the former, the report points to different cultural understandings of violence against women, the use of hallucinatory drugs, and the distrust of authority (9) to demonstrate the potential otherness of ethnic offenders from various (non-Canadian) origins.

The Pacific Region hired a consultant in the 2004-05 fiscal year to review its "ethnocultural population to identify profiles, trends, issues and needs" in relation to the PBC's decision making as a means of enhancing the cultural competency of the hearing process for ethnocultural offenders (PBC 2005e, 2). This study involved an analysis of data extracted from the Offender Management System – a computerized case file management system with information about federally sentenced offenders – to identify the "target groups" of ethnocultural offenders from the "top three communities" in the region based on notions of race (i.e., non-whiteness), country of origin (i.e., outside of Canada), and primary language (i.e., not English or French). The focus on numbers points to the notion of a critical mass, such that an organizational response may be necessary if there are sufficient numbers of offenders from identifiable communities.

The Quebec Region's report examines the experiences of (white) stakeholders in order to assess the "level of general knowledge" among these people in relation to "cultural diversity" (PBC 2005c, 7), presumably to determine whether there was an organizational need or justification for acting on diversity issues. This knowledge is identified as being "limited" as few stakeholders "have received *basic training* on ethnic minorities" (9, emphasis added). Ethnic minorities are simultaneously constituted as an *object* of knowledge and as a *source* of difference. At the same time, the stakeholders are constituted as the homogeneous, non-ethnic majority who "may *encounter* individuals from various cultural origins in their personal lives," yet their gaze upon the other is limited through a low "level of knowledge" about "them" (ibid.). According to the report, "this lack of knowledge gives rise to misunderstanding, mistrust and discomfort" and may work to strain communication between (white) board members and ethnocultural offenders (10). The "appropriate" solution to this problem therefore becomes a matter of increasing knowledge about these offenders and their communities.

Both the Quebec and the Pacific Regions' reports consider the elements involved in the conditional release decision-making process and how these might be modified to attend to the needs of ethnocultural offenders. In relation to information gathering, the PBC (2005c, 11) indicates that ethnocultural offenders need to do "better" at communicating information to board members: "Limited knowledge of the official languages and refusal to or difficulty in expressing oneself openly are barriers that must be overcome so that the offender can clearly express his point of view and initiate change." Ethnocultural offenders are expected to meet the normative criteria of the system. The Pacific Region's report recommends that ethnocultural offenders be allowed assistants at hearings to help ensure a proper flow of communication (PBC 2005e). Likewise, the Quebec Region's report is supportive of formalizing the role of "ethnic minority representatives" as active participants at conditional release hearings (PBC 2005c, 14). This "representative, who belongs to the same ethnic community as the offender, would be able to draw the commissioners' [i.e., board members'] attention to significant elements of his culture in comparison with those of the majority" as well as help ethnocultural offenders "feel more secure" during the hearing process (ibid.). The representative's participation is also seen to "provide supporting information on the home community, monitoring resources and support to which the offender would have access upon release" (ibid.). I examine the PBC's considerations regarding adapting the regular hearing model for ethnocultural offenders later in this chapter.

Concerning risk assessments for decision making, the Quebec Region's report encourages decision makers to recognize the lack of correctional programs for ethnocultural offenders, noting that available programs are run in French or English and "were designed to meet the needs of the majority" (PBC 2005c, 11). Accordingly, board members are advised to "make a distinction between a refusal to participate in programs and difficulty integrating into them" in order "to avoid unfairly penalizing this ethnic clientele" (ibid.). However, it still appears that the onus is placed on ethnocultural offenders to try to participate in programs – even those that may be irrelevant – as their refusal to do so may be used against them as a sign of their resistance to rehabilitative programming.

Last, in relation to parole hearings, the Quebec Region's report indicates that hearings are "uncomfortable" for both ethnocultural offenders and board members (PBC 2005c). The former are said to be "intimidated by the decorum and conduct of a hearing," while the latter believe that ethnocultural offenders "mistrust" the process (12), thereby reducing the "climate of trust and mutual respect" (13). As I show in the previous chapter, similar experiences were reported by Aboriginal offenders, which helped drive the creation of elder-assisted hearings and community-assisted hearings in order to Aboriginalize the hearing format. In keeping with the dominant organizational approach to difference, the report concludes that the PBC does not have to go about altering its "entire decision-making process, but rather, by and large, *making some minor changes* and, above all, *demonstrating an attitude of openness and respect*" (16, emphasis added). In other words, a tweaking of the status quo combined with an "attitude of respect" among board members are viewed as the necessary steps towards "improving the effectiveness of existing mechanisms" (ibid.). For instance, a "greater awareness of the living conditions of the various ethnic minorities would foster greater understanding of the behaviour of offenders and could make mutual interaction easier" (13). In other words, what is required is more knowledge of the other so that (white) board members will know what to do and how to act appropriately when presented with non-white offenders at parole hearings. Training and knowledge acquisition become the appropriate organizational responses in this context.

Similarly, the Pacific Region's report recommends that the organization enhance its cultural competency through orientation and refresher training for board members (PBC 2005e). It also advocates informing offenders that board members receive such training in order to "enhance the confidence of ethnocultural offenders in the Board when offenders prepare for their cases and during the hearing" (8). This step was envisioned as a response to the perception among some ethnocultural offenders "that there is a lack of cultural understanding among Board Members" (ibid.), which is believed to affect their confidence in accessing fair hearings. Similarly, the Quebec Region's report proposes that stakeholders and ethnic minority organizations be educated about the PBC's initiatives to ensure that they are "aware of [the PBC's] open approach and its concern for equity with respect to cultural diversity" (PBC 2005c, 17). In other words, the purpose of educating ethnocultural offenders and their communities is to convey the idea that diversity is being practised at the PBC (Ahmed et al. 2006).

The third report, produced by a consultant for the national office in 2008, stands in stark contrast to the Quebec and Pacific Regions' reports. Although it has a similar focus in terms of providing the organization "with knowledge about [PBC] staff and board member needs pertaining to their work with ethnocultural minority offenders in the hearing process" as a means of informing "the development of training materials, resources and/or other initiatives" (PBC 2009i, ii), the report also draws on external sources that enable a more critical consideration of notions of ethnicity and cultural competency. This report is unique when compared to most PBC documents due to its conceptual exploration of issues related to ethnocultural offenders, including the basic starting point of defining what is meant by the term, some of the advantages and disadvantages of identifying offenders as ethnocultural, and different options for diversity training.

As a knowledge practice, the national office's report provides the PBC with information about the existing legislative frameworks that support diversity and equality (e.g., the *Charter* and *Canadian Multiculturalism Act*) and the development of cultural competency (PBC 2009i). Instead of simply providing knowledge of ethnocultural offenders, the report examines how staff and board members understand and perceive ethnocultural difference and its "place" within the conditional release system. The report is exceptional among other PBC diversity-related documents because it explores how the ethnocultural offender is constituted by the organization and acknowledges the complexities of identifying and responding to ethnic and/or cultural difference.

In sum, the three reports discussed here represent institutional techniques of producing knowledge about ethnocultural offenders as a means of determining how these diversities can be integrated into the PBC's policies and practices. These reports also constitute ethnocultural diversity as pertaining to non-white and non-Aboriginal individuals and communities. Whiteness is the implicit norm against which differences are framed. The reports are illustrative of how the PBC is struggling with the challenge of ethnocultural diversity in the federal offender population.

Knowing the Ethnocultural Offender through Community Consultations

Community consultations are another example of institutional practices focused on ethnocultural difference. In 2004, the Aboriginal and Diversity Initiatives section applied for and received a grant from Canadian Heritage to support its diversity work (PBC 2004d). This funding was intended to support initiatives that formed relationships between the organization and ethnocultural communities, such as forums with these communities and key community leaders (1).[4] According to the Aboriginal and Diversity Initiatives section, the funding provided by Canadian Heritage was met with excitement as it enabled interested regions to "do some of the work that [they] have been wanting to do, for some time now" (2). The section indicated that "a lot" could be accomplished, both nationally and regionally, given "how far [they] have come with minimal financial resources" (ibid.). This statement suggests that such diversity work for ethnocultural offenders had not been funded by the PBC, thereby requiring the Aboriginal and Diversity Initiatives section to seek other government funding to support the work it wanted to carry out.

The Aboriginal and Diversity Initiatives section used some of the funding to support the Ethnocultural Consultation Project, which it started in 2002. The remaining funding was made available to the regions – upon approval of the section – in support of region-specific work with ethnocultural groups (PBC

2004d, 1). The Prairie Region, for example, utilized resources to hold three community forums in March 2005 in Winnipeg, Edmonton, and Calgary, respectively (PBC 2005f). These cities were chosen after a "statistical breakdown" showed that they reflected "diverse offender populations" and had community agencies and services for "ethnocultural people" (n.pag). The aim of the forums was to "provide the Board with a better sense of the programs and services which the agencies offer and ... [to] give [the] National Parole Board an opportunity to inform community agencies and members about [its] role within the criminal justice system" (ibid.). The forums also supported the production of knowledge about these communities as well as the opportunity to build organizational reputation and to download some responsibility for conditional release onto diverse communities.

The Aboriginal and Diversity Initiatives section's Ethnocultural Consultation Project stemmed from the PBC's discussion of "innovative ways that it may be more responsive to offenders from diverse racial, ethnic and cultural backgrounds taking into account their unique cultural heritage and their differential experiences with the criminal justice system" (PBC 2005g, 1). Its advances in the area of hearings for Aboriginal offenders were viewed as having "opened the door to envision the creation of a hearing process which is sensitive to the culture and traditions of offenders from diverse cultural backgrounds" (ibid.). The PBC consulted with ethnocultural offenders, Correctional Service of Canada staff, non-governmental organizations involved in community supervision, and community groups, organizations, and community leaders representing diverse populations. These consultations were conducted in order to fulfill several objectives: to garner feedback about the hearing process and how it could be "enhanced" to better meet the needs of ethnocultural offenders; to gain insight into how to facilitate the release and reintegration of ethnocultural offenders; and to develop partnerships with community organizations and representatives of diverse communities (1-2).

The PBC focused its Consultation Project on ethnocultural offenders – defined as non-white and non-Aboriginal – because it had already conducted a "substantial amount of work" on Aboriginal issues, including consultations with Aboriginal communities and elders (PBC 2005g, 2). Female offenders were excluded from the project because "an extensive consultation" had previously been completed with this population.[5] In this way, culture and ethnicity are artificially separated from gender, such that female offender issues are set apart from those of ethnocultural offenders and deemed to be outside the scope of consultations: the PBC can only look at women *or* ethnicity, not both, even though facets of identity are always multiple, intersecting, and simultan-eously experienced (see hooks 1981; Collins 1990; Crenshaw 1991; Razack 1998; Yuval-Davis 2006). The decision to exclude female offenders also functions to implicitly gender ethnocultural offenders as a male population, while the vary-ing ways masculinities intersect with diverse ethnicities and/or cultures are unrecognized. Yet a consultation project that looks specifically at issues of ethnicity, culture, or race in relation to parole without considering the inter-secting impacts of gender may establish norms for the offender population defined as ethnocultural to the detriment of non-white female offenders. In other words, it raises questions as to how female ethnocultural offenders fit in the conditional release context, such as in relation to their grouping as female offenders, where norms around whiteness may dominate.

The report of the Ethnocultural Consultation Project explores a number of themes related to parole and conditional release for male ethnocultural of-fenders (PBC 2005g) and demonstrates how the PBC is attempting to come to grips with difference. For instance, the issue of the format of release hearings yielded divergent opinions during consultations. On the one hand, the report outlines support – primarily by offenders – for the more informal approach reflected in the EAH model, where the offender's supporters are allowed to speak and the hearing room is organized to enable participants to sit in a circle (5). On the other hand, there was a firm belief, particularly among CSC staff, in the status quo: "The quasi-judicial format is a setting that *most Canadians* are familiar with and comfortable with so there should be no problem in con-tinuing to utilize it for hearings" (ibid., emphasis added). The report does not analyze the assumptions about the status quo for the organization's release hearings. Yet, as this quote indicates, one key assumption among the oppon-ents of a different approach to hearings is that organizational "professionalism" is reflective of a white, masculine, Canadian format that exhibits quasi-judicial formalities (e.g., boardroom set up, official attire, etc.) and demarcates the uneven power relations between board members and offenders.[6]

The Ethnocultural Consultation Project also signalled a desire among deci-sion makers for knowledge about ethnocultural offenders' cultural norms. More specifically, the ways in which various groups' "family dynamics differ from mainstream norms" were seen to "present unique challenges for Board Mem-bers and POs [parole officers]" (PBC 2005g, 10). Knowledge of such norms is linked to the assessment of risk, such that the exploration of cultural issues within release hearings could work to reduce risk within the community. With-out "sufficient information on the cultural norms" of the offender's community, it is feared that board members "may overlook important areas in the hearing" (11). The issue of sufficient information was linked to board member training on "matters of culture" (14). These findings highlight an organizational preference for racialized knowledge of diverse others as a solution to the problems posed by diversity, as though knowing the other will lead to appropriate decisions based upon standard decision-making policies and practices of risk assessment.

The relationship between culture and risk assessment is another area addressed by the Consultation Project, and it illustrates the PBC's attempts to grapple with difference. For instance, the report suggests that risk assessment ought to occur through a consideration of the assorted "cultural factors" underlying a given case, including an analysis of the "cultural implications" of imposing special conditions (PBC 2005g, 10-11). However, the example used – the case of an offender killing his wife – highlights the difficulties associated with inserting culture talk into quasi-judicial settings where gender and multiculturalism intersect.[7] More specifically, the use of cultural knowledges in the context of conditional release hearings raises questions as to what sorts of knowledges are privileged over others, how cultural communities and experts are defined and according to whose terms, and how these knowledges may reduce complex practices and power relations to stereotypes. Given the time pressures and caseloads of board members, there may be a reliance on shorthand information (e.g., reference guides for various cultural or ethnic groups) as well as on cultural fact sheets (discussed later in this chapter).

Knowing the Ethnocultural Offender through Committees

Diversity committees are another strategy for knowing the ethnocultural offender. The Atlantic Region created a committee in response to the perceived needs of ethnocultural offenders, with a specific focus on African Canadian offenders. The African Canadian Offender Project Committee (formerly the Afro-Canadian Committee) was created in 2000 in response to the overrepresentation of African Canadians in the correctional system (PBC 2006b, 9). This committee "examines issues surrounding the African-Canadian population and gathers information to improve the decision-making process for African-Canadian offenders" (ibid.). Knowledge production is a primary aspect of its work. For example, working with community groups in Nova Scotia, the committee has held meetings to "increase [PBC]'s awareness and sensitivity to African-Canadians within the criminal justice system, to increase [PBC]'s knowledge of the communities that ethnocultural offenders will be returning to and how cultural factors impact on the assessment of risk for African-Canadian offenders" (ibid.). One meeting yielded recommendations for the piloting of a CAH within "the African Nova Scotian community" as a way to "allow community members and cultural agencies to be empowered to take a more active role in the hearing process and successful offender reintegration" (12). Other meetings yielded strong support among community groups for alternative approaches to parole hearings for ethnocultural offenders. Such alternatives include allowing for offenders to have assistants present for support and having board members work to establish a "respectful and welcoming" environment for offenders through small talk and the removal of the table (13). The community meetings also yielded calls for a more diverse board that includes representation from various ethnocultural communities, especially for hearings with ethnocultural offenders.

Another initiative of the Atlantic Region entailed holding a mock hearing in March 2005 for community members and those representing cultural and community agencies (PBC 2006b, 15). The mock hearing involved the demonstration of the "regular" hearing model and an "adapted" hearing model that the region developed based on its consultations with community groups. The PBC notes that "the adapted model was selected by participants as the model which should be utilized for African Canadian offenders" (ibid.) This model, termed the "African Canadian Hearing Model," was to be piloted within the Atlantic Region and have the following characteristics: the use of a circle format without tables, a casual style of dress on the part of board members, starting the hearing with small talk to put the offender "at ease," and having board members discuss with the offender "his/her background, upbringing and experiences of racism" (ibid.). Yet board members were still required to assess risk as they do in "all hearings, in accordance with [PBC] policy and legislation" (ibid.). The proposed model reflects the PBC's incorporation and extension of *Gladue* principles to African Canadian offenders, including the consideration of background and systemic factors affecting this population. That the Atlantic Region was able to pilot a hearing model for African Canadians may reflect the unique history of this population in the region (see Nelson 2002). In particular, black Nova Scotian offenders may be easily constituted as an identifiable group of ethnocultural offenders with special needs that can be addressed through an adapted hearing model.

Taken together, the research reports, community consultations, and ethnocultural offender committees represent institutional techniques for producing knowledge about ethnocultural difference and considering how this diversity can be accommodated in conditional release policies and practices. This section shows how the PBC is grappling with ethnocultural difference and its relevance to parole hearing formats and approaches to decision making. As with Aboriginal offenders, gender is partitioned from the institutional discussions about ethnocultural offenders; this population is implicitly constituted as male. Next, I examine in more depth some of the PBC's responses to ethnocultural offenders.

Responding to Ethnocultural Difference

In this section, I consider four examples of the PBC's attempt to accommodate ethnocultural offenders and to respond to their perceived differences. As in the preceding discussion, these institutional responses illustrate how the organization is attempting to address the needs of an increasingly diverse federal offender population. An analysis of these responses shows how discourses of difference work to constitute ethnocultural offenders as non-white and non-Aboriginal, yet as having special needs due to their various racial, ethnic, and/or cultural identities and backgrounds. Ethnocultural offenders are framed as different in relation to an unstated white norm. This framing reinforces their presumed otherness as the targets of inclusion through adapted parole processes.

Reconsiderations of the "Regular" Hearing Format
The preceding discussion of knowledge products, community consultations, and diversity committee work highlights the desire of various stakeholders for the creation of an altered hearing format for ethnocultural offenders. Yet, as noted in previous chapters, the altering of the "regular" hearing format to render it inclusive of "offenders from diverse populations" (PBC 2006b, 17) has been met with some resistance from senior management. Such diverse populations include "cultural, racial, ethnic, women, [and] special interest (i.e. those with mental health concerns, etc.)" offenders (ibid.). The PBC indicates that the EAH format was "identified as the model which stakeholders and key partners would like to see utilized for offenders from diverse cultural backgrounds" (ibid.) This expansion was viewed as "the natural progression of the development of parole decision models which recognize the unique needs and circumstances of diverse groups within the offender populations and diverse communities in Canada" (ibid.) as well as a matter of fairness (i.e., according to the logic that *all* offenders should have a choice, not just those who are Aboriginal) (PBC 2005g). In this context, diverse offender groups implicitly refers to non-Aboriginal and non-white offenders – those who are cultural,

racial, and/or ethnic (but not gendered) others. These groups are understood to need "an open, comfortable atmosphere and tone" for their hearings so that board members can "gather the critical information that is required to make a quality assessment of risk and to enhance [the PBC]'s decision-making ability" (PBC 2006b, 17). As with Aboriginal offenders, ethnocultural offenders were identified as having the potential to benefit through alternative hearing formats and the use of cultural advisors to provide cultural insights to board members about their backgrounds.

According to one informant, a cultural hearings working group was created as a result of pressure for the organization to do something in relation to ethno-cultural offenders (Interview 7). Some work had already been completed on the notion of "alternative models" to the regular hearing format in 2003.[8] The same informant explained that the mandate of the working group was "to look at elder-assisted hearings as a best practice and to see what from that we could learn and transfer to our hearings in general or for offenders from other cultural groups." One of the meeting reports, however, notes that the working group also considered the special needs of female offenders for hearings (PBC 2006c, 1). As the next chapter shows, the offhand inclusion of female offenders in the context of cultural hearings reflects the PBC's confusion around what to do with gender, particularly as gender – coded as relating solely to femininities – is treated separately from issues of culture and ethnicity.

The same informant noted the unwillingness of the PBC to have all conditional release hearings follow the EAH format, despite the prevalence of illiteracy and learning disabilities among the federal offender population (Interview 7). This position was echoed by another informant, who stated that "a less formal, more conversational approach to hearings [was] more successful for every offender" (Interview 8) regardless of her or his gender, ethnicity, or culture. Indeed, as one informant recalled, at a meeting of the working group, participants found that most aspects of the EAH model could be applied to regular hearings:

> So we spent the first day, okay, tell us about what works well with elder-assisted hearings, and the list went on and on. Then we look at, okay, now, what from this is transferable, what could apply to all hearings. And we started pulling everything in effect but the elder and the opening prayer ceremony, right. The respectful environment, the removal of barriers, to facilitate dialogue, you know, more simplistic language, you know, more patience, and so, allowing if there's people from the community there, let them talk if they've got something to add in terms of support upon release or whatever, you know, being more inclusive. So all of this stuff came out. (Interview 7)

According to this informant, the working group "ended up taking all that could be transferred and put it into our proposed hallmarks for a quality hearing [document]." The hallmarks identified by the working group include the following:

1. Respectful of all participants including colleagues, staff, the offender and his/her supports throughout the process.
2. Focused on the statutory criteria relating to the assessment of risk by ensuring a well-managed process for which participants are well prepared, the information is complete and of good quality, and legislation, case law, and policy are adhered to.
3. Conducive to the gathering of information through the use of interview techniques that promote open dialogue, the use of simple written and verbal language to accommodate various literacy levels and language barriers. When required, language and cultural interpretation services are provided by qualified interpreters.
4. Inclusive and flexible in that participants, including victims, have the ability to speak to the important issues regarding the case before the Board and this information is taken into account. Participants, including the offender, feel heard.
5. Cognisant that difference matters and responses which appropriately demonstrate sensitivity and an understanding of who the offender is as an individual in his/her community.
6. Informative and participants, including observers, have a clear understanding of the decision to be made, as well as the hearing and deliberation processes.
7. One in which consideration for the importance of the physical environment is made. Participants are able to hear, tissues and water are provided, the audio equipment used ensures clear recordings of the proceedings, and measures are taken to underscore the independence of the Board. Depending on the type of hearing and physical layout, physical barriers may be removed or minimized through the use of a round table. (PBC 2006c, 2-3)

Similar to the EAH and CAH models, these hallmarks shifted the hearing format but did not alter the structure of parole decision making. Although notions of respect, open dialogue, inclusion, flexibility, and reduced barriers point towards an endeavour to make the hearing format less daunting for all offenders, board members were to stay focused on the assessment of risk, as per the *CCRA* and PBC policy.

Tracking how the working group's hallmarks are operationalized and implemented by the PBC provides an opportunity to see how issues of difference are accommodated and put into practice, and how commitment to diversity changes over time. Following the recommendation of the working group, the above elements were adapted into the "Hallmarks of a Quality Hearing" and included in the organization's Policy Manual, under section 9.2, in August 2007 (PBC 2008a, 221). The hallmarks section of the Policy Manual was implicitly framed in relation to section 151(3) of the *CCRA*; although no specific reference was made to the legislation, the stated commitment reflects its wording. The Policy Manual states: "Hallmarks serve to guide Board members in their responsibility for the conduct and integrity of the hearing and in professionally managing the decision-making process" (PBC 2011c, Ch.9.2, 116). It then lists seven hallmarks said to be reflective of a quality hearing that promotes the organization's duty to act fairly:

- respectful of all those present;
- focused on the statutory criteria for assessing whether or not the offender presents an undue risk to society;
- well managed and that those who are actively participating are well prepared and legislation, case law, and policy are adhered to;
- conducive to the gathering of additional information and facilitating a more accurate understanding of the offender through the use of an interviewing style that uses plain language to accommodate various physical and mental health conditions and literacy levels and facilitates open dialogue. Qualified interpreters provide language interpretation services when required;
- inclusive and flexible allowing Board members to hear from those persons who have information on the case. The offender, and others present, know they are heard;
- responsive to gender and cultural differences demonstrating a sensitivity and an understanding of who the offender is as an individual in his/her community. Qualified cultural interpreters provide services when required; and
- informative and all those present have a clear understanding of the decision to be made, as well as of the hearing and deliberation processes. (PBC 2011c, Ch.9.2, 117)

These hallmarks were similar to the recommended elements proposed by the Cultural Hearings Working Group, with some minor changes. In particular, the working group's seventh proposed element, regarding the physical environment of hearings, was not included as a hallmark but, rather, as an additional factor that could be considered (e.g., the removal of physical barriers) (PBC 2011c, Ch.9.2, 117). Reference to gender as a difference to which to be responsive and sensitive was also included in the hallmarks identified in the Policy Manual, but it was not explicitly mentioned in the Working Group's recommendations. The introduction to the policy was framed as addressing issues related to ethnocultural offenders (e.g., PBC 2007b), with gender being a secondary consideration or add-on, without much thought as to why or how it matters.

These hallmarks, however, did not have staying power. The current version of the Policy Manual (PBC 2015) does not include any such visions of creating a quality hearing by including certain phenomena that reflect the diversity of offenders. As noted in the previous chapter, EAHs and CAHs are the only modified hearing models available, and they are oriented strictly towards Aboriginal spiritual and cultural matters. Despite the PBC's attempt to include ethnocultural difference through its hallmarks approach, the status quo has subsequently been reinforced. The removal of the hallmarks from the Policy Manual suggests that inclusion can be temporary and fleeting as organizational priorities change and/ or individual "champions" move on.

Interpretation Issues

Linguistic difference emerges as another marker of diversity under the umbrella of ethnoculturalism and has been recognized within the PBC as an issue affecting decision making. More specifically, several informants identified language interpretation as being associated with ethnic or cultural difference in the offender population and thus as being racialized as something needed by those offenders defined as ethnocultural. Offenders whose first language is not English or French are largely constituted along racial or ethnic lines. Under section 140(9) of the *CCRA*, offenders have a right to interpretation at conditional release hearings: "An offender who does not have an adequate understanding of at least one of Canada's official languages is entitled to the assistance of an interpreter at the hearing and for the purpose of understanding materials provided to the offender." This right is also set out in section 11.4 of the Policy Manual (PBC 2015). For the PBC (2015, Ch. 11.4, 1), "the use of interpreters ensures that the offender understands the information provided to the Board for the review, the proceedings of the hearing and the decision, and that the offender is able to provide representations." In addition to being a right for offenders, language interpretation reduces the possibility of legal and reputational risks to the organization in cases in which linguistic minority offenders do not receive fair hearings because of a failure to address their language needs.

The Ethnocultural Consultation Project (PBC 2005g, 8) identified language as a "significant problem" for "many ethnocultural offenders, particularly those from Asian or South Asian backgrounds as well as Inuit offenders" who are not English or French speakers. Relying on racialized stereotypes, concerns were raised that, because "Asian offenders come from backgrounds where it is important to be deferential to elders and those in authority," they may "essentially agree to anything without knowing or understanding what they are agreeing to" (ibid.). Language barriers interact with culture and race to the potential detriment of ethnocultural offenders. To address language concerns, the Aboriginal and Diversity Initiatives section applied for and received funding from the "Inclusive Institutions Initiative" of Canadian Heritage in the 2007-08 fiscal year (PBC 2008f). This funding supported an interpretation project to assess "the existing interpretation services provided at [PBC] hearings nationally to ensure that offenders from diverse ethnocultural/ethnoracial backgrounds, whose maternal language is not English or French, receive accurate and precise interpretation services upon which Board Members rely to conduct an assessment of risk and to make a conditional release decision" (1). An offender's inability to speak either official language was identified as a source of her or his exclusion from the normal process of conditional release decision making, with accurate and precise interpretation services working to include her or him.

As explained by the PBC (2008f), language interpretation at panel hearings is important because hearings provide opportunities for offenders to make representations to board members about their cases and for board members to examine issues or concerns and pose questions to offenders about information that may not be contained in their files. Board members rely on language interpretation for hearings with offenders who do not speak or understand English or French in order "to obtain accurate information upon which to base conditional release decisions" (1). Likewise, interpretation helps ensure that offenders are aware of their rights and allows them to understand and respond to the questions posed by board members. One informant noted that interpretation was necessary in order to "ensure every offender has a fair hearing" (Interview 10). The PBC (2008f, 1) indicates that many offenders who do not speak English or French are from racialized groups and may be disadvantaged at their parole hearings due to language interpretation issues.[9] In this context, language emerges as a marker of ethnocultural difference and as an additional issue to be addressed in hearings for ethnocultural offenders.

In 2009, the PBC published a pamphlet providing tips for board members when conducting interpreter-assisted conditional release hearings (PBC 2009j).

Akin to other institutional techniques of managing difference and knowing offenders defined as different (e.g., EAHs, CAHs, training, etc.), these tips reflect diversity as something that can be accommodated within existing organizational structures and practices. The pamphlet is also an auditable product that can show diversity is being accommodated within the organization. And, as with the institutional approach to ensuring appropriate decisions, these tips help responsibilize decision makers for being sensitive to and aware of difference and its application in practice.

The pamphlet explicates the legal basis and communications needs for interpretation at hearings, the extent of Canada's linguistic diversity, and the role of interpreters. In particular, the document notes that, "without interpretation, many linguistic-minority offenders might be disadvantaged at parole hearings," while improper interpretation "might hamper quality decision making" (PBC 2009j, 2). Good interpretation is linked, first, to the protection of the public and, second, to the rights of the offender. The selection of interpreters therefore emerges as a key factor in achieving fair hearings. Initially, the PBC opted for community interpreters who "are often members of the same ethno-linguistic communities for which they are interpreting"; in some cases, "the interpreter and the offender may belong to the same social or geographic community" (5). For this reason, community interpreters were supposed to be aware of and to disclose potential conflicts of interest (e.g., previous interactions or relationships with the offender) and "make special efforts to maintain neutrality" (ibid.). However, later the PBC specified in the Policy Manual that an "interpreter is a neutral third party who is not involved in the decision-making process," someone who, when possible, should "be certified" and not someone known to the offender, such as her or his spouse, friend, or assistant (PBC 2015, Ch. 11.4, 1). As with the selection of elders for contracts with the PBC, it is probable that the organization prefers interpreters who can meet normative criteria reflecting Euro-Canadian values and standards (Waldram 1997).

The pamphlet characterizes "good" interpretation extending beyond the verbal as including non-verbal cues. These are deemed culturally specific and may differ from those that would be easily understood by (white) French and English Canadians (PBC 2009j, 9). For instance, body language, eye contact, and tone of voice are flagged as affecting communication and interpretation within parole hearings (10). However, due to the variety of cultural differences around non-verbal communication, the pamphlet cautions board members against interpreting such cues, presumably in case they get it wrong. Anglo- and Franco-Canadian culture is used as the norm against which to describe standard examples of non-verbal communication and from which others differ. Nor is there any consideration of how gender intersects with culture and other facets of identity to affect communication. The ethnocultural offender imagined as in need of interpretation is implicitly gendered as masculine. The lack of attention to gender is illustrative of the challenge of creating policies and practices that can account for multiple differences simultaneously.

African Canadian Cultural Liaison Project

The African Canadian Cultural Liaison Project is a third example of the PBC's attempts to accommodate ethnocultural offenders' difference. African Canadian offenders have been identified as a specific group of ethnocultural offenders with special needs. The project, based in the Atlantic Region, was the result of funding received through the federal government's Inclusive Institutions Initiatives,[10] the purpose of which was "to ensure that federal programs, policies and services reflect the needs and realities of ethno-racial and ethno-cultural communities" (Canadian Heritage 2005, 25). The notions "ethnoracial" and "ethnocultural" reflect multicultural discourses that racialize difference as belonging to non-white bodies, communities, and cultures (Razack 1998; Dhamoon 2009). Aboriginal peoples are not included in the constitution of difference as being ethnoracial or ethnocultural; rather, these terms are used to define non-Indigenous people of colour, marking them with race, ethnicity, and culture vis-à-vis the unmarked, unstated white norm. Ethnocultural and Aboriginal offenders may share similar needs in the context of parole, but the organizational separation of these groups suggests a recognition of Aboriginal peoples as a distinct population, likely due to their unique constitutional status.

The African Canadian Cultural Liaison Project involves contracting an African Canadian cultural liaison officer to work with the PBC (PBC n.d.-e). According to one informant, the cultural liaison officer's "role is essentially the same in principle as an elder, in terms of he's there at the hearing as a support to the board members" (Interview 10). This informant also explained that hearings with the cultural liaison officer are similar to EAHs or CAHs in that "it's the offender that makes the request to have that type of hearing." The liaison officer also conducts training sessions with regional PBC staff on "the black community in Halifax" (ibid.) and meets with African Canadian prisoners to help prepare them for their hearings and release (Interview 8). The cultural liaison officer's activities echo the role of the Aboriginal elder as s/he functions as an "interpreter" of ethnicity and culture for board members, as a "bridge" between African Canadian communities and the PBC, and as an appropriate support for African Canadian offenders.

The African Canadian Cultural Liaison Project has four goals: (1) improved release plans, (2) better preparation for hearing and release, (3) improved information sharing at hearings, and (4) provision of expertise on matters of culture to board members in order to improve information upon which to make conditional release decisions (PBC n.d.-e). These goals mirror concerns around Aboriginal offenders and the rationale for establishing EAHs and CAHs. To improve African Canadian offenders' release plans, the cultural liaison officer provides "information on community accessibility and activities to help enhance offender[s'] release plans to their home communities" and to improve "their chances of successful release" (n.pag). To better prepare African Canadian offenders for their hearings and release, the cultural liaison officer offers these offenders information about the hearing process. The PBC contends that the increased awareness means offenders "are better equipped to answer the questions they face at these hearings" and "are more at ease with the process" (ibid.) This approach helps the organizational management of difference by orienting African Canadian offenders to the dominant hearing process. It does not, however, fundamentally alter the structure of the hearing: to do so would be seen as compromising the integrity and validity of the process. A similar pattern was observed in the Aboriginalization of parole policies, whereby selective notions of Aboriginal difference were incorporated into existing practices (see Chapter 4).

The cultural liaison officer is expected to accomplish the third goal of enhanced information sharing through improved communication at hearings and the provision of cultural information in relation to community accessibility, the availability of services, and community activities (PBC n.d.-e). Ostensibly, this strengthens African Canadian offenders' release plans. This expertise also addresses other issues related to this target population of offenders. As one informant explained: "Let's say the offender is released to a community outside of Halifax and the board members might have questions about that community, and this person [i.e., the cultural liaison officer] is from ... that area where the bulk of the black offenders in [the Atlantic] Region come from and are released to, so he provides that real cultural awareness to board members about specific communities" (Interview 10). African Canadian offenders and their communities are framed in essentialist terms that gloss over differences and present them as objects that can be known and managed (Dhamoon 2009). The lack of attention to gender raises further questions about who speaks for racialized communities. The rationale for this project follows other organizational techniques of knowing the other through cultural awareness, whereby the cultural liaison officer serves an elder function to translate racialized knowledges and experiences into formats the (white) board can understand and use to make appropriate decisions. In this context, diversity is subject to a regulated accommodation (Razack 1998; Bannerji 2000; Dhamoon 2009).

Cultural Fact Sheets

The final example of organizational approaches to constituting and managing ethnocultural difference concerns cultural fact sheets. The PBC produced a number of "country insights" handouts for several countries, including Pakistan, Vietnam, China, and Jamaica (PBC n.d.-f, n.d.-g, n.d.-h, n.d.-i). These fact sheets contain a variety of information covering demographics, society, and culture. The latter two categories speak to issues related to family, language, religion, politics, education, communication and interpersonal relations, and drug and alcohol use. This information is compiled from several websites, such as those of Citizenship and Immigration Canada and Foreign Affairs and International Trade Canada as well as the Central Intelligence Agency, Wikipedia, the British Broadcasting Corporation, and the countries' government websites. These fact sheets can be understood as techniques of producing knowledge about ethnocultural others, much like the newsletters discussed in Chapter 2. Similar to the newsletters, the cultural fact sheets demonstrate an awareness of difference; however, unlike the newsletters, these facts sheets were created to aid decision making, although it is not clear exactly how this information is to be used.

The concept of a cultural fact sheet appears to have emerged from a meeting of the Cultural Hearings Working Group (PBC 2006c). According to the meeting report, the information contained in the fact sheets was intended to "assist decision-makers on a more basic level to identify possible elements that may affect the offender's case," such as "the impact of participation in a family violence program on an offender whose cultural values and beliefs may *differ from ours*" (4, emphasis added), in cases of deportation, or for cross-cultural understandings of family and religion (e.g., PBC n.d.-e, 1). The lines between "us" and "them" are drawn through the assumption that certain offenders, as cultural others, are different from us and our culture and values. This "our" is not defined, although the implicit assumption is that the "us" is white Canadians while the "our" is Anglo- and/or Franco-Canadian culture. "Our" culture becomes the reference point by which other cultures and countries are described, producing a sense of foreignness and a lack of belonging. Previous research on the assessment of non-white offenders within the justice system points to the use of racialized knowledges of difference that draw upon and reproduce stereotypes of those deemed other (e.g., Hudson and Bramhall 2005; Silverstein 2005; Bramhall and Hudson 2007). In particular, certain characteristics of otherness become constituted as targets for intervention, such as family and community relationships in the case of South Asian offenders in the United Kingdom (Hudson and Bramhall 2005; Bramhall and Hudson 2007).

The working group meeting report cautions that the information provided in the fact sheets "would not be intended to encourage Board members to go to a hearing with any generalizations or preconceptions about race and culture" (PBC 2006c, 4). However, the very format of a fact sheet necessitates some degree of simplification and short-handing of information so that the products are helpful for the user. If the volume of facts is too onerous or the information is too detailed, then the point of the fact sheet would be lost, rendering the product unusable. The framing of the information works to reinforce generalizations and preconceptions through the othering of various cultural or racial groups as different from us. The cultural fact sheets provide shorthand information about their differences, thereby reducing complex cultural, social, political, and economic issues into generalized bits of information about the habits, values, and traditions of people from certain countries. It is unclear the degree to which such information would be applicable to offenders who are first-, second-, or third-generation immigrants to Canada. The cultural fact sheets do not explain to board members how they are to use the information provided to inform their decision making. The responsibility of using this information properly appears to be downloaded to individual board members, thereby shielding the institution from possible scrutiny in instances when cultural information is used inappropriately.

Conclusions

In this chapter, I analyze how institutional discourses of difference constitute the ethnocultural offender as a distinct other (i.e., different from Aboriginal and female offenders) and as a target for accommodation within the broader context of institutionalized multiculturalism. I identify the strategies the PBC uses to know, rationalize, and respond to this offender population with ethnicized parole policies and practices. I argue that these responses are based on an organizational understanding of ethnocultural offenders as other and as illustrative of a liberal multicultural discourse that racializes ethnic and cultural difference as belonging to non-white individuals. At the same time, gender is not considered in the production of knowledge about, and practices for, offenders defined as ethnocultural.

In relation to my larger themes, I point to the productive power of knowledge and the potential to create culturalized and racialized regimes of punishment

Discourses of Difference

in the pursuit of fair and sensitive parole decisions. I also shown how the PBC discursively imagines and constitutes particular offenders' identities based on notions of race, culture, and ethnicity, while whiteness remains the unacknow-ledged and unmarked point of comparison against which this difference is produced. Additionally, I demonstrate that, in contrast to Aboriginality, ethno-cultural difference poses a more challenging set of diversities to be negotiated into conditional release policies and practices because it is tougher to concep-tualize in concise and simple terms. Ethnocultural diversity represents a greater complication to inclusion and accommodation than does Aboriginality be-cause penal institutions must select particular identities (e.g., African Canadian offenders) in order to rationalize and develop diversity initiatives. In the final chapter, I focus on the issue of gender – an issue entirely absent from institutional discourses around ethnocultural difference.

6

Conceptual Silos and the Problem of Gender

In Chapters 4 and 5, I show how issues of gender are largely ignored in parole policies and practices dealing with diversity. For racialized women, penal diversity policies rarely frame gender as intersecting with other forms of difference. When they do, most responses reflect an additive approach whereby racial discrimination adds to gender discrimination so that racialized women are doubly oppressed (Yuval-Davis 2006). The norm for racialized penal populations is implicitly constituted as male. My analysis of organizational documents demonstrates that the recognition of gender (i.e., femininities) within the context of diversity initiatives remains underdeveloped both conceptually and practically. Although criminological knowledges about female offending are used by the Parole Board of Canada, the organizational approaches to female difference reflect the complexities associated with addressing exactly how conditional release processes can be made gender responsive. Additionally, how (or if) parole policies and practices can consider intersecting facets of identity so that penal subjects are understood holistically rather than as singularly (e.g., Aboriginal or female) remains unclear. Put simply, there seems to be an impediment to the creation of policies or approaches that can "gender" diversity. These challenges exist in an organizational context within which the female offender population is a small but growing (see OCI 2014) and increasingly diverse portion of offenders appearing before the board.

In this final chapter, I examine the PBC's responses to female offenders, including informants' perspectives on how gender matters, the institutional process of developing a commitments document, and the creation of a special parole hearing project at Nova Institution in the Atlantic Region. These initiatives are illustrative of the incorporation of feminist and criminological knowledges about female offending into organizational understandings of female offender issues and the management of risk. I conclude the chapter by presenting two main arguments based on my findings regarding how the PBC has dealt with gender difference: first, the organizational approach to gender is one of conceptual silos – that is, gender tends to be treated as an entity that is separate from other aspects of identity. My analysis of PBC texts demonstrates an organizational inability to treat gender as one facet of many intersecting, co-occurring identities. Second, I argue that gender is a "problem" for this organization. Although the PBC recognizes that gender influences criminal offending and parole outcomes, it struggles with the practical application of exactly how gender figures into conditional release decision making. There is a working assumption that "women" (as a category) are different from "men" (as a category) and therefore have special needs. Organizational understandings of, and approaches to, gender reflect the coding of this construct as relating solely to female offenders, such that gender is not seen as mattering for male offenders. There is little consideration of gender as a relational construct or the ways in which policies, practices, or processes themselves are gendered. I conclude the chapter by identifying some of the implications of these findings, including the reproduction of (white) male offenders as the norm and the subsequent othering of female offenders and their essentialization as a homogenous group.

Responses to Female Offenders

The development of special or different penal approaches for female offenders because of their gender is not a new phenomenon. As several scholars show, notions of gender differences have always informed the punishment of women, albeit in different ways based on historically contingent understandings of gender, race, class, and sexuality (e.g., Rafter 1990; Howe 1994; Zedner 1995; Hannah-Moffat 2001; Zaitzow 2004). Penal law and norms are viewed as both gendered and gendering (Bertrand 1999). The gendered nature of punishment has been explored largely in relation to imprisonment, including the structures and experiences of the prison (e.g., Britton 1997, 2000; Sim 1994; Bosworth 1996; Bosworth and Carrabine 2001; Comack 2000; McCorkel 2004), prison programming (e.g., Carlen 1983; Morash et al. 1994; Pollack 2005), and practices of risk assessment (e.g., Hannah-Moffat 1999, 2004b, 2005; Pollack 2007). A smaller body of work considers gender in the context of parole and conditional release (e.g., Hannah-Moffat 2004a; Pollack 2007, 2008, 2009; Turnbull and Hannah-Moffat 2009; Morash 2010).

As discussed in Chapter 1, the Task Force on Federally Sentenced Women's (1990) report, *Creating Choices*, encouraged the creation of a women-centred model of punishment for female prisoners in federal penitentiaries, with specific focus on Aboriginal female offenders through the building of a healing lodge. The recognition of feminist criminological scholarship on the ways and reasons that women and men differ in terms of criminal offending, pathways to crime, experiences of violence and trauma, treatment and reintegration needs, and experiences of imprisonment has supported the development of so called gender-responsive approaches to assessment and treatment within Canada's prisons for women. The extent to which the current model of imprisonment of federally sentenced women is gender responsive or reflects an understanding of diverse women's needs and experiences has been contested, both by scholars (e.g., Hannah-Moffat 1995, 2001; Shaw 1999; Hannah-Moffat and Shaw 2000; Hayman 2006) and by public entities such as the Arbour Commission (Canada 1996a), the Canadian Human Rights Commission (2003), and the Office of the Correctional Investigator (through its annual reports).[1]

Responses to female offenders at the PBC have occurred alongside those for Aboriginal offenders and, more recently, ethnocultural offenders. These responses are also linked to a broader context of social change in the women's movement and the enactment of legislation prohibiting sex-based discrimination (e.g., the *Charter*, the *Canadian Human Rights Act*, etc.). Two informants also had ideas about the origins of organizational responses to female offenders at the PBC. According to one informant, both *Creating Choices* and the Arbour Report propelled the issue of female offenders forward (Interview 7). The same informant explained that organizational attention to female offender issues was bolstered in 2002 or 2003 when this became "part of the standing agenda item in the Aboriginal and Diversity reporting" – at least for a time (see Chapter 2). According to the other informant, the *CCRA* was the main driver for the recognition of gender within PBC policies and practices. However, the informant was sceptical about the impact of the *Act* because "there's virtually nothing in [it] for women" (Interview 13). The same informant speculated that the absence of specific clauses for female offenders was due to a lack of research about their needs at the time and the belief that "the *Charter* was there to protect them." In this way, the *CCRA* helped drive issues related to female offenders forward, but other pieces of legislation, such as the *Charter*, were available to compel organizational responses if needed.

Conceptual Silos and the Problem of Gender

Most informants interviewed indicated that gender mattered in the context of correctional programming and issues related to conditional release. They believed that it was important for the PBC and board members to be aware of the differences in programs for female offenders, the different criminal trajectories and patterns of female offending, and female offender needs in relation to release on parole and reintegration. Several mentioned that female offenders have different needs and risk factors that board members ought to know about to ensure more fair and appropriate decision making. In this regard, a number of informants deemed training for board members on gender issues an important organizational response. According to one informant, some board members needed training on female offenders because they lacked experience with women who were not privileged and who came from disadvantaged backgrounds – women to whom many board members could not relate (Interview 8). Increased sensitivity and awareness was thus viewed as necessary for fair decision making. Another informant noted that board members required training when there were changes in policy or programming at women's prisons (Interview 10) so that they could be kept aware of the factors shaping women's imprisonment.

A minority of informants believed, conversely, that gender was not relevant to parole decision making. For instance, one informant stated that gender was not germane to the assessment of risk, noting instead that female offenders comprise a small segment of the federal offender population and would not necessarily share a common set of generalizable features (Interview 6). Presumably, the small number of female offenders could justify or explain the lack of a need for different approaches or knowledges when it came to decision making (see Adelberg and Currie 1987). Another informant said that the criminal justice system did not hold female offenders as accountable as male offenders and that, in effect, the system was "bending backwards" for them (Interview 12). Gender-responsive penal practices were subsequently viewed as special forms of treatment that diminished women's accountability.

Compared to its other diversity initiatives, the PBC's diversity work related to female offenders is limited in scope. The following considers how the PBC developed its corporate strategy for female offenders and the eventual operationalization of this strategy in the form of a set of commitments. I then examine one of the diversity initiatives developed for female offenders in the Atlantic Region. I suggest that these practices work to produce and circulate gendered knowledges of female offenders and to shape the types of responses deemed appropriate and actionable. The apparent lack of gender-specific parole policies and practices reflects the challenge of including gender as an aspect of difference. The following reveals institutional disagreement about how and when gender matters in the context of conditional release.

Creating a Corporate Strategy for Federally Sentenced Women

In the early 2000s, the PBC undertook a process to create a corporate strategy for federally sentenced women, a result of having made a commitment to do so (PBC 2002c, 2). The organization also produced a corporate strategy for Aboriginal offenders in 1996, although this strategy did not factor in any "gender issues" and was eventually rolled into the PBC's Policy Manual. The process for creating a corporate policy for federally sentenced women began with a discussion paper that outlined female prisoners' issues, followed by a meeting with stakeholders to garner feedback to shape the strategy. Yet, as is discussed below, the corporate strategy never materialized; instead, the organization fashioned a commitments document, which was adopted by the Executive Committee in 2003. The consultations and stakeholder meetings represent institutional processes of negotiating how gender is relevant to parole and the sorts of accommodations permissible to address gender differences.

The initial intention of the corporate strategy for female offenders was "to address specific issues related to the assessment of risk" and "the Board's decision-making process for the conditional release" with regard to this population (PBC 2002c, 2). The strategy was to be based in large part on consultations with various groups from all five PBC regions, including PBC personnel, representatives from the Correctional Service of Canada, inmate committees, and advocacy groups like the Elizabeth Fry Societies as well as incarcerated and conditionally released federally sentenced women (PBC 2002d). According to the PBC, the impetus for the consultation process "was to gather outsider input and to gain insight into how the National Parole Board can facilitate release and reintegration in more innovative and productive ways and to determine if it needs to enhance its credibility, particularly in relation to female offenders" (2). Consistent with other forms of diversity work at the PBC, the focus here was on producing knowledge about female offenders to serve the dual purpose of being more responsive to their needs and improving organizational reputation.

In 2002, the PBC released a discussion paper that reported on the results of the cross-country consultations. This paper was intended to provide a "foundation for the discussion and development" of the strategy (PBC 2002d, 3). It raises several issues related to federally sentenced women at both national and regional levels. The consultations were broad in scope, covering the topics of incarceration, release, and reintegration; as a result, the paper conveys subjects

Conceptual Silos and the Problem of Gender

beyond the purview of the PBC, such as those pertaining to the CSC. In relation to parole, the issue of differential and discriminatory treatment emerges as a prominent theme within the discussion paper. Improved training and more gender-responsive parole processes are the main solutions raised to help address the needs of female offenders.

The differential treatment of women and men is an issue that has received a significant amount of attention within feminist legal scholarship (see Young 1990; Jhappan 1998). Differential treatment was perceived by many respondents during the consultations (PBC 2002d). These perceptions reflect the complexities surrounding the formal equality-versus-substantive equality debate: Does equality (for women) involve their receiving the same treatment (as men) or does it involve their receiving different treatment than men? In the former case, formal equality is said to be achieved if "women" are treated the same as "men";[2] in the latter case, equality is said to be attained if women are treated differently than men, with gender (and other) differences being taken into account and recognized in law or policy (Young 1990; Jhappan 1998). Discrimination may occur in cases in which (1) the same treatment approach disadvantages women and/or (2) the different needs of women are not recognized or accommodated. For the PBC (2002d, 10), "differential treatment, whether real or perceived, needs to be addressed in creating a fair and equitable strategy for the release and reintegration of women offenders." However, this statement does not clarify whether fairness or equity would be best achieved through a formal equality approach or a substantive equality approach.

The issue of differential and discriminatory treatment is discussed in relation to multiple contexts. For example, it pertains to release decisions that facilitate the reintegration of female offenders. According to the discussion paper, respondents raised concerns about a perceived lack of resources and supports within communities for the gradual and structured release of female offenders, including access to programs and halfway houses in women's home communities. The lack of community options was believed to result in the denial of parole for female offenders. Some respondents called on the PBC "to be more flexible and open-minded, particularly when it [came] to release plans that [were] a little different than the standard course of action" (PBC 2002d, 7). Concerns were also voiced about the imposition of release conditions by board members. The discussion paper indicates that conditions may interfere with female offenders' release if they are too restrictive and remove women's sources of support (e.g., through non-association requirements) (9). The concerns expressed within the discussion paper have also been raised by Canadian scholars and advocacy organizations over the past several decades (e.g., Shaw 1999;

CHRC 2003; Pollack 2008). It draws upon and reflects feminist knowledges of female offending and reintegration needs to support arguments for a more gender-responsive approach to parole for female offenders, including different release planning options and conditions of release.

The difference between female and male offenders is also relevant to how parole hearings are conducted. There are divergent views on how gender ought to be integrated into hearings and decision-making processes. The discussion paper notes respondents' belief that the PBC is "harder on women than it is on men," resulting in female offenders dreading their parole hearings while male offenders are viewed as "often eager for this opportunity" (PBC 2002d, 10). Some respondents felt that female offenders were unfairly judged in parole hearings because they had broken societal norms and gender role expectations through their criminal offending, and board members did not consider the gendered dimensions of their lives, such as family and spousal violence (12-13). In contrast, the paper reports that consultations with board members "revealed a belief that women [offenders were] prepared by correctional staff to have expectations about the Board" that it could not meet (10). In particular, it identifies the perception among board members that the CSC takes a "touchy/ feely" approach towards female offenders that it does not take towards male offenders (ibid.). This results in hurt feelings or things being "blown out of proportion" during parole hearings when board members are trying to be "objective" (ibid.). The discussion paper notes the perception among consulted board members that CSC staff side with female offenders and reinforce their "victim status," which serves to make them weak and unable to stand on their own, especially during parole hearings. Consulted board members also gave their opinions as to the nature of women's punishment, including the belief that "the boundaries between the women [offenders] and staff have faded" due to the approach taken by the CSC (ibid.). The "correct" approach for corrections was believed to be reflected in men's institutions as the punishment meted out there was "objective and detached," with clear demarcations between staff and offenders (ibid.). For these respondents, differential treatment was viewed as further disadvantaging women by differentiating them from male offenders.

These views, however, were not shared by other consultation respondents. The discussion paper indicates that staff working with female offenders be-lieved that board members needed to receive training on women and crime because their views were outdated and the "tone and content of questions posed at hearings display[ed] a gender, race and class bias" (PBC 2002d, 11). It dis-cusses how these respondents argued for making changes to parole policies and practices that would reflect "an understanding of women's criminality as

Conceptual Silos and the Problem of Gender

it is situated within the context of social power, gender relations and economic position" (ibid.). Respondents also believed that board members should question women differently from the way in which they questioned men. For example, they should not barrage women offenders with questions or adopt "aggressive tones" towards them; instead, they should allow them to "express themselves in their own way" (ibid.). For these respondents, differential treatment would contribute to more fair and equitable treatment of female offenders as long as conditional release processes were based on feminist criminological knowledges of female offending and involved the proper training of board members. The challenge, as previous research has shown, is how alternative knowledges are then taken up in existing processes, including the selective integration of knowledges that complement dominant framings of female offenders' needs (see Snider 2003; Hannah-Moffat 2005; Moore 2008; Russell and Carlton 2013).

Other indicators of differential treatment raised by the consultations pertain to greater program availability and staffing levels at penitentiaries for male offenders, which were said to result in more opportunities for temporary absences and earlier access to parole (PBC 2002d). Some respondents also opined that female offenders were subjected to a greater number of psychological assessments than were male offenders and that risk assessment tools designed for men were being used for women, even though "the issues that relate to risk of recidivism for the two groups are very different" (11). These respondents believed that, as a result of unfair risk assessment practices, female offenders were also assigned higher levels of supervision while on parole. These concerns around differential treatment highlight the tensions related to the most suitable approach for ensuring equity and fairness in corrections and conditional release processes. In the case of access to programming, staffing, and supervision levels, the implicit assumption is that female offenders should have similar treatment, at least in terms of access, to that received by male offenders. Regarding the risk assessment of female offenders, there is an apparent preference for different tools and practices that reflect gender differences in risk and criminal offending. The PBC is called upon to address forms of differential treatment that disadvantage oppressed groups, while simultaneously pursuing practices and approaches that may counter those disadvantages. The lack of clarity around the "best" way to address gender difference (i.e., similar versus different treatment) may contribute to institutional inertia with regard to addressing the needs of female offenders as a group.

Respondents also voiced concerns about the discriminatory treatment of certain segments of the female offender population. For example, the discussion paper indicates that consultations brought up "the ongoing concern that the

Board is not racially and ethnically diverse," that it is "representative of the female offender population or the public in general" (PBC 2002d, 12). As a result, there was a perception that, due to this lack of representation, the PBC's decision-making process was unfair and biased – an assumption that ignores power relations among women by presupposing that women are oppressed or disadvantaged in the same way (Razack 1998). The consultations revealed support for the use of "cultural assistants" to "clarify misunderstandings and raise Board members' awareness of cultural variations" (ibid.). Concern was also raised regarding the need for the hearing process to respond to female offenders who experience language or educational barriers when being questioned. Respondents' misgivings about the PBC's treatment of diverse female offenders reflect the challenge of capturing and integrating multiple differences into policy. Drawing artificial lines around particular differences, such as the partitioning of gender from ethnicity, simplifies the offender for decision makers.

Some of the regional issues detailed in the discussion paper also spoke to the discriminatory treatment of certain groups of female offenders. For instance, in the Ontario/Nunavut Region, the dominance of Christianity in prison programs at Grand Valley Institution and a lack of openness to non-Christian spirituality were identified as unfair practices. Consultations with the Black Inmate and Friends Alliance revealed a belief that black women offenders tend to be labelled violent, thereby affecting how the CSC and the PBC viewed this group. In the Atlantic Region, consultations at Nova Institution raised concerns that board members were "uncomfortable with same-sex relationships" (PBC 2002d, 18), resulting in "derogatory and judgmental" questioning during hearings (19). It was felt that board members should not question "same-sex relationships as part of a woman's release potential" (ibid.). In the Prairie and Pacific Regions, CSC staff were seen as being unaware of sections 81 and 84 of the CCRA and therefore failing to inform Aboriginal offenders of these culturally oriented options for parole (21). Together, these concerns speak to the diversity of the female offender population and the difficulties of addressing multiple forms of difference simultaneously and in ways that do not privilege gender as the primary target of discrimination.

The discussion paper highlights the importance of acting on the gender-specific needs of female offenders. Respondents' calls for improved gender-responsive approaches were viewed as making parole processes fairer for female offenders. In relation to hearings, some respondents suggested the organization needed "to undertake a more holistic approach to women's parole hearings," such that their life circumstances and responsibilities as mothers be considered

Conceptual Silos and the Problem of Gender

(PBC 2002d, 12). Training on gender-specific issues was viewed as necessary for increasing the gender responsiveness of board members, including in the areas of "cultural differences, addiction, family and spousal violence, women's obligations as mothers and women with special needs" (12-13). Another recommendation was for the PBC to have a "presence" at women's prisons to help inform prisoners about the hearing process, thereby working to demystify the PBC for prisoners and allowing the organization to "get to know" the prisoners (13). Although the discussion paper notes that improvements to how the organization responds to female offenders still need to be made, many respondents acknowledged that the PBC had "improved significantly in being sensitive to women's issues and [was] more aware of appropriate ways to treat women" (14). Within this context, women are framed as a homogeneous group presumed to share similar experiences and needs based on their gender (Razack 1998; Yuval-Davis 2006).

In March 2002, the PBC held a meeting with stakeholders to help in the development of its corporate strategy for federally sentenced female offenders (PBC 2002c). The participants included representatives from the PBC, the CSC, and the British Columbia Parole Board as well as academics, the director of an inmate committee, and a former offender. The meeting report documents the discussions and recommendations and is framed around three main areas: reintegration issues, risk assessment issues, and policy and training issues. According to the report, these discussions and recommendations were intended to "serve as the framework for [the PBC]'s future movement and direction in regard to the development of its corporate strategy" (2). It concludes with a total of thirty-six recommendations for the PBC, many of which focus on issues of training, the needs of female offenders, concerns about cultural and/or ethnic diversity, and the clearer articulation of policy for decision making (25-28). The report echoes many of the issues raised by the preceding discussion paper while advancing the conversation through its recommendations. Like the discussion paper, the meeting report frames advocates' perspectives on how gender issues matter to parole and represents an institutional process of negotiating how gender can be included in policy and practice.

The meeting report summarizes a number of issues raised by participants in relation to reintegration, including the lack of housing for female offenders on parole or conditional release, the difficulties related to finding employment, access to culturally appropriate programs, and the release needs of Aboriginal women offenders (PBC 2002c, 3-9). Participants recommended that the PBC look to "diverse ethno-cultural community agencies" for input on how the organization could better meets the needs of diverse women offenders (6). The report indicates "strong support among participants" for piloting the use of "cultural assistants/interpreters" at parole hearings, with the potential for expanding such an approach to other groups of offenders, such as those with mental health issues or female sex offenders (ibid.). Participants also recommended that the PBC help increase the use of section 81 and section 84 releases for Aboriginal women offenders (9). Support was also given for the extension of these types of releases to "other communities and for other ethno-cultural offenders" (8).

The discussion of risk assessment focused on decision-making issues related to female offenders. For instance, the meeting report notes that the CSC and the PBC have different understandings of risk, with the latter largely concerned about risk of reoffending (PBC 2002c, 10), as mandated by the *CCRA*. It was recommended that the PBC create a protocol on how board members are to assess risk for this group while also ensuring that "creativity" be used for granting release (11). These recommendations are based on a shared understanding among participants that female offenders are generally better risks for release than male offenders (e.g., they are less likely to recidivate and are not as threatening to public safety) (9). Because of these differences, it was argued that female offenders should be given opportunities for more creative releases in support of gradual and structured release plans. The report highlights participants' concerns that the lack of board member diversity may result in limited "sensitivity to specific ethno-cultural groups as well as the unique issues related to women" (12). According to participants, board members' assessment of risk must "be multi-layered with a view to both cultural and gender issues" such that assessments can appropriately capture female offenders' "diverse needs" and experiences (ibid.). Examining female offenders' cultural backgrounds was consistent with the *Gladue* decision, which supports a contextual approach to decision making. It recommended that "cultural interpreters" be involved in hearings to help board members clarify issues related to culture and ensure that they avoid "aggressive, confrontational or offensive" lines of questioning or language (ibid.). Participants also recommended that all hearings follow the "approach and atmosphere engendered at hearings for Aboriginal offenders" (16). The EAH model was thought to "provide a cooperative rather than an adversarial environment" for hearings (ibid.), which was considered a more gender responsive approach.

The meeting report also indicates that participants' support for PBC policy should be "validated for its applicability to gender and ethno-cultural diversity," including the recommendation that the PBC develop working relationships with community agencies to help raise awareness and enhance knowledge of various issues related to diversity (PBC 2002c, 18). Participants also identified the issue of board members' "flexibility," endorsing a move "away from traditional ways of thinking and be[ing] inventive and open to unconventional release plans," albeit within the existing legislative framework (ibid.). This flexibility for approaches to the release plans of female offenders was to be put into policy "to ensure its longevity and its application by Board Members across the country" (19), thereby ensuring institutional accountability. The report also notes the view that board member training was not providing adequate depth on "the unique issues faced by women and ethno-cultural offenders" (ibid.). Participants were concerned that not enough time was allotted during training to "address the diverse issues facing FSW [federally sentenced women] and to increase Board Member awareness and sensitivity" (ibid.). For these participants, board members required in-depth knowledge and awareness of female offender and diversity issues in order to make appropriate release decisions.

In September 2003, the Executive Committee adopted several commitments to federally sentenced women (PBC 2003b), and an action plan was developed to ensure follow through (Interview 7). As one informant noted, these commitments are not the intended corporate strategy that was originally planned during the consultation process and meeting with stakeholders (ibid.). This informant explained that one senior staff member had really pushed for a corporate strategy, but that, largely due to changes in senior management and resistance from individuals within the organization "that's not really what [the PBC] ended up with." My research efforts did not produce any materials that outlined the difference between a corporate strategy and a commitments document. However, it is likely that the former would require action and thus greater organizational accountability to address female offender issues than would the latter.

The commitments document outlines the steps taken by the CSC towards addressing the specific needs of female offenders. Noted initiatives include the building of new regional prisons and a healing lodge, the appointment of a deputy commissioner for women at the CSC, and the closing of the Prison for Women (PBC 2003b, 2). The commitments document is positioned in the context of gains for female offenders and is rationalized as follows:

> In order to continue to progress in a consistent and effective manner and also in concert with our partners who share in our vision we must clearly state our organizational position with regards to FSW [federally sentenced women]. The

[PBC] Commitments are a means to that end and will serve as the foundation and direction of future Board activities dedicated to being responsive to the special needs of women. (PBC 2003b, 2)

Additionally, the document references two pieces of legislation that support the PBC's commitments to federally sentenced female offenders. The first is section 151(3) of the *CCRA*, which requires the organization to respect gender and other differences and be responsive to the special needs of female offenders. The second is the *Charter* and, more specifically, section 15(1), which requires equal protection and equal rights under the law (PBC 2003b). The production of a document that states its objectives and vision in this way speaks to issues of institutional accountability and the management of organizational reputation – albeit less forcefully than a corporate strategy. This type of document works to portray the PBC as a certain type of organization (i.e., one committed to federally sentenced women) while simultaneously making it accountable (e.g., through litigation or public embarrassment) for following through on its commitments.

Through this document, the PBC (2003b) made seven commitments to federally sentenced female offenders. These commitments display a melding of (liberal) feminist and criminological knowledges with dominant organizational approaches to managing difference. They represent a formal recognition that "what works" for female offenders is often different from what works for male offenders, with feminist and criminological knowledges being used as a guide. In this way, the commitments reflect – at least on paper – a substantive equality approach that accepts gender differences as guiding the treatment of female offenders within the context of conditional release. Yet it is important to consider how gender is defined and operationalized, particularly as it may come to signify "a uniform category of difference" (Hannah-Moffat 2008, 198) that captures neither female diversity nor how gender intersects with other facets of identity (see also Russell and Carlton 2013).

The first commitment is to adopt a gender-specific approach at hearings for federally sentenced women. This is based on the idea that female offenders are unique in relation to criminality and needs and "require a gender-sensitive environment that promotes trust and openness and is conducive to information gathering" (PBC 2003b, 3). No further explanation is given as to what might constitute a gender-specific hearing or why issues of trust or openness are related to femininity. However, following from the consultation paper and report of the stakeholder meeting, this commitment may reflect the view that, as they are for Aboriginal offenders as a group, regular parole hearings are difficult for female

Conceptual Silos and the Problem of Gender

offenders as a group, thereby requiring board members to adjust their behaviour and communication styles to ensure accurate information gathering (PBC 2002c, 2002d). These documents also reveal stakeholder preferences for the elder-assisted hearing model and its possible adaptation for use with female offenders. This model was positioned as contributing to a holistic treatment of female offenders and a hearing milieu that promotes openness, trust, and a non-adversarial relationship between board members and offenders. In this context, there is an implicit gendering of the parole hearing, whereby the regular hearing is viewed as masculine and the alternative hearing is constituted as feminine. Following my analysis of EAHs in Chapter 4, the notion of a gender-specific hearing may draw upon and reproduce normative assumptions of femininity and, in the process, establish unspoken expectations around how female offenders – framed as a homogeneous group – behave at hearings and engage with board members.

The second commitment is to forge partnerships with community organizations, academics, researchers, and community leaders to enhance "collective knowledge and awareness of available resources and women's issues" (PBC 2003b, 3). This commitment stems from an acknowledgment of existing knowledge and expertise related to female offenders and the imperative for the PBC to engage with "all relevant and interested partners in new initiatives, policy development and training pertaining to FSW to ensure comprehensive and appropriate measures are undertaken" (ibid.). This commitment appears to follow from the standard organizational practice of consultation as a means of building institutional knowledge and of representing the organization as one that is open, inclusive, and responsive to diversity issues.

The third commitment relates to "the concept of individual, creative and gender-specific options for release, which addresses the re-establishment, where appropriate, of familial relationships and incorporate[s] accommodation options such as Private Home Placements and Satellite Apartments, which meet CSC guidelines" (PBC 2003b, 3). The organization indicates that successful re-integration for female offenders is impeded by a lack of accommodation options upon their release. In this context, private home placements and satellite apartments (that meet CSC guidelines) are viewed as gender-specific accommodation options because they enable women to re-establish familial relationships. This commitment reflects the recommendations put forth in the consultation paper and stakeholder meeting report for the PBC to consider creative options for release so that female offenders are not unfairly disadvantaged by the limited community-based accommodations (PBC 2002c, 2002d). The organization also indicates that "access to positive familial relationships and strong social support networks facilitates" successful reintegration (PBC 2003b, 3). This commitment displays an institutional understanding of the central tenets of relational theory, including the view that relationships are the defining feature of women's lives and selves (Hannah-Moffat 2008) and, thus, a key to their successful reintegration. With this commitment, the PBC supports the re-establishing of certain kinds of familial relationships "where appropriate," thereby suggesting that relationships and supports that are institutionally defined as "positive" may be made relevant to parole decision making (see Hannah-Moffat 2007; Pollack 2007).

The fourth commitment is to ensure that decision makers are equipped with a "comprehensive understanding of women's issues" due to the "potential for poverty and disenfranchisement" to present barriers to meeting basic needs (PBC 2003b, 3). This commitment echoes feminist knowledges about the oppression of women as well as the recommendations emerging from the consultation paper and report of the stakeholder meeting to enable board members to understand how gendered adversities produce and sustain female offending. Presumably, a "comprehensive understanding of women's issues" would reduce unreasonable expectations among board members about who female offenders are (e.g., largely poor, under-educated, low-skill) and how poverty influences their reintegration (PBC 2002d). To make gender-responsive parole decisions, board members would need to understand the social context of female offending and utilize their knowledge to support creative release plans.

The issue of cultural diversity within the female offender population is the focus of the fifth commitment. The PBC (2003b, 3) "acknowledges" that this diversity "exists" and recognizes that there are "resources within [these] communities that could assist decision-makers by contextualizing the crime and its cultural meaning." The organization makes the rather vague commitment to develop "policies and practices that address the ethnocultural diversity" of this population (ibid.). The notion that ethnocultural communities have "resources" to help board members likely relates to using cultural interpreters or assistants in hearings as a means of reducing board member confusion or uncertainty in the face of diversity and of providing knowledge of the cultural contexts of offending. However, the notion of ethnocultural diversity is not defined; it is therefore unclear whether the term includes Aboriginality as a marker of ethnocultural difference or refers to non-white, non-Aboriginal diversity – the implicit institutional framing as discussed in the previous chapter. Additionally, the partitioning of cultural diversity in one commitment works against an intersectional approach, such that racial or cultural difference is added on to the list of elements for decision-makers to consider.

The sixth commitment stems from the acknowledgement that (1) actuarial risk assessment tools do not exist for female offenders and that (2) despite this "deficiency," female offenders still do "well" while on parole (PBC 2003b, 4). The PBC's commitment is to examine "specific issues related to the assessment for release of Federally Sentenced Women and the Board's decision-making process for their conditional release in collaboration with researchers, academics and our partners" (ibid.). That there are no actuarial risk scales for female offenders to be used in decision making, particularly those assessing the risk of recidivism, sets female offenders apart from male offenders in the context of the standard conditional release process.[3] Board members cannot draw on risk scores for their decision making for female offenders. Additionally, as highlighted in the consultation paper and stakeholder meeting report, there is concern that risk tools are being used to assess and guide the treatment of female prisoners even though these tools do not recognize or account for the ways in which risk and need are gendered. The implication here is that correctional decisions based on these tools may affect female offenders in the parole process, whereby their file information influences decision making (PBC 2002d). The organization's commitment to explore risk assessment issues for female offenders suggests that it has accepted the views of stakeholders and gender-informed researchers for more work in this area. Yet this commitment reaffirms actuarial tools as a desirable end goal of ongoing research on risk assessments for female offenders.

The seventh and final commitment to federally sentenced female offenders relates to the creation of "comprehensive training materials to provide the foundation for quality decision-making" for this population (PBC 2003b, 4). This commitment is derived from the acknowledgment that board members need "women-centred" training that includes "a thorough understanding of the particular criminogenic circumstances" of this population (ibid.). The need for gender-responsive training was identified in both the consultation paper and stakeholder meeting report and was linked to more effective conditional release decision making for female offenders. The final commitment also ties together the preceding six commitments as training would inevitably be required to bring them to fruition. As I show in Chapter 3, training is also a standard organizational practice linked to quality decision making and deemed to be particularly relevant to female and non-white offender populations.

The PBC (2003b, 4) indicates that its adoption of the seven commitments to federally sentenced female offenders would "ensure their longevity as well as consistency in their application nationally." Although the commitments document may differ from a corporate strategy, it can be understood as a move towards institutional accountability in the area of female offenders. The document is also noteworthy for the rejection of a gender-neutral approach to parole and the acceptance of different strategies and approaches for female offenders, albeit largely based on an understanding of gender as a homogeneous category. However, as Ahmed (2007b) cautions in relation to the production of commitments documents, "saying" is not necessarily "doing." Bringing about organizational change in relation to diversity is complicated and challenging (Kalev et al. 2006; Dobbin et al. 2011).

Although my research did not trace whether these commitments were actualized, some observations are possible. First, there are no written principles or guidelines for a gender-specific model. However, the Atlantic Region appears to have attempted a gender-responsive approach by adapting its hearing format to remove barriers (Interview 7; Interview 10) and to involve more "questioning on the individual's background and history," including "issues of victimisation, family violence, prostitution, and substance abuse" (PBC 2006c, 2). Second, there were no policies or information detailing how the PBC would address the issue of ethnocultural diversity among federally sentenced women. The initiatives for ethnocultural offenders described in the previous chapter do not consider gender or specific issues pertaining to female offenders. Finally, the training materials on female offenders and gender issues, as shown in Chapter 3, appear incomplete and under-developed rather than comprehensive in nature or scope. Momentum on female offender issues appears to have waned since the early 2000s; the only additional gender-related practice evident was an initiative developed in the Atlantic Region.

Demystifying the Parole Hearing: Information Sessions for Female Offenders

The preceding discussion highlights several perspectives on the needs of female offenders during the conditional release process. In particular, female offenders (as a group) are identified as having more challenging and negative experiences of parole hearings and board members than male offenders (as a group). One regional response to these sorts of concerns was the establishment of the Atlantic Region's Female Offender Committee in September 2000. The purpose of the committee was to identify "issues relating to female offenders that can improve decision-making" (PBC 2006b, 7). In the 2006-07 fiscal year, the committee started an initiative to provide information sessions for female prisoners at Nova Institution (PBC 2007f). These information sessions involved PBC staff, such as communications and hearing officers, screening a video of a parole hearing for female offenders and providing time to answer questions about the hearing process. The sessions were created in response to the concern "that female offenders do not feel prepared for their hearings" (n.pag) and "generally were not opening up" during their hearings (Interview 10) as the PBC had expected. In order to carry out the information sessions, the Atlantic Region sent invitation letters to female prisoners scheduled for hearings and also posted invitation notices about upcoming sessions on bulletin boards throughout the penitentiary. In order to increase participation, the invitations indicated that prisoners were permitted to ask their employers for time off to attend the session and that coffee would be offered (PBC 2007f).

The information sessions were piloted on a monthly basis starting in 2007. However, at a meeting of the Female Offender Committee in November 2008, it was decided that the sessions would be held "every two months instead of monthly due in part to budget restraints and operational requirements" (PBC 2009k, n.pag). According to the committee, the information sessions were viewed positively by Nova Institution (PBC 2007f) and the prisoners who attended them (PBC 2010i). In July 2009, the committee decided it would film a new video of a mock parole hearing using PBC staff as actors because the existing video was "long and a bit outdated" (n.pag). According to one informant, the information sessions helped demystify the hearing by showing female offenders "what to expect," thereby decreasing "their anxiety level" (Interview 10). This diversity initiative assumes that female offenders, as a group, have greater needs in preparing for their hearings than do other offenders. The information sessions represent the inclusion of knowledge about female offenders into an initiative that aims to improve their experiences of the hearing process. That the frequency of the initiative was reduced due to budgetary and operational issues underscores the challenge of pursuing alternative practices, particularly for small segments of the offender population. The staying power of such practices is reflective of the challenge of doing things differently based solely on the construct of gender difference.

The Challenge of Doing Things Differently

As shown above, the institutional discourse around female offenders reproduces a general understanding of women centredness or gender responsiveness that is based on a set of ideas around the different needs of women – needs that cannot be addressed by a correctional system designed for men (Shaylor 2009; Russell and Carlton 2013). According to two informants, in an attempt to be responsive, the Atlantic Region has pursued a different approach to hearings for female offenders. More specifically, hearings for female offenders, regardless of Aboriginal status, involve the removal of barriers (e.g., tables) and the use of a circle format (Interview 7; Interview 10). Yet, as one informant indicated, the removal of barriers at hearings for women offenders was not entirely embraced by all segments of the organization, particularly as some questioned why this should only occur for women (Interview 7). Despite the lack of consensus, the same informant explained that the removal of barriers became part of the hearing policy within the region and therefore constitutes a gendered modification of the standard hearing format.

The debate within the Atlantic Region around how the hearing is set up and the degree to which it should be a gender-responsive approach or should be normalized throughout the region is illustrative of the shaky foundation upon which some ideas about gender responsiveness are based. The previous chapter's discussion of the institutional approach to developing an alternative hearing format also touches on the degree to which adapted formats are responsive to ethnicity or culture. Unlike with EAHs and CAHs, for which Aboriginal knowledges and practices are used to justify the production of a different hearing format, there does not appear to be a solid rationale for why the removal of barriers or the use of a circle format constitutes a "gender issue." The challenge of doing things differently may be dependent upon how gender is operationalized within institutional policies and practices (Hannah-Moffat 2008).

Conclusions: Conceptual Silos and the Problem of Gender

The organizational approaches to female difference discussed in this chapter illustrate the complexities of developing gender-responsive parole processes. The following summarizes my findings on how the PBC has dealt with gender difference by presenting two main arguments. First, the organizational approach to gender is one of conceptual silos; that is, gender tends to be treated as separate from other aspects of identity. Second, gender is a problem for the organization in the sense that it struggles with the practicalities of exactly how gender factors into parole decision making. This institutional approach to gender difference works to both reproduce (white) male offenders as the norm and to essentialize female offenders as a homogenous group.

PBC documents illustrate an organizational inability to treat gender as one facet of many intersecting, co-occurring identities; rather, gender is treated as distinct from race or ethnicity as the main markers of organizationally recognized difference. One of the key implications of the particular way that difference has been institutionally identified and defined – as Aboriginal, female, and ethnocultural – is that a "false unity" has been imposed on these three groups by way of their difference and a "false emphasis" has been placed on a single facet of identity (Hudson 2008b, 279). Individuals are known and defined by one aspect of identity, such as being female, Aboriginal, black, or Asian, and are assigned group membership on the basis of this aspect. Organizational responses have largely been tailored in response to generalized group attributes that imply a "false homogeneity," thereby glossing over substantial diversity within these groups, including their pathways into and out of prison. As Hudson observes, this means "that individuals are too readily assumed to have the values, beliefs, aspirations and dilemmas that are attributed to the group – values, beliefs, aspirations and dilemmas that might or might not be application to their own lives and personalities" (ibid.).

Essentialist constructions of identity are challenged by anti-racist feminist scholars (e.g., hooks 1981, 1992; Collins 1990; Crenshaw 1991; West and Fenstermaker 1995; Razack 1998; Yuval-Davis 2006). The treatment of gender as a unitary category fails to recognize how race, class, sexuality, and ability intersect with gender to differently position women (Razack 1998; Russell and Carlton 2013). Nor do additive approaches (e.g., racism plus sexism equals double oppression) allow for an understanding of intersecting facets of identity (Razack 1998; Yuval-Davis 2006). At various times throughout *Parole in Canada*, I highlight how the additive approach tends to be used when issues of race or ethnicity are considered in relation to female offenders. Aboriginal and racialized female offenders are first identified within the category "woman," and racial or ethnic difference is then added on to gender such that they are doubly disadvantaged or face twice the challenges. In addition, the institutional tendency to define offenders by a single facet of identity means that offenders marked by multiple institutionally identified differences are often left out. This is especially the case among Aboriginal and racialized female offenders; the category of "woman" is implicitly constituted as white, while the Aboriginal and ethnocultural constructs are produced as masculine.

The simultaneity of various facets of difference has evaded policy thinking and the development of practices for "women" as a diverse population. West and Fenstermaker (1995, 13) summarize the problem this way:

Capturing [the simultaneity] compels us to focus on the actual mechanisms that produce social inequality. How do forms of inequality, which we now see are more than the periodic collision of categories, operate together? How do we see that all social exchanges, regardless of the participants or the outcome, are simultaneously "gendered," "raced," and "classed"?

The complexity of an intersectionality analysis makes its transfer to practical settings (e.g., decision making, training, policy development, etc.) challenging. Similar to Hannah-Moffat (2010), my research findings suggest that penal policies are only capable of addressing one form of difference at a time. Feminist reformers have been (largely) successful at putting "woman" on the penal agenda, albeit in an essentialized form.[4]

Second, I argue that gender is a problem for the PBC in the sense that the organization struggles with the practical application of exactly how gender figures into parole decision making. My analyses of various PBC documents pertaining to diversity suggest that the organization has grappled, and continues to grapple, with how gender matters to conditional release. Although gender is officially acknowledged as being important in the context of punishment and relevant to parole, understandings of exactly *how* gender matters and ought to be operationalized within policies and practices are limited (Hannah-Moffat 2008, 2009). Even with an agreed upon assumption in PBC documents that "women" (as a category) are different from "men" (as a category) and therefore have different or special needs, the understanding tends to stop there (see also Hannah-Moffat 1995). There is also little consideration of gender as a relational construct or the ways in which policies, practices, or processes themselves are gendered; instead, gender is code for women and gender difference is unitarily understood as pertaining to femininity. The dominant institutional conceptualization of gender works to reinforce (white) male offenders as the (genderless) norm against which female difference is constituted. My research suggests gender is not as easily operationalized within institutional policies and practices as are notions of Aboriginality.

Conclusion

In *Parole in Canada*, I examine two main questions: How are certain "differences" and categories of offenders constituted as targets for "accommodation" or as having "special needs"? How do penal institutions frame "culturally relevant" or "gender-responsive" policy and, in so doing, use normative ideals and selective knowledge of gender, race, culture, ethnicity, and other social relations to constitute the identities of particular groups of offenders? By analyzing various official and internal government documents and drawing on interviews with informants, I explore these questions by tracing the penal transformations that led to the recognition of gender and facets of diversity within legislation and organizational policies and practices since the 1970s, focusing specifically on present-day approaches to accommodating difference at the Parole Board of Canada. I show how notions of diversity are constituted as relating to non-whiteness and non-maleness, with Aboriginal, female, and ethnocultural offenders identified as populations in need of accommodation. I examine in detail the sorts of organizational approaches and initiatives developed for these three offender groups in order to demonstrate how issues of difference are selectively incorporated and framed as relevant to particular aspects of the parole process. I show how the PBC has negotiated what diversity means and its relevance to parole and release decision making and, in doing so, highlight the challenges and complexities of accommodating offender diversities in the pursuit of a more "fair" and "appropriate" penality.

The institutionalization of diversity at the PBC has involved the inclusion of selective understandings, which ultimately fail to recognize the complexities and nuances of this construct. The exclusive reading of gender as women and diversity as non-whiteness has reinforced the othering of these groups while maintaining masculinity and whiteness as the normative frames and standards within conditional release policies and processes. The implication is that the organizational inclusion of gender and diversity becomes a "special project," one that is peripheral to the "real work" of the institution. At the same time, the organizational tendency to think about differences as separate, rather than as intersecting, results in the prioritization of one facet of identity over others. Gender and diversity are thus made to "fit" within dominant penal logics and approaches, including risk assessment.

I show that the incorporation of diversity into the federal parole system addresses a variety of organizational objectives and interests. These include fulfilling the legislative mandate of the *Corrections and Conditional Release Act* to recognize and respond to diversity; addressing expectations of fairness; observing human rights ideals and, increasingly, the interests of victims; managing reputational risk and conforming to managerial logics as a means of measuring and tracking diversity and showing that it is being done at the organization; instituting "effective" correctional practice in order to reduce risk and increase public safety; and addressing issues of representation such that board members and staff reflect the diversity of the Canadian population. At the same time, the recognition of gender and diversity produces new penal subjectivities, discourses, and sites upon which to govern. More broadly, these research findings indicate that institutional approaches to gender and diversity draw upon and circulate gendered, culturalized, and racialized knowledges of offenders and offending as a way to know certain populations and to develop "responsive" methods that take these differences into account. This is significant because the focus on knowing about various differences does not clearly translate into what to do about these differences in practice.

This analysis of institutional policies, training materials, research reports, corporate documents, and internal records demonstrates the challenge of recognizing and responding to complex and multifaceted identities, histories, and experiences. The incorporation of gender and diversity into the PBC and its parole policies and practices is not a straightforward undertaking. The PBC's various approaches to recognizing and responding to difference – from its implementation of the *Gladue* decision to the development of cultural fact sheets about ethnocultural offenders – are illustrative of how the organization is grappling with offender diversities and their relevance to decision making.

Yet how issues of gender and diversity are initially defined has important implications for the ways in which these constructs are understood and integrated into policy and practice directed at offenders defined as different along lines of gender, race, ethnicity, and culture. Selective and narrow understandings of diversity can limit the scope of penal change when diversity becomes a "special issue" that is seen to affect only certain offenders, policies, or approaches. This research also illustrates the challenge of reconfiguring Canadian penality to accommodate substantive equality approaches (i.e., those that recognize and respond to certain differences and allow for different treatment) in an organizational context that is based on white male offenders as the norm and standard for parole policies and practices. Gender and diversity are appended to dominant structures and approaches as peripheral, rather than as integral, to the PBC's work.

The reconfiguring of parole policy in Canada to be more inclusive of diversity appears, at first glance, as a progressive (liberal) step. Yet, as I show in this book, the institutionalization of diversity as a means of bringing about change has many pitfalls. As a technique of governing difference, the politics of diversity can alternatively be understood as regressive as deeply entrenched historical and systemic factors are glossed over in favour of focusing on certain gender, cultural, or ethnic differences that can be "accommodated" by the penal system. Through the language of diversity, key factors connected to criminalization and punishment – racism, colonialism, poverty, and so on – fade into the background through the "celebration" of difference. As noted in Chapter 2, the politics of diversity encourages a muted discussion and consideration of differences, disconnecting issues of "race" or "gender" from their historical roots and present-day manifestations. As a framework, diversity can work to inadvertently support systems of inequality through processes that fail to upset the dominant systems of privilege and penalty upon which the Canadian penal system is based. In *Parole in Canada*, I demonstrate that it is important to think through the limitations of the politics of inclusion and the framework of diversity in the context of penal reform. We need to contemplate the attendant risks associated with the development and integration of so-called "culturally appropriate" and "gender-responsive" policies and practices, considering what is both gained and lost in the process.

The critical analysis of diversity initiatives at the PBC that I present in *Parole in Canada* invites the question: What do you propose instead? Legally and practically, I would not advocate that we abandon provisions of the CCRA such as 151(3) or parole practices like elder-assisted hearings or community-assisted hearings. In arguing that the institutional integration of gender and diversity concerns is challenging and fraught with difficulties does not suggest that such work is unimportant or does not have the potential to improve offenders' experiences of the parole process or their parole outcomes. Through interviews with informants and countless hours spent reading various documents, it became clear that many people have been, and are, committed to social justice ideals and to improving the lives and life chances of offenders defined as different along lines of gender, race, ethnicity, culture, and so forth. My purpose in this book is not to detract from these beliefs, commitments, and efforts: it is to focus on the processes and implications of how gender and diversity are constituted and institutionalized in the context of penal reform, punishment, and risk. This critical examination of how notions of gender, race, and culture inform penal policies and practices of governing offenders on the basis of difference does not suggest that such approaches have no value or have not improved the lives of those who are punished in Canada. That these policies and practices have, at times, been requested by, or developed in conjunction with, marginalized groups does not preclude an analysis of the official representations of these developments or the discourses upon which they are based.

There may also be limits to the ways in which the federal parole system can respond to issues of racial, cultural, and gender difference. As the last "stop" in an offender's carceral journey, there may be little that the parole process can do to respond to or to address the factors contributing to her or his incarceration in the first place. The challenges of implementing *Gladue* principles at the PBC highlight this point, suggesting that the penal system is a less than ideal locale in which to address systemic discrimination and attempt to ameliorate and repair historical injustices in the contemporary (post)colonial context. This is especially the case when the guiding legislation and decision-making policies support the status quo, thereby restricting what can be done "differently."

It is also important to acknowledge that the way in which I assemble this book, and the analytical approach I take, may work to reinforce the "othering" of Aboriginal, female, and ethnocultural offenders by treating them as different (in comparison to the white, male norm) and distinct (thereby glossing over the intersections among gender and race). In recognizing this contradiction, I suggest that this approach is not necessarily negative as it allows the analysis to follow how notions of difference are produced and taken up within law and organizational policies and practices. For instance, I have separate chapters on Aboriginal, female, and ethnocultural offenders because these are the three groups that the PBC identifies and treats separately in its approaches and practices. I allow my analysis to follow this framing of difference. Additionally, although I look critically at how understandings of gender are taken up within parole policies and practices, I do not specifically examine male offenders, masculinities, or the gendered nature of organizations. Such analytical elements are beyond the scope of this book and may again reflect the contradictions and limitations associated with my analytical approach.

Looking Forward

In writing *Parole in Canada*, I am aware of the organizational constraints in which gendered and diversified parole policies and practices are developed and implemented. This study by no means intends to detract from the work of committed individuals to improve offenders' treatment within the penal system. My research does, however, have some implications for the PBC's policies and practices, and for those who work in the organization, with regards to how diverse offenders are evaluated and how decisions are made. The primary implication relates to the importance of taking care in defining concepts such as gender and diversity as well as being aware of the limitations of these constructs in terms of how they can be incorporated into policy and practice. This type of critical reflection is evidenced by at least one internal document (see PBC 2009i), which considers both the advantages and limitations of the term "ethnocultural" with regard to how it is applied to certain racial minority offenders. This report presents a more sophisticated understanding of ethnic and racial diversity. The challenge for the PBC is how to incorporate a nuanced understanding of difference, one that recognizes the multiplicity and simultaneity of various identities, experiences, and social contexts that shape the individuals appearing before board members. At the same, it is crucial that normative processes and policies are understood as such, enabling critical reflections on the norms of whiteness and masculinity as an essential part of institutional responses to offender diversities.

A potential challenge to such "diversity work" relates to the broader context of criminal justice policy in Canada. The former Conservative government passed a number of legislative reforms that are likely to increase the federal offender population due, in part, to restrictions on parole eligibility. These reforms, and accompanying punitive rhetoric, raise questions about the staying power of current diversity initiatives at the PBC, and throughout the correctional system more generally, as well as the ability of these systems to continue to address issues of difference. If, as I suggest, diversity initiatives tend to be framed as "special projects" and as peripheral to the "real work" of penal organizations or above and beyond that which is legally mandated, there is a possibility that these initiatives could be targeted for cost-saving cuts or abandoned for political reasons. Yet, at the same time, the reforms may work to further increase the rates of incarceration of Aboriginal and other racialized offenders, thereby raising the possibility of future legal challenges of discriminatory treatment. It is hoped that *Parole in Canada* advances the conversation about gendered and racialized penal regimes while encouraging critical reflection on the complexities and challenges of incorporating gender and diversity within penal policies and practices.

Notes

Introduction

1 Because it is awkward to put quotation marks around terms such as "diversity," "difference," and "gender" each time they are employed, I do so only upon their first usage in each chapter. It is hoped that, with or without these quotation marks, the reader will consider these concepts as social constructions.

2 More recently, in Canada mentally ill offenders are increasingly viewed as a special population; however, mental health is not marked as different in the same way as are race or ethnicity, culture, and/or gender.

3 I make reference to the "(post)colonial" context of Canada to draw attention to the unsettled nature of the country as an independent nation-state characterized by ongoing colonial practices, uneven efforts towards liberal multiculturalism, and marked and persistent gender, racial, and socioeconomic inequality.

4 In 2010, the applied title of the National Parole Board was changed to the Parole Board of Canada as a result of the government's Federal Identity Program. For the sake of consistency and clarity, I use the organization's new title throughout.

5 Ontario and Quebec are the only provinces with their own provincial parole boards. British Columbia had its own parole board, but was disbanded on April 1, 2007 (PBC 2008a).

6 The *CCRA* allows for both full- and part-time board members but restricts the number of full-time members to forty-five.

7 Following Larsen and Piché (2009, 206), I provide the ATI reference numbers in the bibliography to enable other researchers to retrieve information obtained through the request by citing the appropriate number.

8 Interestingly, and perhaps unsurprisingly, most informants and the PBC staff with whom I dealt in order to gain access to information repeatedly referred me to the organization's website, as if it contained all the material necessary to conduct a "proper" study of my topic. Given the bureaucratic and political influences on what information actually gets posted

on government websites, the *ATIA* is an important tool for gaining access to information.

Chapter 1: Putting Gender, Race, and Culture on the Penal Agenda

1 The Canadian *Charter* is an important constitutional document that outlines various human rights and associated protections, including those related to Aboriginal peoples.

2 As I indicate in Chapter 5, discussions around ethnocultural offenders emerge much later, primarily beginning in the late 1990s and early 2000s.

3 For example, in 1984, Aboriginal peoples comprised 9.5 percent of the federal prison population, yet made up only 2 percent of the general population (Solicitor General 1988b). In 2013-14, Aboriginal peoples accounted for 22.8 percent of the incarcerated federal offender population, compared to 4 percent of the adult Canadian population (OCI 2014).

4 The Task Force consisted of representatives from the CSC, PBC, Department of Secretary of State, Solicitor General of Canada, Department of Indian and Northern Affairs, and Native Counselling Service of Alberta. To carry out its mandate, the Task Force consulted with Aboriginal inmate groups and Aboriginal communities, staff at federal penitentiaries, PBC staff and board members, as well as other organizations involved in aftercare services for Aboriginal offenders (Solicitor General 1988a).

5 In September 1991, the CSC responded to the Task Force's Final Report via its *Year-End Implementation Report, 1990-1991* (see Solicitor General 1991). It does not appear that the PBC produced a similar document.

6 For example, in 1998, 2.5 percent of the federal prison population were women (Hannah-Moffat and Shaw 2000). In 2013-14, female offenders constituted 4.9 percent of the federal prison population and were among the fastest-growing subpopulations (OCI 2014).

7 The notion of gender justice is attributable to Carlen (2002b).

8 This discussion of *Charter* rights focuses mainly on fundamental human rights issues affecting prisoners; no reference is made to *Charter* equality provisions around sex (or gender), ethnic, racial, and/or cultural discrimination.

9 See O'Connor (1985) for a discussion of the early impacts of the *Charter* on the parole system.

10 This green paper outlines ten issues to be addressed with policy and legislative reform: rebuilding public trust in the justice system; increasing equity and predictability in sentencing and decision making; ensuring greater integration among criminal justice components to make the system work more smoothly; providing more effective sentencing and sentence administration; improving the reintegration of offenders and public protection; increasing fairness and accountability within the justice system; reducing the over-reliance on incarceration and creating alternatives; attending to special classes of offenders; addressing the concerns of victims; and clearly articulating the purposes and principles of sentencing, corrections, and conditional release (Canada 1990b).

11 The sentencing reforms to the *Criminal Code* brought about in 1996 – including section 718.2(e) – were another product of the CLR, although "people often forget" this fact (Interview 1). According to one informant, "it was just because of parliamentary delays and elections that the sentencing stuff was proclaimed later" (Interview 1).

12 The bill's full title is "An Act Respecting Corrections and the Conditional Release and Detention of Offenders and to Establish the Office of Correctional Investigator."

13 See Hayman (2006) for an in-depth study of these penal transformations.

14 Several scholars have expressed doubt about the ability of this provision to reduce the overrepresentation of Aboriginal offenders (see Pelletier 2001; Roberts and Melchers 2003).

15 See, for example, Roach and Rudin (2000), Kramar and Sealy (2006), and Murdocca (2013) for more in-depth analyses of *Gladue*.

Chapter 2: Responding to Diversity

1 Critical race scholars convincingly show how this norm is characterized by its invisibility; that is, to be seen as "normal" and the "universal human," to be without gender or race, is to occupy a privileged position because power is located in this invisibility (hooks 1992; Goldberg 1993; Mohanram 1999; Puwar 2004). Whiteness and maleness are both unmarked normative positions. Whiteness tends to be defined as the absence of race, while the male body is typically invisible as a sexed or gendered entity (Young 1996; Puwar 2004).

2 According to one informant, the Executive Committee "is *the* decision making body" of the PBC (Interview 7).

3 See the listing for the Aboriginal and Diversity Initiatives section of the PBC on the Government Electronic Directory Services: http://sage-geds.tpsgc-pwgsc.gc.ca/en/GEDS/?pgid=009.

4 See the PBC's organizational chart at http://pbc-clcc.gc.ca/org/chart-eng.shtml.

5 This meeting was funded by the Aboriginal Community Corrections Initiative, a part of the federal government's five-year Strategy for Aboriginal Justice.

6 The creation of this type of group mainly comprised of Aboriginal peoples, largely on the basis of ethnic and/or cultural identities, was unique at the PBC.

7 This is not to suggest that such priorities and interests are necessarily or always mutually exclusive.

8 In Canada, the federal cabinet is comprised of ministers selected by the prime minister and is part of the executive function of government (Marleau and Montpetit 2000).

9 This informant indicated that the PBC's written test has been reviewed to assess its "cultural sensitivity" (Interview 5). I filed an ATI request to receive copies of any reviews of the tests, but this request yielded no documents.

10 Albeit in a joking manner, the informant noted that, if representation was based on the *inmate* as opposed to the *general* population, then the PBC would be doing very well in the area of women's representation as board members because the federally sentenced women's population is much smaller than is the general women's population.

11 The issue of reduced communication among Aboriginal offenders is one of the main reasons for the creation of elder-assisted hearings.

12 Other components include making decisions that protect the public while being consistent with the principle of the least restrictive option; reflect an impartial deliberation of the case while being consistent with the duty to act fairly; and is based on pertinent and accurate information and follows the PBC's policies (PBC 2011c, Ch. 2.2: 23-24).

13 I made an ATI request for sections of the *Board Member Risk Assessment Manual* that focus on Aboriginal offenders, women offenders, ethnocultural offenders, and cultural perceptions in order to explore how issues of risk assessment and decision making are articulated in relation to these populations. However, I was informed that the PBC, citing sections 21(1)(a) and 21(1)(b) of the *ATIA*, could not release the manual because the organization was concerned that this would set a precedent and potentially result in offenders learning how board members make decisions (personal communication, January 10, 2011).

Chapter 3: In Pursuit of "Appropriate" Decisions

1 "Talk" about diversity issues does occur (e.g., in the context of diversity committees).

2 Alcoff (1998) suggests that it is important to consider the origins of "sensitivity" training, including the "business case" (i.e., racism impedes workplace productivity) and its development with white people as the target audience.

3 In this context, "expertise" is institutionally defined and may include researchers external to government or representatives from departments such as the CSC.

4 In 2008, the PBC contracted with a consultant to evaluate its program of board member training. Although this evaluation focused broadly on the PBC's board member training regime, some specific comments were made about the need for "further improvement" to training on issues of diversity, including those relating to Aboriginal, ethnocultural, and women offenders (PBC 2008e, 17).

5 The metaphor of carrying a "knapsack" of invisible white privileges was originally created by McIntosh (1992).

6 According to Rozas and Miller (2009, 30), this exercise may also be "evocative for people of color who have *not* had these privileges" as the recognition of such can be validating.

7 Interestingly, the discussion related to empathy is located in the section on gender differences, although there is no indication as to whether or not empathy is considered to be a "gender issue" or a gendered phenomenon.

8 I filed two separate ATI requests with the PBC in 2009 and 2010 regarding training for women offenders. The 2010 request specifically asked for updated materials given the module was listed as "under construction." I was informed that there were no other materials available that would respond to my request (personal communication, December 23, 2010).

9 Of course, this makes sense organizationally, given the division of responsibilities among the CSC and PBC.

10 For example, the report of the Commission of Systemic Racism in the Ontario Criminal Justice System and reports from Statistics Canada.

11 I made a request under the *ATIA* for the "trainer's manual" for APT but was told "there is no current training manual available" (personal communication, December 23, 2010). It is important to note that the version I received under the *ATIA* is identified as a "pilot."

12 Pathways healing ranges (or units) are described as "a traditional environment within CSC institutions for Aboriginal offenders dedicated to following a traditional healing path" and are part of the "Aboriginal Corrections Continuum of Care" model introduced by the CSC in 2003 (CSC 2009a).

13 Other scholars (e.g., Hannah-Moffat 2005; Martel et al. 2011) argue instead that such assessments are inherently flawed (and racialized) because they capture various factors that systematically disadvantage Aboriginal peoples.

14 I submitted an ATI request to access this report but was told that it could not be located (ATI no. A-2010-00027 to the PBC).

Chapter 4: Cultural Ghettos?

1 As I show, the terms used to describe hearings for Aboriginal offenders have changed over time. For the sake of simplicity and consistency, throughout this book I use "elder-assisted hearing" (EAH) to describe this hearing format.

2 Additionally, as of 1997, offenders are asked to confirm on record their request for an EAH (PBC 2006a, 5).

3 In 2000, the federal budget set aside funding over five years for "A Strategy to Advance Effective Corrections and Citizen Engagement" (PBC 2004a). The PBC, along with two

other federal partners (the Solicitor General and the CSC), was granted funding, part of which it used to focus on Aboriginal corrections. Among its commitments was the expansion of EAHs and the implementation of "culturally appropriate hearing models for offenders from the Nunavut Territory" (7). According to the PBC's (2004a) evaluation report, the number of EAHs increased in each region over this time period.

4 In addition to assessing the implementation of the EAH approach, the evaluation report also provides some data on EAHs, including which offenders were using this hearing format. For instance, between June 1996 and September 1999, males accounted for the vast majority (98 percent) of offenders for which EAHs were conducted, with 88 percent of these offenders defined as Aboriginal (PBC 2000b, 6).

5 The exception related to Inuit offenders; PBC-contracted elders interviewed for the evaluation did not think they could provide advice on Inuit traditions (PBC 2000b, 21).

6 See Haslip (2002) for a discussion of attempts to reintroduce traditional principles to contemporary Aboriginal communities.

7 Of course, one could question the cultural appropriateness of secure spaces within penal institutions and the degree to which such spaces are experienced as white and/or colonizing (see, for example, Faith 1995; Waldram 1997; Edney 2002; Martel and Brassard 2008).

8 In one study of PBC decision-making practices, Silverstein (2005) found that board members relied on elders at hearings to confirm whether or not the offender was following traditional ways.

9 The PBC (2007e, 1) notes that this definition is "therefore not necessarily restricted to the Aboriginal community." As I discuss later, this may open up CAHs to non-Aboriginal communities, assuming such communities "fit" within the definition.

10 I could not locate reliable data on the number and frequency of CAHs since 2000. One report (see PBC 2007b) indicates that two CAHs were held for Aboriginal female offenders in 2006, but it is unknown if additional CAHs were held that year. Statistical information about CAHs do not appear to be reported annually, as is the case for EAHs.

11 The latest version of the PBC Policy Manual indicates that CAHs follow the EAH model but are held in an Aboriginal community (see PBC 2015, Ch. 11.1.1: 1).

12 The CSC's workload for parole supervision is subsequently reduced (PBC 2002b).

13 See works by Garroutte (2003) and Raibmon (2005) for thoughtful discussions of how Aboriginal identities and authenticities are negotiated in the context of modernity.

14 A parallel can be drawn here to cases in which Aboriginal offenders do not request an EAH (or CAH) but, rather, proceed with a "regular" hearing. This raises the question of how an offender's status as Aboriginal is seen to matter in the context of the regular hearing format.

15 Section 718.2(e) has been interpreted as requiring a different methodology for determining what is "right" for Aboriginal offenders, not mandating a different result (see, for example, R. v. Wells [2000], para. 44).

16 This extension of Gladue principles has also occurred in other parts of the correctional process, including the preparation of pre-sentence reports in the Province of Ontario (see Hannah-Moffat and Maurutto 2010).

17 My request to the PBC under the ATIA for the Board Member Risk Assessment Manual was denied.

Chapter 5: Discourses of Difference

1 Multiculturalism is a contested concept about which much scholarship has been produced. I do not have the space here to review this debate and discussion. For differing perspectives, see Kymlicka (2007) and Dhamoon (2009), among others. In this chapter, I draw primarily

on the work of Bannerji (2000) and Dhamoon (2009) for their intersectional analysis of multiculturalism.

2 As part of this implementation, federal institutions are supposed to report annually on any internal activities pertaining to the *Canadian Multiculturalism Act* (see Citizenship and Immigration Canada 2009).

3 The report states that, "in spite of their small numbers, [Aboriginal offenders] have had the benefit, for some years, of specific institutional programs and special arrangements for their hearings" (PBC 2005c, 7). This, according to the report, is "understandable" because Aboriginal people "are homogeneous and share many customs, beliefs and cultural values" (ibid.). The assumption here is that it is easier for the organization to accommodate the needs of Aboriginal offenders because they are essentially all the same (i.e., they are all Aboriginal). This is contrasted to those offenders constituted as ethnic minorities who are understood to be made up of "many ethnic groups, races and cultures" (ibid.).

4 This funding could also be used for regional pilots of a hearing model for ethnocultural offenders (PBC 2004d, 2).

5 The organization is referring to its "Federally Sentenced Women's Consultation Report" (see PBC 2002d).

6 Concerns were also raised during consultations in relation to "informal" hearing formats not satisfying victims, the idea being that the PBC would need to "find some balance between the victim's needs and processes that are most beneficial and productive for the offender and the Board Members" (PBC 2005g, 6). This assumes that victims would only be satisfied with a hearing process that reflects white, normative standards.

7 See Razack (1998) and Deckha (2004) for important feminist analyses of the impacts of recognizing cultural identities within legal settings.

8 See PBC (2003a). One informant explained that the regional director at the time was tasked with the job of identifying alternative approaches "as part of his performance agreement" (Interview 7).

9 The PBC (2008f, 6) also indicates that ethnocultural offenders with limited English- or French-language competency are at a further disadvantage as the CSC's core programs are primarily offered in the official languages. Clearly, this reduces their ability to complete the recommended rehabilitative programs.

10 This initiative was a component of *A Canada for All: Canada's Action Plan against Racism*, a federal plan launched in 2005 by the then Liberal government (Canadian Heritage 2005).

Chapter 6: Conceptual Silos and the Problem of Gender

1 However, the bulk of scrutiny of the "handling" of women offender issues appears to be directed towards the Correctional Service of Canada rather than towards the PBC. For instance, the Office of the Correctional Investigator's annual reports document that various failings of CSC in relation to this population. Many of the criticisms were directed towards the housing of women prisoners in maximum security units and in male penitentiaries (e.g., OCI 2000). These reports also highlight the overrepresentation of Aboriginal women among the federal female population and their underrepresentation on conditional release. The high proportion of "visible minority" women incarcerated federally in Canada has also been noted (OCI 2001).

2 I have used quotation marks to signal the gender essentialism produced by the equality model, where men as a class are the assumed reference group and intragroup differences (e.g., race, class, sexuality, etc.) among both men and women are denied (see Jhappan 1998).

3 The exception is Aboriginal offenders (male and female) as the primary risk tool – the Statistical Information on Recidivism scale – upon which the PBC relies to inform decision making is not valid for female and Aboriginal offenders.
4 The privileging of white, middle-class sensibilities in feminist thinking in the context of penal reform can be viewed as the result "from both who did the theorizing and how they did it" (West and Fenstermaker 1995, 10).

References

Adelberg, Ellen, and Claudia Currie, eds. 1987. *Too Few to Count: Canadian Women in Conflict with the Law*. Vancouver: Press Gang.

Ahmed, Sara. 2006. "The Nonperformativity of Antiracism." *Meridians* 7 (1): 104–26. http://dx.doi.org/10.2979/MER.2006.7.1.104.

–. 2007a. "The Language of Diversity." *Ethnic and Racial Studies* 30 (2): 235–56. http://dx.doi.org/10.1080/01419870601143927.

–. 2007b. "'You End Up Doing the Document Rather than Doing the Doing': Diversity, Race Equality and the Politics of Documentation." *Ethnic and Racial Studies* 30 (4): 590–609. http://dx.doi.org/10.1080/01419870701356015.

–. 2012. *On Being Included: Racism and Diversity in Institutional Life*. Durham, NC: Duke University Press.

Ahmed, Sara, Shona Hunter, Sevgi Kilic, Elaine Swan, and Lewis Turner. 2006. *Race, Diversity and Leadership in the Learning and Skills Sector: Final Report*. https://www.researchgate.net/publication/242469110_Race_Diversity_and_Leadership_in_the_Learning_and_Skills_Sector.

Ahmed, Sara, and Elaine Swan. 2006. "Doing Diversity." *Policy Futures in Education* 4 (2): 96–100. http://dx.doi.org/10.2304/pfie.2006.4.2.96.

Alcoff, Linda Martin. 1998. "What Should White People Do?" *Hypatia* 13 (3): 6–26. http://dx.doi.org/10.1111/j.1527-2001.1998.tb01367.x.

Andersen, Chris. 1999. "Governing Aboriginal Justice in Canada: Constructing Responsible Individuals and Communities through 'Tradition.'" *Crime, Law, and Social Change* 31 (4): 303–26. http://dx.doi.org/10.1023/A:1008372610195.

Appadurai, Arjun. 1988. *The Social Life of Things: Commodities in Cultural Perspective*. Cambridge: Cambridge University Press.

Auditor General of Canada. 2003. "Chapter 4 – Correctional Service Canada – Reintegration of Women Offenders." In *April 2003 Report of the Auditor General of Canada*. Government of Canada. http://www.oag-bvg.gc.ca/internet/English/parl_oag_200304_04_e_12910.html.

Bannerji, Himani. 2000. *The Dark Side of the Nation: Essays on Multiculturalism, Nationalism and Gender*. Toronto: Canadian Scholars' Press.

Barlow, David E., and Melissa Hickman Barlow. 1993. "Cultural Diversity Training in Criminal Justice: A Progressive or Conservative Reform?" *Social Justice* 20 (3-4): 69–84.

Benschop, Yvonne. 2001. "Pride, Prejudice and Performance: Relations between HRM, Diversity and Performance." *International Journal of Human Resource Management* 12 (7): 1166–81. http://dx.doi.org/10.1080/09585190110068377.

Bertrand, Marie-Andrée. 1999. "Incarceration as a Gendering Strategy." *Canadian Journal of Law and Society* 14 (1): 47–59. http://dx.doi.org/10.1017/S0829320100005925.

Blumstein, Alfred. 2003. "Stability of Punishment: What Happened and What Next?" In *Punishment and Social Control*, 2nd ed., ed. Thomas Blomberg and Stanley Cohen, 255–69. New York: Aldine de Gruyter.

Bosworth, Mary. 1996. "Resistance and Compliance in Women's Prisons: Towards a Critique of Legitimacy." *Critical Criminology* 7 (2): 5–19. http://dx.doi.org/10.1007/BF02461111.

Bosworth, Mary, and Eamonn Carrabine. 2001. "Reassessing Resistance: Race, Gender and Sexuality in Prison." *Punishment and Society* 3 (4): 501–15. http://dx.doi.org/10.1177/14624740122228393.

Bosworth, Mary, B. Bowling, and M. Lee. 2008. "Globalization, Ethnicity and Racism: An Introduction." *Theoretical Criminology* 12 (3): 263–73. http://dx.doi.org/10.1177/1362480608093307.

Brady, Maggie. 1995. "Culture in Treatment, Culture as Treatment: A Critical Appraisal of Developments in Addictions Programs for Indigenous North Americans and Australians." *Social Science & Medicine* 41 (11): 1487–98. http://dx.doi.org/10.1016/0277-9536(95)00055-C.

Bramhall, Gaynor, and Barbara Hudson. 2007. "Criminal Justice and 'Risky' Masculinities." In *Gendered Risks*, ed. Kelly Hannah-Moffat and Pat O'Malley, 127–44. New York: Routledge-Cavendish.

Brayboy, Bryan McKinley Jones. 2003. "The Implementation of Diversity in Predominantly White Colleges and Universities." *Journal of Black Studies* 34 (1): 72–86. http://dx.doi.org/10.1177/0021934703253679.

Britton, Dana. 1997. "Gendered Organizational Logic: Policy and Practice in Men's and Women's Prisons." *Gender & Society* 11 (6): 796–818. http://dx.doi.org/10.1177/089124397011006005.

–. 2000. "The Epistemology of the Gendered Organization." *Gender & Society* 14 (3): 418–34. http://dx.doi.org/10.1177/089124300014003004.

Brown, Mark. 2005. "Liberal Exclusions and the New Punitiveness." In *The New Punitiveness: Trends, Theories, Perspectives*, ed. John Pratt, David Brown, Mark Brown, Simon Hallsworth, and Wayne Morrison, 272-89. Portland: Willan Publishing.

Buchanan, Nicholas, and Eve Darian-Smith. 2011. "Introduction: Law and the Problematics of Indigenous Authenticities." *Law & Social Inquiry* 36 (1): 115–24. http://dx.doi.org/10.1111/j.1747-4469.2010.01225.x.

Canada. 1974. *Parole in Canada: Report of the Standing Senate Committee on Legal and Constitutional Affairs* (Goldenberg Report). Ottawa: Government of Canada.

–. 1982. *The Criminal Law in Canadian Society*. Ottawa: Department of Justice Canada.

–. 1988. *Taking Responsibility: Report of the Standing Committee on Justice and Solicitor General on Its Review of Sentencing, Conditional Release and Related Aspects of Corrections*. Ottawa: Canadian Government Publishing Centre.

–. 1990a. Parliament. House of Commons. Debates, 34th Parliament, 2nd session, vol. 12, November 27, 1990. Ottawa: Canadian Government Publishing.

–. 1990b. *Directions for Reform: A Framework for Sentencing, Corrections and Conditional Release*. Ottawa: Solicitor General of Canada.

–. 1990c. *Directions for Reform in Corrections and Conditional Release*. Ottawa: Solicitor General of Canada.

–. 1990d. *Directions for Reform in Sentencing*. Ottawa: Solicitor General of Canada.

–. 1991. Parliament. House of Commons. Debates, 34th Parliament, 3rd session, vol. 4, November 4, 1991. Ottawa: Canadian Government Publishing.

–. 1995. *Bridging the Cultural Divide: A Report on Aboriginal People and Criminal Justice in Canada. Royal Commission on Aboriginal Peoples*. Ottawa: Canada Communication Group.

–. 1996a. *Report of the Commission of Inquiry into Certain Events at the Prison for Women in Kingston*. Ottawa: Public Works and Government Services Canada.

–. 1996b. *Report of the Royal Commission Aboriginal Peoples*. Ottawa: Ministry of Supply and Services.

–. 1998. *Towards a Just, Peaceful and Safe Society: Consolidated Report – The Corrections and Conditional Release Act Five Years Later, Report of the CCRA Working Group*. Ottawa: Public Works and Government Services Canada.

–. 2000. *The Corrections and Conditional Release Act. Sub-Committee on Corrections and Conditional Release Act of the Standing Committee on Justice and Human Rights*. Ottawa: Communication Canada.

Canadian Corrections Association. 1967. *Indians and the Law*. Ottawa: Department of Indian Affairs and Northern Development.

Canadian Heritage. 2005. *A Canada for All: Canada's Action Plan against Racism*. Ottawa: Department of Canadian Heritage.

Canadian Human Rights Commission. 2003. *Protecting Their Rights: A Systemic Review of Human Rights in Correctional Services for Federally Sentenced Women*. Ottawa: Government of Canada. http://www.chrc-ccdp.ca/eng/content/protecting-their-rights-systemic-review-human-rights-correctional-services-federally.

Caplow, Theodore, and Jonathon Simon. 1999. "Understanding Prison Policy and Population Trends." In *Prisons*, ed. Michael Tonry, Vol. 26: *Crime and Justice: A Review of Research*, 63-120. Chicago: University of Chicago Press.

Carlen, Pat. 1983. *Women's Imprisonment: A Study in Social Control*. London: Routledge.

–. 2002a. "Women's Imprisonment: Cross-National Lessons." In *Women and Punishment: The Struggle for Justice*, ed. Pat Carlen, 138-51. Portland: Willan Publishing.

–. 2002b. "Women's Imprisonment: Models of Reform and Change." *Probation Journal* 49 (2): 76–87. http://dx.doi.org/10.1177/026455050204900202.

–. 2008. "Imaginary Penalities and Risk-Crazed Governance." In *Imaginary Penalities*, ed. Pat Carlen, 1-25. Cullompton, Devon: Willan Publishing.

Carlen, Pat, and Jacqueline Tombs. 2006. "Reconfigurations of Penality: The Ongoing Case of the Women's Imprisonment and Reintegration Industries." *Theoretical Criminology* 10 (3): 337–60. http://dx.doi.org/10.1177/1362480606065910.

CBC News. 2012a. "Haitian-born Murderer to Receive Aboriginal Parole Hearing" (January 17, 2012). http://www.cbc.ca/news/canada/montreal/haitian-born-murderer-to-receive -aboriginal-parole-hearing-1.1165071.

–. 2012b. "Parole Denied for Haitian-born Murderer at Aboriginal Hearing" (January 19, 2012). http://www.cbc.ca/news/canada/montreal/parole-denied-for-haitian-born -murderer-at-aboriginal-hearing-1.1281765.

Chan, Wendy, and George Rigakos. 2002. "Risk, Crime and Gender." *British Journal of Criminology* 42 (4): 743–61. http://dx.doi.org/10.1093/bjc/42.4.743.

Chiu, Daina. 1994. "The Cultural Defense: Beyond Exclusion, Assimilation, and Guilty Liberalism." *California Law Review* 82 (4): 1053–125. http://dx.doi.org/10.2307/ 3480939.

Citizenship and Immigration Canada. 2009. *Annual Report on the Operation of the Canadian Multiculturalism Act, 2007-2008.* Ottawa: Citizenship and Immigration Canada.

Collins, Patricia Hill. 1990. *Black Feminist Thought: Knowledge, Consciousness and the Politics of Empowerment.* New York: Routledge.

Comack, Elizabeth. 2000. "The Prisoning of Women: Meeting Women's Needs." In *An Ideal Prison? Critical Essays on Women's Imprisonment in Canada,* ed. Kelly Hannah-Moffat and Margaret Shaw, 117–27. Halifax: Fernwood.

Comaroff, John, and Jean Comaroff. 2004. "Criminal Justice, Cultural Justice: The Limits of Liberalism and the Pragmatics of Difference in the New South Africa." *American Ethnologist* 31 (2): 188–204. http://dx.doi.org/10.1525/ae.2004.31.2.188.

Corcoran, Mary S. 2010. "Snakes and Ladders: Women's Imprisonment and Official Reform Discourse under New Labour." *Current Issues in Criminal Justice* 22 (2): 233–51.

Correctional Service of Canada (CSC). 2009a. "Strategic Plan for Aboriginal Corrections: Innovation, Learning and Adjustment, 2006-07 to 2010-11." Ottawa: Correctional Service of Canada. http://www.csc-scc.gc.ca/aboriginal/002003-1001-eng.shtml.

–. 2009b. "Ethnocultural Initiatives." http://www.csc-scc.gc.ca/ethnoculture/index-engs. html.

–. 2010a. "Reintegration Programs for Women Offenders." PowerPoint presentation. Doris Fortin, Correctional Service of Canada. Obtained through ATI request no. A-2010 -00038 to the PBC.

–. 2010b. "Women Offenders." PowerPoint presentation. Kelly Taylor, Correctional Ser- vice of Canada. Obtained through ATI request no. A-2010-00038 to the PBC.

Correctional Service of Canada and Parole Board of Canada (CSC-PBC). n.d. "Pacific Region Ethnocultural Advisory Committee: Terms of Reference." Obtained through ATI request no. A-2010-00033 to the PBC.

Cowlishaw, Gillian. 2003. "Disappointing Indigenous People: Violence and the Refusal of Help." *Public Culture* 15 (1): 130–25. http://dx.doi.org/10.1215/08992363-15-1-103.

Crenshaw, Kimberle. 1991. "Mapping the Margins: Intersectionality, Identity Politics, and Violence against Women of Color." *Stanford Law Review* 43 (6): 1241–99. http://dx.doi. org/10.2307/1229039.

Cunneen, Chris. 2006. "Racism, Discrimination and the Over-Representation of Indigen- ous People in the Criminal Justice System: Some Conceptual and Explanatory Issues." *Current Issues in Criminal Justice* 17 (3): 329–46.

–. 2009. "Indigenous Incarceration: The Violence of Colonial Law and Justice." In *The Violence of Incarceration,* ed. Phil Scraton and Jude McCulloch, 209–24. New York: Routledge.

Day, Andrew. 2003. "Reducing the Risk of Re-Offending in Australian Indigenous Offenders: What Works for Whom?" *Journal of Offender Rehabilitation* 37 (2): 1–15. http://dx.doi.org/10.1300/J076v37n02_01.

Day, Andrew, Kevin Howells, and Sharon Casey. 2003. "The Rehabilitation of Indigenous Prisoners: An Australian Perspective." *Journal of Ethnicity in Criminal Justice* 1 (1): 115–33. http://dx.doi.org/10.1300/J222v01n01_06.

Deckha, Maneesha. 2004. "Is Culture Taboo? Feminism, Intersectionality, and Culture Talk in Law." *Canadian Journal of Women and the Law* 16 (1): 14–53.

Dhamoon, Rita. 2009. *Identity/Difference Politics: How Difference Is Produced, and Why It Matters.* Vancouver: UBC Press.

Dobbin, Frank, Soohan Kim, and Alexandra Kalev. 2011. "You Can't Always Get What You Need: Organizational Determinants of Diversity Programs." *American Sociological Review* 76 (3): 386–411. http://dx.doi.org/10.1177/0003122411409704.

Dyck, Noel. 1991. "Tutelage and the Politics of Aboriginality: A Canadian Dilemma." *Ethnos* 56 (1): 39–52. http://dx.doi.org/10.1080/00141844.1991.9981423.

Edelman, Lauren, Sally Riggs Fuller, and Iona Mara-Drita. 2001. "Diversity Rhetoric and the Managerialization of Law." *American Journal of Sociology* 106 (6): 1589–641. http://dx.doi.org/10.1086/321303.

Edney, Richard. 2002. "Indigenous Punishment in Australia: A Jurisprudence of Pain?" *International Journal of the Sociology of Law* 30 (3): 219–34. http://dx.doi.org/10.1016/S0194-6595(02)00026-6.

Ekstedt, John, and Curt Griffiths. 1988. *Corrections in Canada: Policy and Practice.* Toronto: Butterworth.

Ericson, Richard, and Kevin Haggerty. 1997. *Policing the Risk Society.* Toronto: University of Toronto Press.

Eveline, Joan, Carol Bacchi, and Jennifer Binns. 2009. "Gender Mainstreaming versus Diversity Mainstreaming: Methodology as Emancipatory Politics." *Gender, Work and Organization* 16 (2): 198–216. http://dx.doi.org/10.1111/j.1468-0432.2008.00427.x.

Faith, Karlene. 1995. "Aboriginal Women's Healing Lodge: Challenge to Penal Correctionalism?" *Journal of Human Justice* 6 (2): 79–104. http://dx.doi.org/10.1007/BF02585445.

–. 1999. "Transformative Justice versus Re-entrenched Correctionalism: The Canadian Experience." In *Harsh Punishment: International Experiences of Women's Imprisonment,* ed. Sandy Cook and Susanne Davies, 99–122. Boston: Northeastern University Press.

Feeley, Malcolm, and Jonathon Simon. 1992. "The New Penology: Notes on the Emerging Strategy of Corrections and its Implications." *Criminology* 30 (4): 449–74. http://dx.doi.org/10.1111/j.1745-9125.1992.tb01112.x.

–. 1994 "Actuarial Justice: The Emerging New Criminal Law." In *The Futures of Criminology,* ed. David Nelken, 173–201. London: Sage.

Flavin, Jeanne, and Mary Bosworth. 2007. "Epilogue: Humanizing Difference – Toward a New Penality." In *Race, Gender, and Punishment: From Colonialism to the War on Terror,* ed. Mary Bosworth and Jeanne Flavin, 216–23. Piscataway, NJ: Rutgers University Press.

Fournier, Pascale. 2002. "The Ghettoisation of Difference in Canada: 'Rape by Culture' and the Danger of a 'Cultural Defence' in Criminal Law Trials." *Manitoba Law Journal* 29 (1): 81–119.

Garland, David. 1990. *Punishment and Modern Society: A Study in Social Theory.* Chicago: University of Chicago Press. http://dx.doi.org/10.7208/chicago/9780226922508.001.0001.

–. 1996. "The Limits of the Sovereign State: Strategies of Crime Control in Contemporary Society." *British Journal of Criminology* 36 (4): 445–71. http://dx.doi.org/10.1093/oxfordjournals.bjc.a014105.

–. 2001. *Culture of Control: Crime and Social Order in Contemporary Society*. Chicago: University of Chicago Press.

–. 2003a. "Penal Modernism and Postmodernism." In *Punishment and Social Control*, 2nd ed., ed. Thomas Blomberg and Stanley Cohen, 45–73. New York: Aldine de Gruyter.

–. 2003b. "The Rise of Risk." In *Risk and Morality*, ed. Richard Ericson and Aaron Doyle, 48–86. Toronto: University of Toronto Press.

Garroutte, Eva Marie. 2003. *Real Indians: Identity and the Survival of Native America*. Berkeley: University of California Press.

Giroday, Gabrielle. 2012. "Haitian-born Killer Denied Parole in Aboriginal Hearing" (January 19, 2012). *National Post*. http://news.nationalpost.com/2012/01/19/haitian-born-killer-denied-parole-in-aboriginal-hearing/.

Giroday, Gabrielle, and Katherine Wilton. 2012. "Parole Hearing 'Grave Disrespect'" (January 19, 2012). *Winnipeg Free Press*. http://www.winnipegfreepress.com/local/parole-hearing-grave-disrespect-137654963.html.

Goldberg, David. 1993. *Racist Culture: Philosophy and the Politics of Meaning*. Oxford: Blackwell Publishers.

Grabham, Emily, Davina Cooper, Jane Krishnadas, and Didi Herman, eds. 2009. *Intersectionality and Beyond: Law, Power and the Politics of Location*. London: Routledge Cavendish.

Griffiths, Curt. 1988. "Canadian Corrections: Policy and Practice North of 49°." *Prison Journal* 68 (1): 51–62. http://dx.doi.org/10.1177/003288558806800107.

Hallsworth, Simon. 2005. "Modernity and the Punitive." In *The New Punitiveness: Trends, Theories, Perspectives*, ed. John Pratt, David Brown, Mark Brown, Simon Hallsworth, and Wayne Morrison, 239–55. Portland: Willan Publishing.

Haney, Lynne. 2004. "Introduction: Gender, Welfare, and States of Punishment." *Social Politics* 11 (3): 333–62. http://dx.doi.org/10.1093/sp/jxh040.

Hannah-Moffat, Kelly. 1995. "Feminine Fortresses: Women Centred Prisons?" *Prison Journal* 75 (2): 135–64. http://dx.doi.org/10.1177/0032855595075002002.

–. 1999. "Moral Agent or Actuarial Subject: Risk and Canadian Women's Imprisonment." *Theoretical Criminology* 3 (1): 71–94. http://dx.doi.org/10.1177/1362480699003001004.

–. 2001. *Punishment in Disguise: Penal Governance and Federal Imprisonment of Women in Canada*. Toronto: University of Toronto Press.

–. 2002. "Creating Choices: Reflecting on Choices." In *Women and Punishment: The Struggle for Justice*, ed. Pat Carlen, 199–219. Cullumpton, Devon: Willian Publishing.

–. 2004a. "Losing Ground: Gendered Knowledges, Parole Risk, and Responsibility." *Social Politics* 11 (3): 363–85. http://dx.doi.org/10.1093/sp/jxh041.

–. 2004b. "Gendering Risk at What Cost: Negotiations of Gender and Risk in Canadian Women's Prisons." *Feminism & Psychology* 14 (2): 243–49.

–. 2005. "Criminogenic Needs and the Transformative Risk Subject." *Punishment and Society* 7 (1): 29–51. http://dx.doi.org/10.1177/1462474505048132.

–. 2007. "Gendering Dynamic Risk: Assessing and Managing the Maternal Identities of Women Prisoners." In *Gendered Risks*, ed. Kelly Hannah-Moffat and Pat O'Malley, 229–47. New York: Routledge-Cavendish.

–. 2008. "Re-Imagining Gendered Penalties: The Myth of Gender Responsivity." In *Imaginary Penalities*, ed. Pat Carlen, 193–217. Cullompton, Devon: Willan Publishing.

–. 2009. "Gridlock or Mutability: Reconsidering 'Gender' and Risk Assessment." *Criminology & Public Policy* 8 (1): 221–29.

–. 2010. "Sacrosanct or Flawed: Risk, Accountability and Gender-Responsive Penal Politics." *Current Issues in Criminal Justice* 22 (2): 193–215.

Hannah-Moffat, Kelly, and Pat O'Malley, eds. 2007. *Gendered Risks*. New York: Routledge-Cavendish.

Hannah-Moffat, Kelly, and Paula Maurutto. 2010. "Re-Contextualizing Pre-Sentence Reports: Risk and Race." *Punishment and Society* 12 (3): 262–86. http://dx.doi.org/10.1177/1462474510369442.

Hannah-Moffat, Kelly, and Margaret Shaw. 2000. "Introduction: Prisons for Women: Theory, Reform, Ideals." In *An Ideal Prison? Critical Essays on Women's Imprisonment in Canada*, ed. Kelly Hannah-Moffat and Margaret Shaw, 11–27. Halifax: Fernwood.

Harcourt, Bernard. 2007. *Against Prediction: Profiling, Policing, and Punishing in the Actuarial Age*. Chicago: University of Chicago Press.

Haslip, Susan. 2002. "The (Re)Introduction of Restorative Justice in Kahnawake: 'Beyond Indigenization.'" *E Law: Murdoch University Electronic Journal of Law* 9 (1): 1–61. http://www.murdoch.edu.au/elaw/issues/v9n1/haslip91.html.

Hayman, Stephanie. 2006. *Imprisoning Our Sisters: The New Federal Women's Prisons in Canada*. Montreal, Kingston: McGill-Queen's University Press.

Hedderman, Carol. 2010. "Government Policy on Women Offenders: Labour's Legacy and the Coalition's Challenge." *Punishment and Society* 12 (4): 485–500. http://dx.doi.org/10.1177/1462474510385965.

Herring, Cedric. 2009. "Does Diversity Pay? Race, Gender, and the Business Case for Diversity." *American Sociological Review* 74 (2): 208–24. http://dx.doi.org/10.1177/000312240907400203.

hooks, bell. 1981. *Ain't I a Woman*. Boston: South End Press.

–. 1992. *Black Looks: Race and Representation*. Toronto: Between the Lines.

Hopper, Tristan, and Katherine Wilton. 2012. "Haitian-Born Killer Granted Aboriginal Parole Hearing" (January 17, 2012). *National Post*. http://news.nationalpost.com/2012/01/17/haitian-born-killer-granted-aboriginal-parole-hearing/.

Houchin, Robert. 2003. "Significant Change Is Likely in Our Prisons: The Question Is, Change in What Direction?" *Probation Journal* 50 (2): 142–8. http://dx.doi.org/10.1177/0264550503502005.

Howe, Adrian. 1994. *Punish and Critique: Towards a Feminist Analysis of Penality*. New York: Routledge.

Hudson, Barbara. 1993. "Racism and Criminology: Concepts and Controversies." In *Racism and Criminology*, ed. Dee Cook and Barbara Hudson, 1–27. London: Sage.

–. 2002. "Gender Issues in Penal Policy and Penal Theory." In *Women and Punishment: The Struggle for Justice*, ed. Pat Carlen, 21–46. Portland: Willan Publishing.

–. 2003. *Justice in the Risk Society: Challenging and Re-Affirming Justice in Late Modernity*. London: Sage.

–. 2008a. "Difference, Diversity and Criminology: The Cosmopolitan Vision." *Theoretical Criminology* 12 (3): 275–92. http://dx.doi.org/10.1177/1362480608093609.

–. 2008b. "Re-Imagining Justice: Principles of Justice for Divided Societies in a Globalised World." In *Imaginary Penalities*, ed. Pat Carlen, 275–93. Cullompton, Devon: Willan Publishing.

Hudson, Barbara, and Gaynor Bramhall. 2005. "Assessing the 'Other': Constructions of 'Asianness' in Risk Assessments by Probation Officers." *British Journal of Criminology* 45 (5): 721–40. http://dx.doi.org/10.1093/bjc/azi002.

Hunter, Shona. 2010. "What a White Shame: Race, Gender, and White Shame in the Relational Economy of Primary Health Care Organizations in England." *Social Politics* 17 (4): 450–76. http://dx.doi.org/10.1093/sp/jxq015.

Hyndman, Jennifer. 1998. "Managing Difference: Gender and Culture in Humanitarian Emergencies." *Gender, Place and Culture* 5 (3): 241–60. http://dx.doi.org/10.1080/09663699825197.

Jaccoud, Mylène, and Maritza Felices. 1999. "Ethnicization of the Police in Canada." *Canadian Journal of Law and Society* 83 (1): 83–100. http://dx.doi.org/10.1017/S0829 320100005949.

Jackson, Michael. 1988. *Locking Up Natives in Canada: A Report of the Committee of the Canadian Bar Association on Imprisonment and Release*. Ottawa: Canadian Bar Association.

–. 2002. *Justice behind the Walls: Human Rights in Canadian Prisons*. Vancouver: Douglas and McIntyre.

Jhappan, Radha. 1998. "The Equality Pit or the Rehabilitation of Justice." *Canadian Journal of Women and the Law* 10 (1): 60–107.

Kalev, Alexandra, Erin Kelly, and Frank Dobbin. 2006. "Best Practices or Best Guesses? Assessing the Efficacy of Corporate Affirmative Action and Diversity Policies." *American Sociological Review* 71 (4): 589–617. http://dx.doi.org/10.1177/000312240607100404.

Kemshall, Hazel. 2003. *Understanding Risk in Criminal Justice*. Maidenhead: Open University Press.

Kramar, Kirsten, and David Sealy. 2006. "Cultural Difference and Criminal Sentencing: Critical Reflections on *R. v. Gladue* and *R. v. Hamilton*." In *Locating Law: Race/Class/Gender/Sexuality Connections*, 2nd ed., ed. Elizabeth Comack, 123–45. Halifax: Fernwood.

Kruttschnitt, Candace, and Rosemary Gartner. 2003. "Women's Imprisonment." In *Crime and Justice*, ed. Michael Tonry, Vol. 30: *A Review of Research*, 1–81. Chicago: University of Chicago Press.

–. 2005. *Marking Time in the Golden State: Women's Imprisonment in California*. Cambridge: Cambridge University Press.

Kymlicka, Will. 2007. *Multicultural Odysseys: Navigating the New International Politics of Diversity*. Oxford: Oxford University Press.

LaPrairie, Carol. 1996. "Examining Aboriginal Corrections in Canada." Ottawa: Solicitor General of Canada. http://www.publicsafety.gc.ca/cnt/rsrcs/pblctns/xmnng-brgnl -crrctns/index-eng.aspx.

LaRocque, Emma. 1997. "Re-Examining Culturally Appropriate Models in Criminal Justice Applications." In *Aboriginal and Treaty Rights in Canada: Essays on Law, Equity, and Respect for Difference*, ed. Michael Asch, 75–96. Vancouver: UBC Press.

Larsen, Mike, and Justin Piché. 2009. "Exceptional State, Pragmatic Bureaucracy, and Indefinite Detention: The Case of the Kingston Immigration Holding Centre." *Canadian Journal of Law and Society* 24 (2): 203–29. http://dx.doi.org/10.1017/S0829320100009911.

Lawrence, Sonia. 2001. "Cultural (in)Sensitivity: The Dangers of a Simplistic Approach to Culture in the Courtroom." *Canadian Journal of Women and the Law* 13 (1): 107–36.

Maidment, MaDonna. 2006. *Doing Time on the Outside: Deconstructing the Benevolent Community*. Toronto: University of Toronto Press.

Malkki, Liisa. 1992. "National Geographic: The Rooting of Peoples and the Territorialization of National Identity among Scholars and Refugees." *Cultural Anthropology* 7 (1): 24–44. http://dx.doi.org/10.1525/can.1992.7.1.02a00030.

Marie, Dannette. 2010. "Maori and Criminal Offending: A Critical Appraisal." *Australian and New Zealand Journal of Criminology* 43 (2): 282–300. http://dx.doi.org/10.1375/acri.43.2.282.

Marleau, Robert, and Camille Montpetit. 2000. "House of Commons Procedure and Practice." Ottawa: Parliament of Canada. http://www.parl.gc.ca/MarleauMontpetit/.

Martel, Joane, and Renée Brassard. 2008. "Painting the Prison 'Red': Constructing and Experiencing Aboriginal Identities in Prison." *British Journal of Social Work* 38 (2): 340–61. http://dx.doi.org/10.1093/bjsw/bcl335.

Martel, Joane, Renée Brassard, and Mylène Jaccoud. 2011. "When Two Worlds Collide: Aboriginal Risk Management in Canadian Corrections." *British Journal of Criminology* 51 (2): 235–55. http://dx.doi.org/10.1093/bjc/azr003.

Maurutto, Paula, and Kelly Hannah-Moffat. 2006. "Assembling Risk and the Restructuring of Penal Control." *British Journal of Criminology* 46 (3): 438–54. http://dx.doi.org/10.1093/bjc/azi073.

McCorkel, Jill. 2004. "Criminally Dependent? Gender, Punishment, and the Rhetoric of Welfare Reform." *Social Politics* 11 (3): 386–410. http://dx.doi.org/10.1093/sp/jxh042.

McIntosh, Peggy. 1992. "White Privilege and Male Privilege: A Personal Account of Coming to See Correspondences through Work in Women's Studies." In *Race, Class and Gender: An Anthology*, ed. Margaret Anderson and Patricia Hill Collins, 70–81. Belmont, CA: Wadsworth Publishing.

McKim, Allison. 2008. "'Getting Gut Level': Punishment, Gender, and Therapeutic Governance." *Gender & Society* 22 (3): 303–23. http://dx.doi.org/10.1177/0891243208317826.

McMillan, L. Jane. 2011. "Colonial Traditions, Co-optations, and Mi'kmaq Legal Consciousness." *Law & Social Inquiry* 36 (1): 171–200. http://dx.doi.org/10.1111/j.1747-4469.2010.01228.x.

McPhail, Alison. 1999. "The Development of Corrections and Conditional Release Act." Paper presented at the Changing Punishment at the Turn of the Century: Finding a Common Ground Conference, September 26-29, 1999, Saskatoon, Saskatchewan.

Mills, Sara. 1997. *Discourse*. New York: Routledge.

Minow, Martha. 1990. *Making all the Difference: Inclusion, Exclusion and American Law.* Ithaca, NY: Cornell University Press.

Mohanram, Radhika. 1999. *Black Body: Women, Colonialism, and Space*. Minneapolis: University of Minnesota Press.

Monture, Patricia. 2006. "Standing against Canadian Law: Naming Omissions of Race, Culture, and Gender." In *Locating Law: Race/Class/Gender/Sexuality Connections*, ed. Elizabeth Comack, 73–93. Halifax: Fernwood.

Monture-Angus, Patricia. 1999. "Women and Risk: Aboriginal Women, Colonialism, and Correctional Practice." *Canadian Women's Studies* 19 (1/2): 24–29.

Moore, Dawn. 2008. "Feminist Criminology: Gain, Loss and Backlash." *Sociology Compass* 2 (1): 48–61. http://dx.doi.org/10.1111/j.1751-9020.2007.00052.x.

Morash, Merry. 2010. *Women on Probation and Parole: A Feminist Critique of Community Programs and Services*. Lebanon, NH: Northeastern University Press.

Morash, Merry, Robin Haarr, and Lila Rucker. 1994. "A Comparison of Programming for Women and Men in U.S. Prisons in the 1980s." *Crime and Delinquency* 40 (2): 197–221. http://dx.doi.org/10.1177/0011128794040002004.

Murdocca, Carmella. 2007. "Incarcerating Culture Difference: Race, National Responsibility and Criminal Sentencing." PhD diss., University of Toronto.

–. 2009. "From Incarceration to Restoration: National Responsibility, Gender and the Production of Cultural Difference." *Social & Legal Studies* 18 (1): 23–45. http://dx.doi.org/10.1177/0964663908100332.

–. 2013. *To Right Historical Wrongs: Race, Gender, and Sentencing in Canada.* Vancouver: UBC Press.

Nelson, Jennifer. 2002. "The Space of Africville: Creating, Regulating, and Remembering the Urban 'Slum.'" In *Race, Space, and the Law: Unmapping a White Settler Society*, ed. Sherene Razack, 211–32. Toronto: Between the Lines.

Nielsen, Marianne. 2003. "Canadian Aboriginal Healing Lodges: A Model for the United States?" *Prison Journal* 83 (1): 67–89. http://dx.doi.org/10.1177/0032885502250394.

Nightingale, Margo. 1991. "Judicial Attitudes and Differential Treatment: Native Women in Sexual Assault Cases." *Ottawa Law Review* 23 (1): 71–98.

O'Connell, Anne. 2010. "An Exploration of Redneck Whiteness in Multicultural Canada." *Social Politics* 17 (4): 536–63. http://dx.doi.org/10.1093/sp/jxq019.

O'Connor, Fergus. 1985. "The Impact of the Canadian Charter of Rights and Freedoms on Parole in Canada." *Queen's Law Journal* 10: 336–91.

Office of the Correctional Investigator of Canada (OCI). 2000. *Annual Report of the Office of the Correctional Investigator, 1999-2000.* Ottawa: Public Works and Government Services Canada. http://www.oci-bec.gc.ca/cnt/rpt/annrpt/annrpt19992000-eng.aspx.

–. 2001. *Annual Report of the Office of the Correctional Investigator, 2000-2001.* Ottawa: Public Works and Government Services Canada. http://www.oci-bec.gc.ca/cnt/rpt/annrpt/annrpt20002001-eng.aspx.

–. 2006. *Annual Report of the Office of the Correctional Investigator, 2005-2006.* Ottawa: Public Works and Government Services Canada. http://www.oci-bec.gc.ca/cnt/rpt/pdf/annrpt/annrpt20052006-eng.pdf.

–. 2009a. *Good Intentions, Disappointing Results: A Progress Report on Federal Aboriginal Corrections.* Ottawa: Public Works and Government Services Canada. http://www.oci-bec.gc.ca/cnt/rpt/pdf/oth-aut/oth-aut20091113-eng.pdf.

–. 2009b. *Annual Report of the Office of the Correctional Investigator, 2008-2009.* Ottawa: Public Works and Government Services Canada. http://www.oci-bec.gc.ca/cnt/rpt/annrpt/annrpt20082009-eng.aspx.

–. 2014. *Annual Report of the Office of the Correctional Investigator, 2013-2014.* Ottawa: The Correctional Investigator Canada. http://www.oci-bec.gc.ca/cnt/rpt/annrpt/annrpt20132014-eng.aspx.

O'Malley. Pat. 1999. "Volatile and Contradictory Punishment." *Theoretical Criminology* 3 (2): 175-96.

–. 2004. *Risk, Uncertainty and Government.* London: Glasshouse Press.

Parole Board of Canada (PBC). 1996. *The National Parole Board Corporate Policy on Aboriginal Offenders.* Ottawa: Parole Board of Canada.

–. 2000a. "Aboriginal Issues and the National Parole Board: A Discussion Paper on Where We Are At, Where We Need to Go, and What We Need to Do to Get There" (October 2000), Diversity Issues. Obtained through ATI request no. A-2009-00017 to the PBC.

–. 2000b. *Evaluation of the National Parole Board's Elder Assisted Hearing Approach: Final Report.* Ottawa: Parole Board of Canada.

–. 2000c. "Restorative Justice and the National Parole Board: A Discussion Paper on Policy Implications and Implementation Strategies" (February 2000), Policy, Planning and Operations. Obtained through ATI request no. A-2010-00006 to the PBC.

–. 2001. [title unknown] Myaat Wteeh Consulting. Obtained through ATI request no. A-2009-00022 to the PBC.

–. 2002a. "NWT Meeting" (November 4 & 5, 2002), Aboriginal Unit. Obtained through ATI request no. A-2009-00017 to the PBC.

–. 2002b. "National Parole Board – Prairie Region Evaluation: Community Assisted Hearings" (March 2002). Obtained through ATI request no. A-2009-00017 to the PBC.

–. 2002c. *Report of the Stakeholders' Meeting on the Development of a National Parole Board Corporate Strategy for Federally Sentenced Women.* Ottawa: Parole Board of Canada.

–. 2002d. "The National Parole Board's Federally Sentenced Women's Consultation Report: A Discussion Paper." Ottawa: Parole Board of Canada.

–. 2003a. "Alternatives Models to National Parole Board Hearings" (October 2003), Prairie Region. Obtained through ATI request no. A-2010-00006 to the PBC.

–. 2003b. *Parole and Federally Sentenced Women: National Parole Board Commitments.* Ottawa: Parole Board of Canada.

–. 2004a. *Evaluation Report for the National Parole Board's Effective Corrections and Citizen Engagement Initiatives, 2000-2003.* http://pbc-clcc.gc.ca/rprts/rprt-eng.shtml.

–. 2004b. "Inuit Hearing Model for Inuit Offenders in the Federal Institutes of Canada" by Mary Alainga. Obtained through ATI request no. A-2009-00022 to the PBC.

–. 2004c. *Policy Circular, No. 2004-3.* Ottawa: Parole Board of Canada.

–. 2004d. "Aboriginal and Diversity Initiatives Regional Conference Call" (June 2, 2004). Obtained through ATI request no. A-2009-00017 to the PBC.

–. 2005a. "Diversity Committee Terms of Reference" (August 19, 2005), Ontario Region. Obtained through ATI request no. A-2010-00033 to the PBC.

–. 2005b. "The Aboriginal Circle: Role, Vision, and Priorities" (March 2005). Obtained through ATI request no. A-2010-00030 to the PBC.

–. 2005c. "Needs Analysis – Ethnic Minority Clientele" (February 2005), by BDL, Conseillers en Administration Inc. Obtained through ATI request no. A-2010-00022 to the PBC.

–. 2005e. "Review of the Parole Needs of Ethnocultural Offenders" (March 2005), by Primexcel Consultants. Obtained through ATI request no. A-2010-00022 to the PBC.

– 2005f. "Ethno-Cultural Community Forums Final Report" (March 31, 2005). Obtained through ATI request no. A-2009-00017 to the PBC.

–. 2005g. "Ethnocultural Consultation" (March 2005), Aboriginal and Diversity Initiatives. Obtained through ATI request no. A-2009-00017 to the PBC.

–. 2006a. "Elder-Assisted Hearings: An Historical Perspective" (February 2006), Aboriginal and Diversity Initiatives. Obtained through ATI request no. A-2009-00010 to the PBC.

–. 2006b. "Cultural Hearings Working Group, Phase II: Current Position" (February 2006), Aboriginal and Diversity Initiatives. Obtained through ATI request no. A-2010-00006 to the PBC.

–. 2006c. "Cultural Hearings Working Group, Meeting Report, February 20-21, 2006" (March 2006). Obtained through ATI request no. A-2009-00017 to the PBC.

–. 2007a. *Aboriginal and Diversity Initiatives Newsletter* 1 (1). Obtained through ATI request no. AI-2009-00001 to the PBC.

–. 2007b. *Performance Monitoring Report, 2006-2007.* Ottawa: Parole Board of Canada. http://pbc-clcc.gc.ca/rprts/pmr/pmr_2006_2007/index-eng.shtml.

–. 2007c. "From Confinement to Community: The National Parole Board and Aboriginal Offenders." Obtained through ATI request no. A-2009-00010 to the PBC.

–. 2007d. *Aboriginal Perceptions Training: Participant Workbook* (October 2007). Professional Development and Decision Processes. Obtained through ATI request no. A-2009-00018 to the PBC.

–. 2007e. "Community-Assisted Hearings General Guidelines" (June 1, 2007), Prairie Region. Obtained through ATI request no. A-2009-00010 to the PBC.

–. 2007f. "2006-2007 Year End Report" (March 31, 2007), Female Offender Committee, Atlantic Region. Obtained through ATI request no. A-2010-00032 to the PBC.

–. 2008a. *Performance Monitoring Report, 2007-2008*. Ottawa: Parole Board of Canada. http://pbc-clcc.gc.ca/rprts/pmr/pmr_2007_2008/inex-eng.shtml.

–. 2008b. *Aboriginal and Diversity Initiatives Newsletter* 1(2). Obtained through ATI request no. AI-2009-00003 to the PBC.

–. 2008c. *Aboriginal and Diversity Initiatives Newsletter* 1(3). Obtained through ATI request no. AI-2009-00003 to the PBC.

–. 2008d. "Assessment of the Operations, Efficiency and Effectiveness of the Aboriginal Circle" (March 31, 2008) by Sussex Circle Inc. Obtained through ATI request no. A-2009-00018 to the PBC.

–. 2008e. "National Parole Board Evaluation of Board Member Training," by Richard Rittenberg, Whitehaven Associates. Obtained through ATI request no. A-2010-00031 to the PBC.

–. 2008f. "National Parole Board Interpretation Project Report" (March 2008), Aboriginal and Diversity Initiatives. Obtained through ATI request no. A-2009-00017 to the PBC.

– 2009a. *Diversity Committee Newsletter* (January-March 2009). Prairie Region. Obtained through ATI request no. A-2009-00010 to the PBC.

–. 2009b. "Vision 2020 – Public Safety, Public Service." http://pbc-clcc.gc.ca/infocntr/vision2020-eng.shtml.

–. 2009c. "Board Member Orientation Week, National Office Week" (PowerPoint presentation) (June 1-12, 2009), Aboriginal and Diversity Initiatives. Obtained through ATI request no. A-2009-00009 to the PBC.

–. 2009d. "Aboriginal Circle Terms of Reference" (February 2009). Obtained through ATI request no. A-2010-00033 to the PBC.

–. 2009e. *Performance Monitoring Report, 2008-2009*. Ottawa: Parole Board of Canada. http://pbc-clcc.gc.ca/rprts/pmr/pmr_2008_2009/index-eng.shtml.

–. 2009f. "Aboriginal and Diversity Initiatives" (PowerPoint presentation). Obtained through ATI request no. A-2009-00009 to the PBC.

–. 2009g. "Elder Assisted Hearings [and] Community Assisted Hearings Protocol" (PowerPoint presentation) (March 2, 2009), Aboriginal and Diversity Unit, Prairie Region. Obtained through ATI request no. A-2009-00010 to the PBC.

–. 2009h. "National Parole Board Prairie Region Elder-Assisted Hearings General Guidelines" (February 5, 2009). Obtained through ATI request no. A-2009-00010 to the PBC.

–. 2009i. "Offenders from Ethnocultural Minority Background and the NPB Hearing Process: Exploring Issues with NPB Staff and Board Members" (April 2009), by Gentium Consulting. Obtained through ATI request no. A-2009-00020 to the PBC.

–. 2009j. "Interpreter-Assisted National Parole Board Hearings: Tips for NPB Members" (March 2009), by Gentium Consulting. Obtained through ATI request no. A-2009-00020 to the PBC.

–. 2009k. "2008-2009 Year End Report" (March 31, 2009), Female Offender Committee, Atlantic Region. Obtained through ATI request no. A-2010-00032 to the PBC.

–. 2010a. "Fact Sheet: Types of Release." http://pbc-clcc.gc.ca/infocntr/factsh/rls-eng.shtml.

–. 2010b. "From Confinement to Community." http://www.pbc-clcc.gc.ca/infocntr/cc-eng.shtml.

–. 2010c. "Aboriginal and Diversity Initiatives." http://pbc-clcc.gc.ca/infocntr/ethno-eng.shtml.

–. 2010d. *Performance Monitoring Report, 2009-2010*. http://pbc-clcc.gc.ca/rprts/pmr/pmr_2009_2010/index-eng.shtml.

–. 2010e. "Mission." http://pbc-clcc.gc.ca/about/miss-eng.shtml.

–. 2010f. "Aboriginal Circle Hearings" (August 2010), Ontario and Nunavut Region. Obtained through ATI request no. A-2010-00034 to the PBC.

–. 2010g. "Guidelines for Elder Assisted Hearings," Atlantic Region. Obtained through ATI request no. A-2010-00034 to the PBC.

–. 2010h. "The *Canadian Multiculturalism Act*." http://pbc-clcc.gc.ca/infocntr/multi-eng.shtml.

– 2010i. "2009-2010 Year End Report" (March 31, 2009), Female Offender Committee, Atlantic Region. Obtained through ATI request no. A-2010-00032 to the PBC.

–. 2011a. "Overview." http://pbc-clcc.gc.ca/about/abt-eng.shtml.

–. 2011b. "PBC Board Member (GIC) Qualification Process Overview." http://pbc-clcc.gc.ca/employ/gicqual-eng.shtml.

–. 2011c. "NPB Policy Manual 1(18)" (electronic version).

–. 2015. "Decision-Making Policy Manual for Board Members, 2nd ed., no. 04 – 2015-07-23." http://pbc-clcc.gc.ca/infocntr/policym/polman-eng.shtml.

–. n.d.-a. "*R. v. Gladue*." Obtained via ATI request no. A-2010-00008 to the PBC.

–. n.d.-b. "Community Outreach." Obtained through ATI request no. A-2009-00017 to the PBC.

–. n.d.-c. "Module 1 – Diversity in Offender Population and Other Considerations." Obtained through ATI request no. A-2009-00009 to the PBC.

–. n.d.-d. *The National Parole Board Prairie Region Elder Reference Manual*. Obtained through ATI request no. A-2009-00010 to the PBC.

–. n.d.-e. "Inclusive Institutions Initiative Performance Reporting: A Guide for Project Partners." Obtained through ATI request no. A-2009-00020 to the PBC.

–. n.d.-f. "NPB – Country Insights – Pakistan." Obtained through ATI request no. A-2010-00006 to the PBC.

–. n.d.-g. "NPB – Country Insights – Vietnam." Obtained through ATI request no. A-2010-00006 to the PBC.

–. n.d.-h. "NPB – Country Insights – China." Obtained through ATI request no. A-2010-00006 to the PBC.

–. n.d.-i. "NPB – Country Insights – Jamaica." Obtained through ATI request no. A-2010-00006 to the PBC.

Pavlich, George. 1996a. *Justice Fragmented: Mediating Community Disputes under Post-Modern Conditions*. London: Routledge. http://dx.doi.org/10.4324/9780203428368.

–. 1996b. "The Power of Community Mediation: Government and Formation of Self-Identity." *Law & Society Review* 30 (4): 707–33. http://dx.doi.org/10.2307/3054115.

–. 2005. *Governing Paradoxes of Restorative Justice*. London: Glasshouse Press.

Pelletier, Renée. 2001. "The Nullification of Section 718.2(e): Aggravating Aboriginal Over-representation in Canadian Prisons." *Osgoode Hall Law Journal* 39 (2/3): 469–89.

Petersilia, Joan. 2003. *When Prisoners Come Home: Parole and Prisoner Re-entry*. New York: Oxford University Press.

Phillips, Coretta. 2007. "The Re-emergence of the 'Black Spectre': Minority Professional Associations in the Post-Macpherson Era." *Ethnic and Racial Studies* 30 (3): 375–96. http://dx.doi.org/10.1080/01419870701217431.

–. 2011. "Institutional Racism and Ethnic Inequalities: An Expanded Multilevel Framework." *Journal of Social Policy* 40 (1): 173–92. http://dx.doi.org/10.1017/S004727941 0000565.

Phillips, Coretta, and Benjamin Bowling. 2003. "Racism, Ethnicity and Criminology: Developing Minority Perspectives." *British Journal of Criminology* 43 (2): 269–90. http://dx.doi.org/10.1093/bjc/43.2.269.

Pollack, Shoshana. 2005. "Taming the Shrew: Regulating Prisoners through Women-Centred Mental Health Programming." *Critical Criminology* 13 (1): 71–87. http://dx.doi.org/10.1007/s10612-004-6168-5.

–. 2007. "'I'm Just Not Good in Relationships': Victimization Discourses and the Gendered Regulation of Criminalized Women." *Feminist Criminology* 2 (2): 158–74. http://dx.doi.org/10.1177/1557085106297521.

–. 2008. *Locked In, Locked Out: Imprisoning Women in the Shrinking and Punitive Welfare State*. http://www.wlu.ca/docsnpubs_detail.php?doc_id=30852&grp_id=1067.

–. 2009. "Circuits of Exclusion: Criminalized Women's Negotiation of Community." *Canadian Journal of Community Mental Health* 28 (1): 83–95. http://dx.doi.org/10.7870/cjcmh-2009-0007.

– 2011. "Victimisation and Governance: Gender-Responsive Discourses and Correctional Practice." In *Working with Women Offenders in the Community*, ed. Rosemary Sheehan, Gill McIvor, and Chris Trotter, 110–26. New York: Willan Publishing.

Power, Michael. 1997. *The Audit Society: Rituals of Verification*. Oxford: Oxford University Press.

–. 2007. *Organized Uncertainty: Designing a World of Risk Management*. Oxford: Oxford University Press.

Pratt, John. 2000. "The Return of the Wheelbarrow Men; Or, the Arrival of a Postmodern Penality?" *British Journal of Criminology* 40 (1): 127–45. http://dx.doi.org/10.1093/bjc/40.1.127.

Pratt, John, David Brown, Mark Brown, Simon Hallsworth, and Wayne Morrison. 2005. "Introduction." In *The New Punitiveness: Trends, Theories, Perspectives*, ed. John Pratt, David Brown, Mark Brown, Simon Hallsworth, and Wayne Morrison, xi–xxvi. Portland: Willan Publishing. http://dx.doi.org/10.1016/j.amjcard.2005.03.005.

Puwar, Nirmal. 2004. *Space Invaders: Race, Gender and Bodies Out of Place*. Oxford: Berg.

Rafter, Nicole Hahn. 1990. *Partial Justice: Women, Prisons, and Social Control*, 2nd ed. New Brunswick: Transaction Publishers.

Raibmon, Paige. 2005. *Authentic Indians: Episodes of Encounter from the Late-Nineteenth-Century Northwest Coast*. Durham, NC: Duke University Press.

Rankin, L. Pauline, and Jill Vickers. 2001. *Women's Movements and State Feminism: Integrating Diversity into Public Policy*. Ottawa: Status of Women Canada.

Razack, Sherene. 1998. *Looking White People in the Eye: Gender, Race, and Culture in Courtrooms and Classrooms*. Toronto: University of Toronto Press.

Restoule, Jean-Paul. 2000. "Aboriginal Identity: The Need for Historical and Contextual Perspectives." *Canadian Journal of Native Education* 24 (2): 102–12.

Roach, Kent, and Jonathon Rudin. 2000. "*Gladue*: The Judicial and Political Reception of a Promising Decision." *Canadian Journal of Criminology* 42 (3): 355–88.

Roberts, Julian, and Ronald Melchers. 2003. "The Incarceration of Aboriginal Offenders: Trends from 1978 to 2001." *Canadian Journal of Criminology and Criminal Justice* 45 (2): 211–42. http://dx.doi.org/10.3138/cjccj.45.2.211.

Rozas, Lisa Werkmeister, and Joshua Miller. 2009. "Discourses for Social Justice Education: The Web of Racism and the Web of Resistance." *Journal of Ethnic & Cultural Diversity in Social Work* 18 (1): 24–39. http://dx.doi.org/10.1080/15313200902874953.

Russell, Emma, and Bree Carlton. 2013. "Pathways, Race and Gender Responsive Reform: Through an Abolitionist Lens." *Theoretical Criminology* 17 (4): 474–92. http://dx.doi.org/10.1177/1362480613497777.

Sawchuck, Joe. 2001. "Negotiating an Identity: Métis Political Organizations, the Canadian Government, and Competing Concepts of Aboriginality." *American Indian Quarterly* 25 (1): 73–92. http://dx.doi.org/10.1353/aiq.2001.0012.

Schneiberg, Marc, and Sarah Soule. 2005. "Institutionalization as a Contested, Multi-Level Process: Politics, Social Movements and Rate Regulation in American Fire Insurance." In *Social Movements and Organizations*, ed. Gerald Davis, Doug McAdam, W.R. Scott, and Mayer Zald, 122-60. Cambridge: Cambridge University Press. http://dx.doi.org/10.1017/CBO9780511791000.008.

Schoenfeld, Heather. 2010. "Mass Incarceration and the Paradox of Prison Conditions Litigation." *Law & Society Review* 44 (3/4): 731–67. http://dx.doi.org/10.1111/j.1540-5893.2010.00421.x.

Shaw, Margaret. 1999. "'Knowledge without Acknowledgement': Violent Women, the Prison and the Cottage." *Howard Journal* 38 (3): 252–66. http://dx.doi.org/10.1111/1468-2311.00131.

Shaylor, Cassandra. 2009. "Neither Kind nor Gentle: The Perils of 'Gender Responsive Justice.'" In *The Violence of Incarceration*, ed. Phil Scraton and Jude McCulloch, 145-63. New York: Routledge.

Silverstein, Martin. 2005. "What's Race Got to Do with It? Responsibilization Strategies at Parole Hearings." *British Journal of Criminology* 45 (3): 340–54. http://dx.doi.org/10.1093/bjc/azh102.

Sim, Joe. 1994. "Tougher Than the Rest? Men in Prison." In *Men, Masculinities and Crime*, ed. Tim Newburn and Elizabeth Stanko, 100–17. New York: Routledge.

Simon, Jonathan. 1993. *Poor Discipline: Parole and the Social Control of the Underclass, 1890-1990*. Chicago: University of Chicago Press.

–. 2007. *Governing through Crime: How the War on Crime Transformed American Democracy and Created a Culture of Fear*. New York: Oxford University Press.

Simon, Jonathon, and Malcolm Feeley. 2003. "The Form and Limits of the New Penology." In *Punishment and Social Control*, 2nd ed., ed. Thomas Blomberg and Stanley Cohen, 75–116. New York: Aldine de Gruyter.

Smith, Linda, and Theresa Roberts. 2007. "The Journey to Inclusion: The Role of Diversity Committees in Schools of Social Work ... A Cautionary Tale." *Journal of Human Behavior in the Social Environment* 15 (1): 121–34. http://dx.doi.org/10.1300/J137v15n01_06.

Snider, Laureen. 2003. "Constituting the Punishable Woman: Atavistic Man Incarcerates Postmodern Woman." *British Journal of Criminology* 43 (2): 354–78. http://dx.doi.org/10.1093/bjc/43.2.354.

Solicitor General. 1975. *Report of the National Conference on Native People and the Criminal Justice System: Native Peoples and Justice*. Ottawa: Solicitor General of Canada.

–. 1981. *Solicitor General's Study of Conditional Release: Report of the Working Group*. Ottawa: Solicitor General of Canada.

–. 1984. *Report of the Advisory Committee to the Solicitor General of Canada on the Management of Correctional Institutions*. Ottawa: Solicitor General of Canada.

–. 1986a. "Correctional Philosophy, Correctional Law Review Working Paper No.1." Ottawa: Solicitor General of Canada.

–. 1986b. "A Framework for the Correctional Law Review, Correctional Law Review Working Paper No. 2." Ottawa: Solicitor General of Canada.

–. 1988a. *Final Report: Task Force on Aboriginal Peoples in Federal Corrections*. Ottawa: Solicitor General of Canada.

–. 1988b. "Correctional Issues Affecting Native Peoples, Correctional Law Review Working Paper No. 7." Ottawa: Solicitor General of Canada.

–. 1991. *Task Force on Aboriginal Peoples in Federal Corrections – Year-End Implementation Report, 1990-1991*. Ottawa: Solicitor General of Canada.

Sparks, Richard. 2003. "State Punishment in Advanced Capitalist Countries." In *Punishment and Social Control*, 2nd ed., ed. Thomas Blomberg and Stanley Cohen, 19–44. New York: Aldine de Gruyter.

Spivakovsky, Claire. 2008. "Approaching Responsivity: The Victorian Department of Justice and Indigenous Offenders." *Flinders Journal of Law Reform* 10: 642–62.

–. 2009. "The Construction of the Racially Different Indigenous Offender." In *C3 2009: Proceedings of 2009 Australian and New Zealand Critical Criminology Conference*, 215–27. Melbourne: Monash University. http://artsonline.monash.edu.au/criminology/files/2013/03/anz-critical-criminology-conference-2009-proceedings.pdf.

–. 2013. *Racialized Correctional Governance: The Mutual Constructions of Race and Criminal Justice*. Surrey: Ashgate Publishing Ltd.

Squires, Judith. 2005. "Is Mainstreaming Transformative? Theorizing Mainstreaming in the Context of Diversity and Deliberation." *Social Politics* 12 (3): 366–88. http://dx.doi.org/10.1093/sp/jxi020.

Stanko, Elizabeth. 1997. "Safety Talk: Conceptualizing Women's Risk Assessment as a 'Technology of the Soul.'" *Theoretical Criminology* 1 (4): 479–99. http://dx.doi.org/10.1177/1362480697001004004.

Sudbury, Julia. 2005. "'Mules,' 'Yardies,' and Other Folk Devils: Mapping Cross-Border Imprisonment in Britain." In *Global Lockdown: Race, Gender, and the Prison-Industrial Complex*, ed. Julia Sudbury, 167–83. New York: Routledge.

Swan, Elaine, and Steve Fox. 2010. "Playing the Game: Strategies of Resistance and Co-optation in Diversity Work." *Gender, Work and Organization* 17 (5): 567–89. http://dx.doi.org/10.1111/j.1468-0432.2010.00524.x.

Task Force on Federally Sentenced Women (TFFSW). 1990. *Report of the Task Force on Federally Sentenced Women – Creating Choices*. Ottawa: Solicitor General of Canada.

Tonry, Michael. 2004. *Thinking about Crime: Sense and Sensibility in American Penal Culture*. Oxford: Oxford University Press.

Tonry, Michael, and Joan Petersilia. 1999. "American Prisons at the Beginning of the Twenty-First Century." In *Prisons*, ed. Michael Tonry, Vol. 26: *Crime and Justice: A Review of Research*, 1–16. Chicago: University of Chicago Press. http://dx.doi.org/10.1086/449293.

Turnbull, Sarah, and Kelly Hannah-Moffat. 2009. "Under These Conditions: Gender, Parole and the Governance of Reintegration." *British Journal of Criminology* 49 (4): 532–51. http://dx.doi.org/10.1093/bjc/azp015.

van Dongen, Els. 2005. "Repetition and Repertoires: The Creation of Cultural Differences in Dutch Mental Health Care." *Anthropology & Medicine* 12 (2): 179–97. http://dx.doi.org/10.1080/13648470500140088.

Volpp, Leti. 1994. "(Mis)Identifying Culture: Asian Women and the 'Cultural Defense.'" *Harvard Women's Law Journal* 17: 57–80.

Wacquant, Loïc. 2003. "America's New 'Peculiar Institution': On the Prison as Surrogate Ghetto." In *Punishment and Social Control*, 2nd ed., ed. Thomas Blomberg and Stanley Cohen, 471–82. New York: Aldine de Gruyter.

–. 2005. "The Great Penal Leap Backward: Incarceration in America from Nixon to Clinton." In *The New Punitiveness: Trends, Theories, Perspectives*, ed. John Pratt, David Brown, Mark Brown, Simon Hallsworth, and Wayne Morrison, 3–26. Portland: Willan Publishing.

Walby, Kevin, and Mike Larsen. 2011. "Getting at the Live Archive: On Access to Information Research in Canada." *Canadian Journal of Law and Society* 26 (3): 623–33. http://dx.doi.org/10.3138/cjls.26.3.623.

Waldram, James. 1997. *The Way of the Pipe: Aboriginal Spirituality and Symbolic Healing in Canadian Prisons*. Peterborough: Broadview Press.

Walklate, Sandra. 1997. "Risk and Criminal Victimization: A Modernist Dilemma?" *British Journal of Criminology* 37 (1): 35–45. http://dx.doi.org/10.1093/oxfordjournals.bjc.a014148.

Webb, Janette. 1997. "The Politics of Equal Opportunity." *Gender, Work and Organization* 4 (3): 159–69. http://dx.doi.org/10.1111/1468-0432.00032.

West, Candace, and Sarah Fenstermaker. 1995. "Doing Difference." *Gender & Society* 9 (1): 8–37. http://dx.doi.org/10.1177/089124395009001002.

Williams, Toni. 2009. "Intersectionality Analysis in the Sentencing of Aboriginal Women in Canada." In *Intersectionality and Beyond: Law, Power and the Politics of Location*, ed. Emily Grabham, Davina Cooper, Jane Krishnadas, and Didi Herman, 79–104. London: Routledge-Cavendish.

Wrench, John. 2005. "Diversity Management Can Be Bad for You." *Race & Class* 46 (3): 73–84. http://dx.doi.org/10.1177/0306396805050019.

Young, Alison. 1996. *Imagining Crime: Textual Outlaws and Criminal Conversations*. London: Sage.

Young, Iris Marion. 1990. *Justice and the Politics of Difference*. Princeton, NJ: Princeton University Press.

Yuval-Davis, Nira. 2006. "Intersectionality and Feminist Politics." *European Journal of Women's Studies* 13 (3): 193–209. http://dx.doi.org/10.1177/1350506806065752.

Zaitzow, Barbara. 2004. "Pastel Fascism: Reflections of Social Control Techniques Used with Women in Prison." *Women's Studies Quarterly* 32 (3/4): 33–48.

Zedner, Lucia. 1995. "Wayward Sisters: The Prison for Women." In *The Oxford History of the Prison*, ed. Norval Morris and David Rothman, 328–61. Oxford: Oxford University Press.

Zellerer, Evelyn. 2003. "Culturally Competent Programs: The First Family Violence Program for Aboriginal Men in Prison." *Prison Journal* 83 (2): 171–90. http://dx.doi.org/10.1177/0032885503083002004.

Court Cases

R. v. Borde, [2003] 172 C.C.C. (3d) 225 (Ont. C.A.)

R. v. Hamilton, [2004] O.J. No. 3252, 186 C.C.C. (3d) 129 (Ont. C.A.)

R. v. Gladue [1999] 1 S.C.R. 688

Legal Statutes

Access to Information Act, R.S.C., 1985, c. A-1

Canadian Charter of Rights and Freedoms, Part I of the *Constitution Act*, 1982, being Schedule B to the *Canada Act* 1982 (U.K.), 1982, c. 11

Canadian Human Rights Act, R.S.C. 1985, c. H-6

Canadian Multiculturalism Act, R.S.C. 1985, c. 24 (4th Supp.)

Corrections and Conditional Release Act, S.C. 1992, c. 20

Criminal Code of Canada, R.S.C. 1985, c. C-46

Parole Act, R.S.C. 1985, c. P-2

Penitentiary Act, R.S.C. 1985, c. P-5

Index

Aboriginal and Diversity Initiatives section, 12, 39, 48, 53–57, 59, 77–78, 83, 159–60, 169, 205n3; creation and role of, 53–57; and "diversity work," 55–57

Aboriginal Circle: creation of, 63–66; as diversity work, 64; purpose of, 64; role in supporting diversity work, 121, 132

Aboriginal communities: authenticity of, 140; responsibilization of 37–38, 138–39; *Corrections and Conditional Release Act (CCRA)* definition of, 132; as distinct, 37, 67, 132; and diversity training, 93–95; elder knowledge of, 23; and *Gladue*, 45; resource guides about, 67; role in community-assisted hearings, 131–32, 135–37; as target of diversity initiatives, 21–24, 26, 33, 35, 39, 62–63, 68, 137–38, 160, 204n4, 207n6

Aboriginal corrections, 34, 83, 206n12, 206nn3–4

Aboriginal identity: authenticity, 140–43, 207n13; and "birth right," 98–99; constituted through paradigm of difference, 100–01 (*see also* cultural difference); and co-optation by penal

system, 142. *See also* Aboriginality; healing

Aboriginal offenders, as a special offender population, 33–36, 42, 113. *See also* Aboriginal peoples; Aboriginal women offenders

Aboriginal peoples: and failure of the criminal justice system, 15, 17, 20, 24, 33, 44; greater involvement in the penal system, 21, 37–38, 130–35; producing knowledge about, 85–86, 94–95, 98–99, 102–03; and multiculturalism, 153–54; self-determination of, 24, 30, 133; special constitutional identity of, 33–34, 171, 204n1; as targets of corrections and parole policy, 39, 45–46, 64, 68, 78, 105–49; as victims, 63–64, 105, 131, 135, 137; "worldviews" of, 100–01, 103. *See also* Aboriginal communities; Aboriginal identity; Aboriginal offenders; Aboriginality; Aboriginal women offenders; elder-assisted hearings (EAHs); community-assisted hearings (CAHs)

Aboriginal women offenders: and community-assisted hearings, 136,

186, 207n10; in diversity training, 92; as "doubly disadvantaged," 25, 28, 37; as having different needs, 43, 178, 185; exclusion of in policy, 97; punishment of, 29, 208n1

Aboriginality, 4, 13, 15, 25, 29, 35, 39–40, 46, 92, 100–01, 105–06, 112, 114, 117, 127, 133, 141–44, 149, 151, 155, 175, 190, 196; and authenticity, 141–43. *See also* Aboriginal identity; healing; Indigeneity

Access to Information Act (ATIA), 11, 85, 92, 114, 120, 154, 155, 203n8, 205n13, 206n11, 207n17

African Canadian offenders, 13, 46, 57, 145, 147, 151, 162–63, 171–72, 175; African Canadian cultural liaison officer, 57, 171–72; African Canadian Cultural Liaison Project, 171–72; African Nova Scotian community, 163; parole hearings for, 163, 171–72. *See also* black offenders; ethnocultural offenders

Ahmed, Sara, 7, 48–49, 53–54, 72, 104, 192

Andersen, Chris, 52, 142

anti-racism, and language of diversity, 49–50

Arbour, Louise, 43,

Arbour Report, 43, 178

Atlantic Region, 9, 57–58, 63, 67, 84, 111, 112–13, 125, 145, 162–63, 171–72, 177, 179, 184, 192–93; Aboriginal community resource guides, 67; "African Canadian Hearing Model," 163; African Canadian Cultural Liaison Project, 171–72; community outreach, 63; diversity committees, 57–58, 162–63; diversity training, 84; elder-assisted hearings in, 112–13, 125; information sessions for female offenders, 192–93; parole hearings for female offenders, 177, 192–94

Auditor General of Canada, 136

Bannerji, Himani, 88, 153, 207n1

black offenders, 58, 152–53, 163, 172, 195; "black community," 147, 171; Black

History Month, 60; black women offenders, 184. *See also* African Canadian offenders; ethnocultural offenders

Brassard, Renée, 100, 119, 142

Bromby, Gregory, 3

Buchanan, Nicholas, 143

Canadian Bar Association (CBA), 24, 43; CBA Committee on Imprisonment and Release, 24–25; *Locking up Natives in Canada* report, 24

Canadian Charter of Rights and Freedoms, 15, 28–33, 36, 159, 178, 188, 204n1, 204n8, 204n9

Canadian Heritage, 159, 169

Canadian Human Rights Commission, 43, 136, 178

Canadian Multiculturalism Act, 151–52, 159, 208n2

Carlen, Pat, 204n7

colonialism, 19, 88, 91, 104, 134, 141; and Canadian identity, 88; as causing social disorders, 24, 98–99, 147; as connected to contemporary incarceration rates, 24, 44; contemporary legacy of, 24, 44, 86, 101–03; and multiculturalism, 153; reparative and restorative justice, 7, 134, 140–42, 207n7; residential schools, 94; and rhetoric of diversity, 8, 199; "60s scoop," 95. *See also* Aboriginal peoples; cultural difference

community-assisted hearings (CAHs): and "Aboriginal community," 132; for African Canadians, 163, 171–72; as alternative parole hearing model, 106, 143–45, 168; and authentic Aboriginal identity, 140–43, 207n14; as building reputation, 138; and Correctional Law Review (CLR), 131; definition of, 207n9; as diversity initiative, 76, 106, 130–31, 157; elder involvement in, 121, 135; and *Final Report: Task Force on Aboriginal Peoples in Federal Corrections*, 131; history of, 131–33; implementation challenges, 135–36; as knowledge practice, 137–38, 170; policy for, 123, 134, 207n11;

responsibilization of Aboriginal communities, 138–40; as restorative justice, 136–37; role of Correctional Service of Canada (CSC) in, 132–34, 136; section 79, 132; section 84, 131–33; statistics about, 207n10; as target of community outreach, 62–63

Correctional Law Review (CLR), 30–36, 38, 131, 204n11

Correctional Service of Canada (CSC), 9, 22, 92, 101, 150, 160, 180–82, 184–87, 189, 208n1; diversity training by, 92; and *Gladue*, 98–99, 145–46; relationship to Parole Board of Canada, 9, 180; role in community-assisted hearings, 132–34, 136, 146

Corrections and Conditional Release Act (CCRA): creation of, 38–40; five-year review of, 41–42; as impetus for elder-assisted hearings, 111; and institutional recognition of diversity, 15, 38, 48, 68, 80; limits of in relation to gender and diversity, 39–40; Part I, 39; Part II, 39; section 79, 132; section 84, 62, 131–33, 136, 186; section 151(3), 9, 39, 41, 48, 53, 68, 80, 121–22, 145, 167, 188, 199. *See also* section 84; section 151(3)

Cowlishaw, Gillian, 141

Creating Choices. See Task Force on Federally Sentenced Women (TFFSW)

Criminal Code: amendments to, 32, 204n11; review of, 31–32; section 718.2(e), 44–46, 76, 147, 204n11, 207n15. *See also* section 718.2(e)

Criminal Law Review, 30–31

criminalization, 14, 199

cultural advisors, 66, 122–23, 165. *See also* elders

cultural difference, 6, 9, 14, 39, 47–48, 52, 73, 80; and Aboriginality, 17–22, 28, 33, 37; in advisory groups, 61; cultural "ghettos," 148–49; cultural loss, 28; in diversity newsletters, 59–60; in diversity training, 81–83; in fact sheets, 67; production of knowledge about, 75,

151, 154–64; and "worldviews," 90–91. *See also* ethnocultural

culturally appropriate: and parole process, 13, 68, 104, 116, 125, 128–30, 132–33, 139, 148–49, 206n3; and penal policy, 7, 52, 117, 199; and punishment, 17, 21–22, 44, 52, 100, 141–42, 185; and risk assessment, 102, 126–27

Darian-Smith, Eve, 143

Daubney Committee, 19, 21–22, 24, 27–28, 36; *Taking Responsibility* report, 19

decision making, 9–10, 13–14, 18, 22–23, 41, 46, 52, 67, 73, 79–84, 86–87, 94–96, 126, 148, 164, 185, 205n13; "appropriate" decisions, 23, 74–76, 89–90, 104, 157, 179; and cultural fact sheets, 173–74; and gender, 177, 179, 186, 190–91, 194, 196–97; and *Gladue*, 97–98, 101; "hallmarks" of, 166–68; and language interpretation, 167–70; risk of bias, 82, 90; and role of elders, 114, 119. *See also* Parole Board of Canada (PBC); reputational risk; risk assessment

Dhamoon, Rita, 208n1

diversity: and additive approach, 28, 176, 195; "business case" for, 206n2; celebration of, 49, 60, 152, 154, 199; commitment to, 54–56, 58, 68, 77–78, 80, 83, 152–53, 167, 177, 179–80, 187–88; compartmentalization of, 35, 37, 39, 47, 56; and corporate culture, 50, 54–55; definition of, 5–6, 51; diversity champions, 58, 152, 168; institutional inertia, 71, 183; institutionalization of, 6, 47, 50–53, 78, 104, 126, 151, 153, 198–99; language of, 49–50, 199; and organizational change, 50, 54, 82, 192; and othering, 55, 59, 79, 85–88, 144, 174, 177, 198, 200; in penal populations, 5–6, 12–17, 39–40, 47, 49, 51, 55, 85, 150–54, 159–60, 164–65, 168, 174; as peripheral to penal reform, 31; and political will, 53–54, 57; responsibility for, 53, 58, 66; and representation, 48,

69–70; social construction of, 203n1. *See also* cultural difference; diversity initiatives; diversity training; diversity work; gender; risk assessment

diversity initiatives, 5, 50, 53–54, 56–57, 75–77, 83, 105–07, 116–17, 150–51, 154, 176, 179, 199, 201. *See also* community-assisted hearings (CAHs); diversity work; elder-assisted hearings (EAHs)

diversity training (for parole board members), 81–97, 104, 158; Aboriginal Perceptions Training (APT), 92–97; challenge of, 84–85; and cultural difference, 82; cultural perceptions, 81, 90–91; and evidence base, 83; female offenders, 91–92; focus on awareness and sensitivity to diversity, 89–90; and knowledge production, 81–82, 85–86; and othering, 85–87; regional differences, 83–84; role of elders in, 84; reproduction of institutional whiteness, 87–89; white knapsack exercise, 88–89, 206n5

diversity work: advisory communities, 60–62; community outreach, 62–63; diversity committees, 57–59; forms of at Parole Board of Canada, 57; newsletters, 59–60; resource guides, 67; Sara Ahmed's definition of, 53. *See also* Aboriginal and Diversity Initiatives section; Aboriginal Circle; diversity training

Dyck, Noel, 133

Ekstedt, John, 26

elder-assisted hearings (EAHs): and Aboriginal identity, 109, 121–24, 140–43; as an "alternative" hearing model, 143–45; attendees, 125; cost of, 125; cultural protocols for, 110, 119, 124–25; and decision making, 126–28; definition of, 124; history of, 107–12; impetus for, 107–08; Inuit hearings, 112–14; "mainstreaming" of, 121–24, 144–45; and non-Aboriginals, 109,

121–24, 144–45; physical format of, 110, 113, 115–16, 124–25; policy for, 124–25, 128–29; production of "authentic" Aboriginality, 140–43; regional differences, 112, 114–15, 117; and as removing barriers, 108, 110, 124; role of elders, 128–30; selection of elders for, 115, 118–20; tensions associated with development, 114–21. *See also* Aboriginal identity; cultural advisors; elders; Inuit offenders

elders: and Aboriginal cultural advisors, 123; and community-assisted hearings, 121, 135; as decision-makers, 22–23; definitions of, 107, 118, 123; hiring of by Parole Board of Canada, 118–20; role in diversity training, 84; role in elder-assisted hearings, 128–30. *See also* cultural advisors; elder-assisted hearings (EAHs)

equality: as aim of diversity work, 58–59, 159; "diversity" instead of, 49–50, 133; formal equality, 48, 181, 208n2; substantive *vs* formal, 48, 181; substantive equality, 7, 48, 90, 181, 188, 199

ethnocultural: definition of, 42, 61–62, 152, 201; *vs* non-ethnocultural, 61–62

ethnocultural offenders: and African Canadian Cultural Liaison Project, 171–73; and board member representation, 69; as a "challenge," 55; committees on, 61; community consultations on, 159–62; constitution of as "different," 6, 10, 13, 61–62, 83, 85, 150–55, 164–75; and *Corrections and Conditional Release Act*, 39–40, 42; and cultural fact sheets, 173–74; cultural hearings for, 164–68; diversity committees on, 162–64; and elder-assisted hearing approach, 121; and female offender population, 190; and institutional multiculturalism, 151–54; interpretation issues, 168–71, 208n9; research reports on, 155–59. *See also* Aboriginal and Diversity Initiatives section; African Canadian offenders;

Kingston, Ontario, 25
Kymlicka, Will, 207n1

LaRocque, Emma, 86, 96, 117, 141
Larsen, Mike, 11, 203n7

Martel, Joane, 100, 119–20, 139, 142
masculinity: and definition of gender,
   87; institutional, 13, 51, 82, 85, 201;
   and intersectionality analysis, 161,
   195; as normative, 51, 61, 82, 87, 97,
   161, 171, 198, 201, 205n1; and parole
   hearings, 189. *See also* gender;
   whiteness
Maurutto, Paula, 99
McPhail, Alison, 31
methodological approach, 11–12, 200–01
Métis, 18, 44, 113, 122; and elder-assisted
   hearings, 115
Minow, Martha, 79
Monture-Angus, Patricia, 102, 128
multiculturalism, 5, 13, 203n3, 207n1;
   as framework for organizing racial,
   ethnic, and cultural difference, 60,
   153–54, 162, 174; and Parole Board of
   Canada, 61, 150–53. *See also Canadian
   Multiculturalism Act*
Murdocca, Carmella, 47, 205n15

O'Connell, Anne, 153–54
Office of the Correctional Investigator,
   136, 178, 204n12, 208n1
Ontario/Nunavut Region, 58, 112–13,
   124–25, 184; Diversity Committee,
   58; elder-assisted hearings in,
   124–25
overrepresentation in penal system: of
   Aboriginal peoples, 15, 17, 19–20,
   24–25, 29, 33, 36, 42, 44–46, 53, 55,
   62, 64, 93, 105, 204n3, 205n14; of
   Aboriginal women, 42–43, 208n1; of
   African/black Canadians, 152, 162

Pacific Region, 9, 61, 109, 111–12, 114–
   18, 126, 148, 155–58, 184; elder-
   assisted hearings in, 109, 111–12,
   114–18, 126; Ethnocultural Advisory

Committee, 61–62; ethnocultural
   offender report, 148, 155–58, 184
parole: and conditional release, 8; conditions of, 9, 181; definition and purpose
   of, 8, 10; types of parole hearings,
   8. *See also* Parole Board of Canada
   (PBC); elder-assisted hearings (EAHs),
   community-assisted hearings (CAHs);
   *Corrections and Conditional Release
   Act (CCRA)*
Parole Board of Canada (PBC):
   Aboriginal board members, 21, 56, 64,
   66, 68, 84, 108, 111; background and
   purpose, 9–10, 80; *Board Member Risk
   Assessment Manual*, 205n13; board
   members as target of diversity initiatives, 59–60, 67, 73–75, 101, 105, 107,
   161–63, 165–74, 188–92; board member participation in diversity initiatives, 58, 61, 63–68; commitments to
   federally sentenced women, 188–92;
   Executive Committee, 53, 64, 66, 72,
   77, 112, 121, 146, 187, 205n2; hallmarks of quality parole hearing, 165–
   68; hiring of board members, 69–71,
   77; need to be "representative," 8, 10,
   33, 35, 51, 56, 69–71, 157, 198, 205n10;
   number of board members, 9, 203n6;
   offices, 9; Policy Manual, 9, 101, 113,
   121–26, 128, 146–47, 167–68, 170, 180,
   207n11; presumed whiteness/maleness
   of board members, 154, 156, 158;
   "quality" decision making, 10, 73–76,
   80, 108, 129, 137, 165, 170, 191; relationship to Correctional Service of
   Canada, 9; training of board members,
   10, 38, 56, 80–100. *See also* Aboriginal
   Circle; Aboriginal and Diversity Initiatives section; Atlantic Region; community-
   assisted hearings (CAHs); diversity
   training; elder-assisted hearings (EAHs);
   institutional whiteness; masculinity;
   Ontario/Nunavut Region; Pacific Region; Prairie Region; Quebec Region
Pavlich, George, 136
penal reform, 4–5, 7, 15–16, 18, 15, 31,
   199–200, 209n4

Printed and bound in Canada by Friesens

Set in Myriad and Minion by Artegraphica Design Co. Ltd.

Copy editor: Joanne Richardson